DEATH
OF AN EMPIRE

THE PRINCE OF SALEM. Salem's foremost merchant and civic leader after the War of 1812–1815, the fabulously wealthy Stephen White (1787–1841) pursued his vision of both a world-class seaport and a modern city.

DEATH
OF AN EMPIRE

THE
RISE AND MURDEROUS
FALL OF SALEM,
AMERICA'S RICHEST CITY

ROBERT BOOTH

Thomas Dunne Books
ST. MARTIN'S PRESS
NEW YORK

THOMAS DUNNE BOOKS.
An imprint of St. Martin's Press.

DEATH OF AN EMPIRE. Copyright © 2011 by Robert Booth. All rights reserved. Printed
in the United States of America. For information, address St. Martin's Press, 175 Fifth
Avenue, New York, N.Y. 10010.

www.thomasdunnebooks.com
www.stmartins.com

Library of Congress Cataloging-in-Publication Data

Booth, Robert.
    Death of an empire : the rise and murderous fall of Salem, America's richest city /
Robert Booth. — 1st ed.
        p. cm.
    ISBN 978-0-312-54038-8
    1. Salem (Mass.)—History—19th century. 2. Salem (Mass.)—Economic conditions—
19th century. 3. Salem (Mass.)—Biography. 4. Murder—Massachusetts—Salem.
5. Trials (Murder)—Massachusetts—Salem. I. Title.
    F74.S1B66 2011
    974.4'5—dc22   2011005078

First Edition: August 2011

10 9 8 7 6 5 4 3 2 1

Dedicated to my mother,

Joyce McKay Booth,

a lover of history,

and to the memory of my friend

John Pickering Jr. of Salem

CONTENTS

III. INTO THE DARKNESS

IV. BLOWN AWAY

Lo! in the magic mirror I uphold,

thou seest thy ripening greatness; wide thy bounds

extend, temples and palaces arise,

arts flourish, and pomp of luxury

rolls through thy gorgeous streets. But in the heavens

behold the appalling sign! And on it writ

in characters of fire—'Carthage is not,

nor Tyre, nor Sidon—and their fate is thine!'

—HENRY PICKERING OF SALEM,

FROM HIS POEM "THE HUDSON," C. 1830

PREFACE

E. Hasket Derby, of Salem, Massachusetts, was America's first million-aire. As a pioneer of his nation's commerce with the Orient, he accumu-lated property on a scale so vast that at his death in 1799, he was the wealthiest man on earth; and to this day he remains one of "the seventy-five richest people in human history," rated at $31.4 billion in adjusted net worth.[1] Amid emperors, bankers, railroad tycoons, and oil barons, he is the only one whose business was shipping. And all of his shipping was done from the seaport of Salem.

Derby bequeathed an empire including two hundred wooden ships and fa-vored positions in major markets from the Caribbean to the South China Sea. His successors were deeply grateful. Salem, the sixth-largest population center with about 9,500 inhabitants, was by far the richest place, per capita, in the United States; and so it stayed for another thirty years. In truth, it had few resources other than confidence, aggressiveness, and intelligence, but these were enough for its vessels to be the first to carry the flag into the seaports of India, Sumatra, Java, and Arabia and for its shipowners to remain the dominant Americans in those markets for many years.

Salem's merchants, operating within the larger white male political system, ruled the town as autocrats, but also as sons of the Enlightenment. Their drive to prosper was matched by their scientific interests and their fascination with foreign cultures. Although their ships bristled with cannon, they established a worldwide commerce without resorting to coercion or violence toward other

peoples. For decades, Salem was the center of American multicultural conscious-
ness. In its streets were the goods and aromas of far-off places; at the heart of
its downtown was the museum of another world. Salem was not like the rest
of America.

Salem's commerce with the peoples of the Indian Ocean was achieved without the arrogance and exploitation that were typical of Europeans. Salem men
deplored the behavior of the British, French, and Dutch, and they and their
government were not interested in overseas colonizing, nation-building, or imposition of values or politics on others. Americans were guests in the East. Since
America produced nothing of any value to their hosts, most of Salem's East India
vessels sailed "in ballast," with cavernously empty holds. This daunting lack of
an outward cargo—cold cash was the only medium of exchange on board—was
both real and symbolic: Salem merchants relied on the resourcefulness of their
agents to fill those huge spaces and did not presume to send unwanted exports,
including notions of cultural or military superiority. When it became the fashion to dispatch American missionaries to the East, most Salem merchants ac-
tively opposed them. In foreign ports, Salem men dressed down, spoke the lingo,
ate the chow, mixed with the crowd, and took pride in their republican ways, so
different from the British and French. While selling and buying ashore in the
great trading cities, most Salem captains and business agents roomed in the native neighborhoods and negotiated directly with the local suppliers. It turned
out to be a very good formula for success.

The eastward empire of maritime commerce made rich men richer and
filled the nation's coffers with the duties of foreign trade. But a newly independent America also began pursuing a manifest destiny westward, throwing waves
of settlers onto the frontier, killing the Indians along the ever-changing borders,
expanding slaveholding agriculture into new states and territories. The western
empire of internal conquest and development, with steamboats plying the rivers
and cities springing up to consume and manufacture, eventually challenged the
wealth and influence of the seaports. In the collision of the two imperial movements, one would be overwhelmed by the values and ambitions of the other, with
profound consequences for the future of the United States.

This book focuses on a typical ambitious Salem family, the Whites, and what they tried to accomplish in the seaport, the nation, and the world. It is a story of people and power, and the evolution of America into a modern country, and who won and lost in the process. The Whites belonged to a class of immensely wealthy, well-educated, entrepreneurial, globally oriented merchants who would disappear from the scene in the years between the War of 1812 and the 1830s. In their heyday, they served in the federal and state governments at the highest levels, and they connected the new republic to the markets and cultures of other peoples.

What happened? Why have we heard about the lurid witchcraft trials but not about Salem's golden empire? One answer is that it existed long ago and far away, out on foreign oceans, before the Civil War, before germ theory and railroads and telegraphs, in a period that has remained obscure except for the War of 1812. Another answer is that it ended abruptly and did not relate to what came after: a reorganization of society based on industrial capitalism, immigration, urbanization, and westering progress. Finally, there was a cover-up: Salemites suppressed the memory of their empire's sordid demise, a trauma involving murder, executions, and disgrace. Their conspiracy succeeded: modern Salem has no memory of the Whites and their many achievements.

Once the tall ships left in the 1830s and 1840s, the seaport joined the ranks of midsized American manufacturing cities, and its leaders had its beautiful rivers and inner harbor filled in and covered over with buildings, tracks, roadbeds, and freight yards. Many of the people formerly involved in commerce moved away, and new people moved in, and the decades of legendary wealth and global seafaring came to seem like a dream, except for a few upscale old neighborhoods and a collection of dusty stuff that the sailors had brought home. Salem accepted its fate and remained obscure until recently, as the fascination of the witchcraft episode of 1692 has given the city a different sort of historical celebrity. That an American empire could have risen and fallen in Salem in the decades before 1830 seems improbable; but an empire did, and with some help and the passage of time, it has been forgotten.

This book is also the story of a new way of being in the world. At the height of its commerce, Salem did what had never been done in the history of western expansion: it sent out its seafarers in peace and friendship, seeking from others only mutual regard and a fair exchange of goods. The impact of their arrival in foreign seas was felt as a moral force, in stark contrast with bloody-minded explorers and the armies and navies of the Europeans' East India monopoly companies. By the early 1790s, Salem shipmasters, welcome everywhere, had broken the hold of the Dutch and the British on the best markets of South Asia. Among peoples in the Orient, Salem was imagined to be its own nation, overflowing with genial inhabitants, grand vessels, and treasure chests full of silver and gold.

Hasket Derby, the prime mover, had found the Calcutta textiles trade to be three times more profitable than the China trade. His Yankee captains made other Oriental discoveries as they took on freights for all comers and roamed at will, opening new markets, making new friends, loading rich cargoes of indigo, sugar, pepper, spices, and coffee. The United States officially kept out of it: no naval vessels were sent, and no forts or settlements were built.[2] The merchants were entirely responsible for the safety of their vessels, cargoes, crews, and captains—if something went wrong, they could not expect the government to intervene or retaliate. But very little did go wrong, and British observers in the Orient could admit, "Of the utter failure of monopoly projects [like the British East India Company] we have too many examples. Of the success of free trade we have one great one, in the Indian commerce of the Americans."[3]

Wealth was the result, and wealth transformed the old colonial town into a beautiful world capital, with elegant landscaped parks and boulevards of new mansions and an extended waterfront of wharves, warehouses, and tall-masted ships. This book is, therefore, also a story of wealth and the difficulty of possessing it without being possessed by it. Salem's wealth was dynamic, constantly put at risk in the high-stakes export-transport-import game known as commerce. Wealth raised up a merchant aristocracy with many dependents. Wealth also gave merchants great leverage in Washington, for seaport duties on foreign imports paid for most of the expenses of the federal government.

And wealth spawned great jealousy. Within a year of Hasket Derby's death, his family split into two tribes: his brother-in-law George Crowninshield organized a merchant house that engaged the Derbys in a struggle for dominance. Unable to quell their leaders' rivalries, Salem's people remained devout in their churchgoing and keen in their awareness of the corrupting influences of money. They relied on their ministers to temper the feuding parties and to teach them all how to be rich and good. Charity was strongly encouraged as an antidote to vanity and selfishness. Virtue was self-consciously practiced. Much of the merchants' money was plowed back into the work life of Salem and environs rather than invested in institutions or stock markets, which did not yet exist: and it was deployed abroad to fuel endless enterprises and interactions in which people of unlike cultures cooperated. Among other things, then, Salem's global enterprise had the effect of creating a de facto foreign policy for the United States, carried out in the positive interactions of merchant mariners and their native partners.

Salem, less a place in America than a presence in the world, was peculiarly vulnerable. When epochal change swept the planet in 1815, Salem merchants, among the richest and smartest of men, scrambled to puzzle out its meaning and to adjust and reinvent in the face of the new conditions: the Pax Britannica, the worldwide economic depression, and the tariffs that accompanied the onrushing Industrial Revolution.

In the end, Derby's Salem could not be sustained. Sailors had to give up their dreams and adventures and find work ashore. Most of the merchants, holding tight to their fortunes, became industrial capitalists and even tried to transform Salem into a manufacturing center. So this is also a story of internal collapse, in the form of efforts that fell short, people who failed or gave up, amusements that turned sinister, and casual criminality that devolved into robbery, plunder, and finally murder. Out in the world, Salem's humanistic values were eroded by its own commercial overreaching—the trade in opium, high-risk extended voyages, intrusion into hostile cultures—and by the takeover of the nation's foreign policy by the racist militarists of the Jackson administration.

By the late 1820s, imperial Salem was breaking its promises to its sons and daughters. One young sea captain, drunk in his boots and cut off from the career that he had thought would make him rich, wondered aloud if anyone had the grit to kill a man for money. From a dark corner of the seaport's night town, he received a fateful answer. Its portent of murder and vengeance was repeated on the far side of the planet along the coast of Sumatra, as a Salem vessel figured in an incident that would forever change America's relations with other peoples.

Although much has been forgotten, Salem and its seafaring commerce were astonishing creations of young America—worldwide in scope, revolutionary in impact, colored with high adventure and vaulting ambition, and worthy of a place in the national story.

WHITE

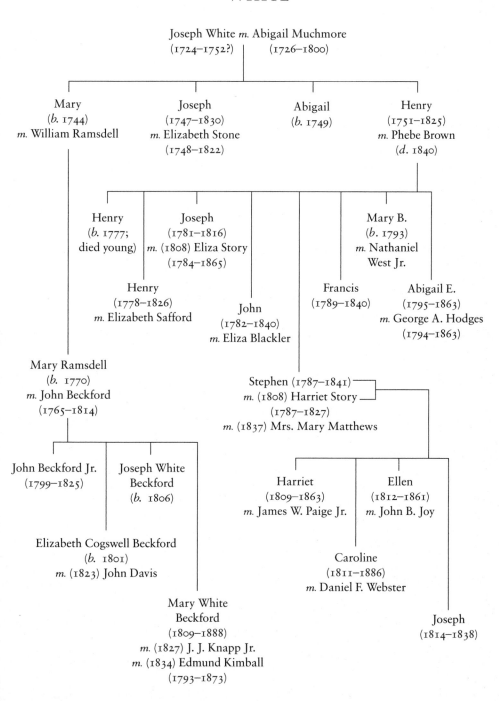

Joseph White *m.* Abigail Muchmore
(1724–1752?)   (1726–1800)

Mary
(*b.* 1744)
m. William Ramsdell

Joseph
(1747–1830)
m. Elizabeth Stone
(1748–1822)

Abigail
(*b.* 1749)

Henry
(1751–1825)
m. Phebe Brown
(*d.* 1840)

Henry
(*b.* 1777;
died young)

Joseph
(1781–1816)
m. (1808) Eliza Story
(1784–1865)

Mary B.
(*b.* 1793)
m. Nathaniel
West Jr.

Henry
(1778–1826)
m. Elizabeth Safford

John
(1782–1840)
m. Eliza Blackler

Francis
(1789–1840)

Abigail E.
(1795–1863)
m. George A. Hodges
(1794–1863)

Mary Ramsdell
(*b.* 1770)
m. John Beckford
(1765–1814)

Stephen (1787–1841)
m. (1808) Harriet Story
(1787–1827)
m. (1837) Mrs. Mary Matthews

John Beckford Jr.
(1799–1825)

Joseph White
Beckford
(*b.* 1806)

Harriet
(1809–1863)
m. James W. Paige Jr.

Ellen
(1812–1861)
m. John B. Joy

Elizabeth Cogswell Beckford
(*b.* 1801)
m. (1823) John Davis

Caroline
(1811–1886)
m. Daniel F. Webster

Mary White
Beckford
(1809–1888)
m. (1827) J. J. Knapp Jr.
m. (1834) Edmund Kimball
(1793–1873)

Joseph
(1814–1838)

STORY

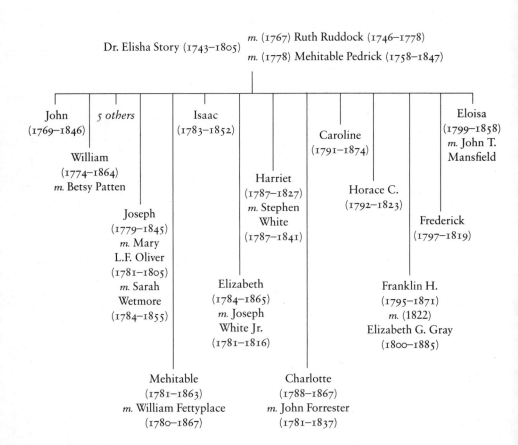

Dr. Elisha Story (1743–1805)

m. (1767) Ruth Ruddock (1746–1778)
m. (1778) Mehitable Pedrick (1758–1847)

John (1769–1846)

5 others

Isaac (1783–1852)

Caroline (1791–1874)

Eloisa (1799–1858)
m. John T. Mansfield

William (1774–1864)
m. Betsy Patten

Harriet (1787–1827)
m. Stephen White (1787–1841)

Horace C. (1792–1823)

Joseph (1779–1845)
m. Mary L.F. Oliver (1781–1805)
m. Sarah Wetmore (1784–1855)

Elizabeth (1784–1865)
m. Joseph White Jr. (1781–1816)

Frederick (1797–1819)

Franklin H. (1795–1871)
m. (1822) Elizabeth G. Gray (1800–1885)

Mehitable (1781–1863)
m. William Fettyplace (1780–1867)

Charlotte (1788–1867)
m. John Forrester (1781–1837)

STONE

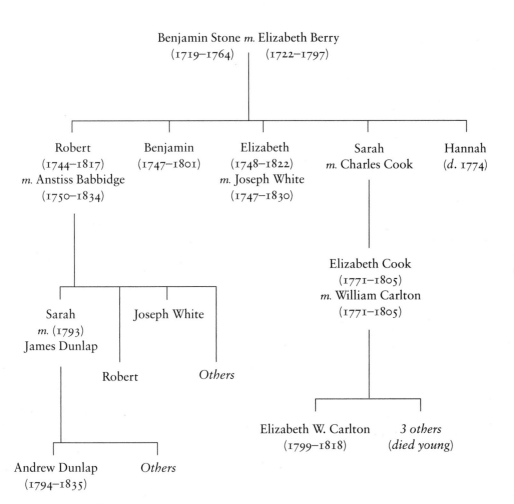

Benjamin Stone *m.* Elizabeth Berry
(1719–1764)   (1722–1797)

Robert
(1744–1817)
m. Anstiss Babbidge
(1750–1834)

Benjamin
(1747–1801)

Elizabeth
(1748–1822)
m. Joseph White
(1747–1830)

Sarah
m. Charles Cook

Hannah
(*d.* 1774)

Sarah
m. (1793)
James Dunlap

Joseph White

Robert   *Others*

Elizabeth Cook
(1771–1805)
m. William Carlton
(1771–1805)

Andrew Dunlap
(1794–1835)

Others

Elizabeth W. Carlton
(1799–1818)

3 others
(*died young*)

CROWNINSHIELD

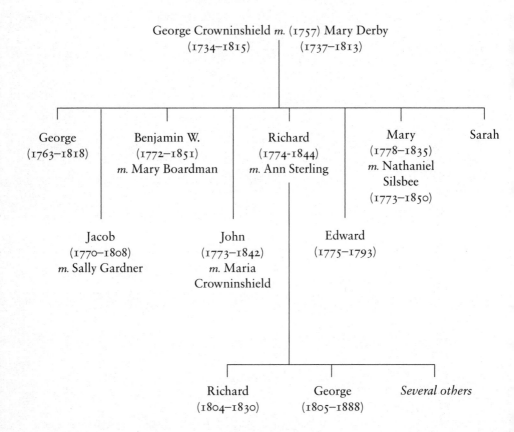

George Crowninshield *m.* (1757) Mary Derby
(1734–1815)   (1737–1813)

George
(1763–1818)

Benjamin W.
(1772–1851)
m. Mary Boardman

Richard
(1774-1844)
m. Ann Sterling

Mary
(1778–1835)
m. Nathaniel
Silsbee
(1773–1850)

Sarah

Jacob
(1770–1808)
m. Sally Gardner

John
(1773–1842)
m. Maria
Crowninshield

Edward
(1775–1793)

Richard
(1804–1830)

George
(1805–1888)

Several others

DEATH
OF AN EMPIRE

A BOULEVARD OF MANSIONS. Foreign trade was the most lucrative business in young America, and no one did it better than Salem. Chestnut Street, overarched by elms, was an exclusive West End enclave for the wealthiest Federalist merchant shipowners.

PART ONE

MASTERS
OF THE UNIVERSE

THE GRAND TURK *SALUTING MARSEILLES AT WAR'S END.* The large privateer brig Grand Turk, owned principally by the White family, was a very successful predator on British shipping, second only to the Crowninshields' great ship America in the profits she reaped for her owners and crew.

I.

AT WAR

August 1814

Two years into America's war with England, Salem was suffering. Death and loss stalked the famous seaport, transforming the once bustling waterfront into a forlorn landscape of empty wharves and gaunt warehouses and skeletal masts of unsailing ships. In the houses along the dirt lanes of the seafaring East Parish, men and boys were scarce, as in peacetime. But now, instead of sailing to foreign ports, hundreds were crewing on naval vessels and privately owned warships known as privateers, hundreds more were languishing in crowded, disease-ridden hulks and prisons overseas, and several dozen were dead, killed in action, or fatally wounded.

From time to time, a Salem privateer would make a run for the open sea; but such forays were now rare, and rarer still were the arrivals of prize vessels captured from the English. The problem was the British naval blockade, generally effective against the shipping of Massachusetts, including the Salem Bay towns of Gloucester, Manchester, Beverly, Marblehead, and Salem. Rumors of peace wafted in every week, blasted by alarms of invasion from Halifax, the Nova Scotian home base to 130 British warships and several regular army regiments. Invasion now seemed much more likely than armistice, as the United States faced defeat.

In the heat of August, British battleships cruised among the islands off Salem Neck.[1] For the second straight month, neither privateers nor captured prizes arrived; and dark rumors and false reports buzzed in the sweltering air. The discouraged Republicans had not bothered to sponsor an orator or hold a parade on the Fourth of July, leaving the field to the antiwar harangues of the Federalists.

Most of the town's large merchant vessels lay careened on the beaches and sat leaking in the docks, and the privateers rode at their anchors. Out at Salem Neck, Colonel Joseph White Jr., thirty-three, the jaunty leader of the militia regiment, was supervising the final phases of rebuilding Fort Lee and the construction of a new battery at the point called the Juniper, to command the mouth of the harbor. White doubted the ability of his men or the federal garrison at nearby Fort Pickering to resist a serious British attack. And the British were known to be on the move: their recent capture of Eastport, Maine, was an indication that London was out of patience and would authorize all-out aggression against New England to end this half-fought American war.

Colonel White, a staunch Republican, did all he could to prepare Salem for the coming confrontation. Others, not so brave, had left on long trips or removed to new homes in the countryside.[2] White himself wished to join them; he was heartily sick of war and disease and death. In February 1813, his infant daughter, Charlotte, had died; and in July of that year, he and his brother Stephen and their brother-in-law Judge Joseph Story had jointly purchased a large tomb. Colonel White's other two children had been sick all that summer, and he himself had fallen so ill as to have gone off to Saratoga Springs for a cure, returning via New York City "quite recovered" by September.

With Salem's Republican leaders caught up in illness, military duties, and privateering, the local Federalists had managed to win the district's congressional seat for their candidates since 1809, including the incumbent Timothy Pickering, formerly a senator and cabinet member. The seaport was hardly a Federalist stronghold—its (absent) sailors made up a majority, and most voted Republican—but that was not the view from the outside. Salem had long been envied as a bastion of wealth and privilege by the rest of the nation, in whose imagination its people lived like lords and ladies off the accumulated wealth of the world. But money seemed to have made them mad: the pro-British antiwar ferocity of the Federalists was regarded as verging on treason.

If the British stormed ashore at Salem Neck, Joseph White and his brother Captain Stephen White, twenty-seven, would do their best, although it would not be enough. They had no experience of combat, and their gunners were not particularly accurate, as they kept proving in rare target practice hampered by lack of ammunition. White had been watching the handsome British warships in the bay, one of them an immense seventy-four-gun ship of the line; through his telescope he could make out the colors of the sailors' whiskers and count the muskets stacked on the deck. Two of these ships, a few frigates, and a dozen transports full of troops would reduce Salem's forts to rubble in an hour—Essex County would be conquered, and he would be dead.

For Colonel White, who retired each day to a beautiful new mansion and his wife, Eliza, and little girls, death was not a welcome thought. He and his brother, colonel and captain, loved their lives and their shipping partnership, which they had managed profitably through some very difficult years. Joseph, a specialist in the importation of fine wines, was a lover of the high life and the elegance and gaiety of Salem's social scene. His interest in the military arose more from a fondness for pomp and circumstance than a taste for blood. Not that he lacked resolve, or that Salem would not be defended honorably, for Joseph and Stephen White both lived in it as princes, fully partaking of its great wealth and imperial lifestyle, willing to fight as princes must.

More than anything, as they prepared for battle, they yearned for peace and a chance to resume the commerce of a place that now seemed only a dream of former magnificence. The people of that Salem had built an imperial capital with boulevards of brick mansions and beautiful parks and cobbled streets of handsome stores and high-steepled churches.[3] From their grand houses, White and his fellow shipowners in high beaver hats and cutaway coats had headed downtown to the insurance offices to hear the morning news and perhaps find a cargo or lease space on a freighter before going off to their respective counting-houses. Salem had been the most relentlessly commercial place in the country, at a time that "commerce" meant "trade across the waters" and when "merchant" meant "shipowner importing and exporting goods." Represented in the overseas markets by their shipmasters and supercargoes (business agents), these merchants had the knowledge and judgment to compete successfully in international trade, with its shifting markets and currencies, embargoes and wars, pirates, privateers, and rival merchant fleets. Great wealth had been their reward, and would be again, if only peace would come.

Two years before, in June 1812, as Congress had declared war, Salem had declared its own refusal to fight. At a town meeting, the voters of both parties had passed a resolution instructing Congress not to engage in an "unnecessary, impolitic and unjust" contest with England.[4] The merchants' great fear had always been war with either of the European superpowers, Britain or France, which had been fighting each other worldwide since 1793.

In Salem, neutrality meant prosperity. For twenty years, the American policy of neutrality had enabled shippers to extend their trade around the world. In spite of losses and insults, American merchants had the largest and most lucrative trading fleet on earth. Others might resent bullying by France or Britain enough to rattle sabers, but not the merchants: as long as profits were high, vessel seizures and ransom negotiations were acceptable parts of the game; and they gladly paid for insurance coverage, which they also underwrote, as their hedge.

The Federalists were, in fact, not opposed to war, but their preferred enemy was Napoleon's France. Before 1812, the French had impounded hundreds of American ships and cargoes worth millions of dollars and had offered no reparations. Britain's Royal Navy had also harassed and sometimes captured American vessels and impressed some of their crewmen. But London had apologized for its worst insults and had paid for its thievery; and the seaport Federalists excused the British as long as they thwarted Napoleon—no Federalist had forgotten the emperor's 1802 invasion of the Caribbean with an army of sixty thousand fever-doomed French soldiers.

By the summer of 1812, Salem was out of business—its commerce had ceased. Regarding the war as a matter of partisan politics rather than patriotism, the Federalist merchants had withheld their ships and money from the war effort and had defiantly proclaimed that "no allegiance is due, where no protection is afforded."[5] Their position would not soften over time; they despised the fomenters of the war, their values, and their ambition to rule in America, and many hoped—some prayed—for a speedy British victory.

At first, people in other regions of the country had not understood, for British attacks on shipping had been cited as the main cause for going to war. But the Federalists had set them straight in speeches and newspapers, blasting away at mad President Madison and his suicidal friends. So deep was their antipathy that the Massachusetts governor, a Federalist, backed by the legislature, refused to place the state militia under General Henry Dearborn, federal commander in New England.

Salem's Republicans dutifully answered the call of their country, and the richest—Crowninshields, Silsbees, and Whites—created partnerships to spread the risk of privateering. Their efforts soon paid off, as Salem became the terror of British commerce: in the first six months of war, eighteen Salem privateers captured eighty-seven English freighters and transports.[6] These encounters resulted in few casualties and in much new property. The prizes, sent into Salem to be sold at auction, resulted in profit for the owners, pay for the sailors, and new vessels and valuable provisions for the town.

Risking their fortunes, the youthful White brothers, Joseph and Stephen, partners in a shipping firm, gradually outfitted a total of nine privateers. Their large brig, the 310-ton *Grand Turk,* mounting eighteen guns, was a fast sailer and a good predator. Under Captain Holton Breed, forty-one, she captured many prizes, as did the Whites' schooner *General Stark* and their ship *Alfred.* They experimented with new models for speed. To Baltimore, famous for its fast clipper-style schooners, they sent their friend Joseph J. Knapp to supervise construction of a 172-ton privateer schooner, *Growler,* which went to sea by Thanksgiving 1812 and made several captures on her first cruise.[7]

Throughout the year 1813, the British increased their naval presence in the North Atlantic, but some privateers still beat the odds. By the end of 1813, one of the Salem Crowninshields, Benjamin W., chief owner of the privateer ship *America,* had raked in more than $1 million in prizes, and he had risked most of his winnings in loans to the federal government. In defiance of the ever-tightening blockade, the Whites, the Crowninshields, and their Republican friends continued to send out their vessels: privateers on their cruises, coasters making trips along the shore, and a class of privateers known as letters of marque, laden with freight and looking for trade overseas.

The merchants of the Federalist Party, dominant in Massachusetts, watched from the sidelines as the American military campaigns failed on the northern and western fronts. They smiled, too, at the news of the decimation of Napoleon's army in Russia during the winter of 1812–13. The French collapse could only mean a larger British war effort in North America and the likely defeat of the Republicans' war machine.

The anticipated British victory could not come soon enough. When some of Salem's Republican merchants ventured in 1814 on high-risk commerce with the embattled ports of southern Europe, a few younger Federalists joined in. Among others, George Nichols, thirty-five, and his brother-in-law Benjamin Peirce assembled valuable cargoes and fitted out three of their best vessels. They could get only a little insurance coverage on such perilous voyages, but these men could no longer sit idle in their mansions, retired from the great game of trade. One after another, their beautiful ships sailed out from Salem Harbor and over the horizon.

None would ever return.

In the summer of 1814, English warships sailed unchallenged in Salem Bay, ominous precursors of the nightmare fleet. "Our seacoast was defenseless," wrote one Salemite, "and British ships were all the time cruising up and down as near the shore as they could safely get. Every little while they landed somewhere or chased a coaster or fisherman, or made a pretense of intending to bombard some town. Merchants who had stocks of goods on hand moved them into the country. Many families that were able took themselves away. The whole community was in a state of terror and agitation . . ."[8]

Weeks passed without any big news, but with a mounting sense of dread; then, at the end of August, word came that the English army had captured Washington and burned down the White House and the United States Capitol. Some Federalists were glad. Without a functioning federal government, New England could make a settlement with Britain. But soon rumors flew that a fleet had sailed from Halifax to punish Salem and Marblehead for their privateering. Panic set in, and Salem families swarmed into the countryside. On September 9, Salem learned that the British had captured Penobscot Bay in Maine and set up a naval base at Castine. Next day an express rider gave the alarm that British commandos had landed only twelve miles from Salem at the fishing village of Sandy Bay. Salem's panic turned into full-blown frenzy, with "people tumbling over one another" to escape the onrushing disaster.[9]

With their wives and children safely departed, the White brothers and their volunteers held on at Fort Lee, posting lookouts on the highlands, scanning the horizon for the first sign of apocalypse. Early on September 15, Salem's would-be defenders received the joyful news of Commodore MacDonough's great victory over the British on Lake Champlain. Within a week, the families flooded back into town. At a grand regimental review on the Common, Colonel Joseph White Jr.'s militia turned out in uniform, along with the artillery, the cavalry, and Stephen White's elite cadets, very handsome in new caps and shortened red coats.[10]

That marked the turning point. The churches filled on Sundays; the children played in the lanes; the men and boys shipped out on board the Republican merchants' privateers. Defeated at Baltimore, the British abandoned the Chesapeake "by the rocket's red glare" and broke off their campaigns in Florida and New York. By the end of November, as a large rum-laden prize entered Salem Harbor, not even the tremors of a mild earthquake could disturb the Salemites in their Thanksgiving rites. The worst, they felt, was over.

In December, the most successful of the Crowninshields, Benjamin W., was appointed secretary of the navy, which gave Salem a presence in the highest counsels of war policy.[11] At that moment, Parson William Bentley, of the East Church, Unitarian, noticed that Crowninshield's prodigal brother, Richard, had returned from an absence of several years. Bentley rode out the three miles to South Danvers to visit his former parishioner, once an East India shipmaster and then a New York banker for his family's Salem shipping firm. Richard, cross-eyed and impetuous, had married a volatile young Irish widow, Ann Sterling, and with her had a family of young children. Eager to profit from wartime textile shortages, he had tried manufacturing; but his Connecticut woolen factory had burned down upon completion, and his next one had made him a bankrupt.[12] Despite these failures, Richard had fallen in love with machinery and the idea of making first-class woolen broadcloth, and he had the support of his very rich old father.

Back in the vicinity of Salem, Crowninshield resided with his wife and children—the eldest, Richard Jr., was ten—on the farm formerly of his uncle Hasket Derby, where he had a large flock of imported merino sheep. Richard was convinced that his was the way of the future: pre-war, Americans had relied on importers for almost all of their textiles; but the cessation of commerce had created a new American industry, as workshops and cloth factories were built along the falls of swift-moving rivers. There were no such rivers in Salem; but in nearby Danvers a Captain Foster had set up a cotton-cloth mill, and certain rich Boston Federalists had clubbed together to build an English-style textile complex at suburban Waltham. The marketplace's acceptance of the Boston Associates' cotton sheeting signaled the rise of a capitalist class—formerly shipping merchants—at the head of the new industrial order envisaged by Richard Crowninshield.

At Buxton Hill, Bentley found him building a large brick factory to be powered by water from a new dam. Bentley, "very hospitably received," entered a barn housing the unfamiliar forms of textile equipment—"carding and spinning machines, and looms with spring shuttles," and a prototype shearing machine—like pieces of exotic sculpture, inert and disparate. The man of God was much impressed by this ambitious Crowninshield and his wonderful machinery, awaiting the jolt that would bring them to life.

No doubt Bentley was familiar, also, with the work of Sarah Savage, a Salem teacher who had just published a novel called *The Factory Girl*, examining millwork and its impact on young women and society.[13] The author had observed in the courtroom of her father, Justice Ezekiel Savage, the fate of unmarried women who had turned to thievery or prostitution rather than submit to societal constraints. Her main character, Mary, welcomes the Industrial Revolution as a life-changing opportunity. Escaping from the closed-in drudgery of domestic service—the typical employment of that time—a young woman might enter a spacious factory, where her spinning and weaving were transformed into real wages.[14]

Savage fearlessly explored social structures and stereotypes and showed factories as places where young women might assert themselves, learning from one another and making their own choices. Most of her readers, however, saw factories as hives of corruption, not unlike Salem's own ropewalks, the low, long, dirty buildings where drunks made cordage for the ships. For those readers, factory work denied the American ideal of the self-reliant worker—the craftsman or farmer, or the hardy sailors and their captains faring bravely around the world. Work was not supposed to be degrading; people were not to be herded like animals into oversize buildings and yoked to machines, as they were in England.

Following the American victory at Lake Champlain, the British leaders decided to end this war that the Americans had started. Both nations' representatives signed a truce in December in the Belgian town of Ghent. But news traveled slowly across the ocean, and therefore hostilities would continue. On January 8, 1815, with their commanders unaware of the proceedings at Ghent, two armies came together at New Orleans. General Andrew Jackson's artillery serenely blew apart whole companies of General Sir Edward Pakenham's British regulars, and the battle became a rout.

After a war made up of many losses, America celebrated the victorious finale. In Washington, the congressmen, without a Capitol, partied harder than anyone; and President Madison, long and widely derided, was toasted as a hero along with Jackson, MacDonough, Decatur, Perry, and other commanders. Amid the snow-drifts, Salem celebrated, too, with artillery barrages and fizzling fireworks and nighttime illuminations and feasts in the taverns, minus most of the Federalists and all of the hundreds of seafaring men still locked up in British prisons.

The war was over: the war in America and the war in the world. Britain had won everywhere and would impose a Pax Britannica. None of the war aims of

President Madison and Speaker Henry Clay had been achieved: impressment of sailors, the main casus belli, was not even discussed, and Canada proudly kept flying the British flag. But Jackson or New Orleans had given the propagandists what they needed, and America went forward with a new sense of unity as a nation—indivisible, with slavery, Indian clearances, industrial development, and manifest destiny for all.

Judge Story of Salem saw this as the moment to "extend national authority over the whole extent of power given by the Constitution." Regional differences would dissolve, and Americans would come together under a federal government "endeared to the people," while "the factions of the great states will be rendered harmless."[15] America was united in a Republican vision. The Federalists, not the British, had been completely defeated. For misjudging their country, they had forfeited their standing as a national political force.

Absent from the world for three years, Salem was left in a very difficult position. The Federalists had been right about the disastrous consequences of war, for Salem had surrendered its commerce to other nations, suffered further sundering of its politics, and endured the terrorizing of its citizenry and the imprisonment of hundreds of men and the deaths of dozens more. As manufacturers asserted their claims to the future, the British battleships sailed away, and the oceans were opened to free trade and fierce competition among all nations.

The White brothers, the Crowninshields, George Nichols, and other Salem merchants sent smallish schooners to Baltimore and Norfolk and on to Havana and awaited more clarity regarding overseas trade. As months passed, and as liberated sailors came home from prison, a euphoric spirit swept the town. Optimism—a belief that the future would prove prosperous, that voyages would bring profits—was essential to the conduct of a large commerce; and optimism now reigned. Voyages were planned. New partnerships were formed; huge sums of money were put at risk on great expectations. The reality of peace, and the desire to take advantage of it, finally overcame wartime paralysis and exhaustion, and the very process of refitting the great ships helped to restore a belief in good times to come. Joseph L. Tillinghast's "Ode to Commerce," printed in the *Essex Register* in the spring of 1815, captured the moment.

By freedom roused from death's cold sleep
Again see Commerce cheer the deep;
Peace to her shining vesture clings
And treasures load her spreading wings.
Hail, returning Commerce, hail!
Ride the billow, rule the gale!

Columbia's flag again unfurled
Shall wave her honors thro' the world;
Once more her eagle's flaming eye
Shall pierce the clouds in Europe's sky.
Hail, returning Commerce, hail!
Ride the billow, rule the gale!

These are the boons we Yankees boast,
And neither singly shall be lost:
Freedom and Commerce shall be ours
While life supplies resisting powers!
Hail, returning Commerce, hail!
Ride the billow, rule the gale!

2.

THE LOST PRINCE

Colonel Joseph White Jr. stood, smiling, at the pinnacle of Salem's postwar social and economic order in 1815, with assets that made him one of the richest men in New England. At thirty-four, he commanded the town militia regiment, served in the state legislature, held directorships in a bank and an insurance company, and ran the Story-White political machine. He and his brother Stephen owned a worldwide shipping firm; separately, Joseph had a private banking portfolio and shares in another six trading vessels.

Joseph White Jr. and his brother-partner, Stephen, twenty-eight, were extremely close. They had married the Story sisters of Marblehead, and both now had families of three little girls, and Stephen had a fourth child, two-year-old Joseph. They owned adjoining mansions; and now they purchased a wharf and buildings and began the urgent business of outfitting ships and finding cargoes. In April, the White brothers sent out a small schooner, followed in June by the sturdy brig *Mary & Eliza,* the schooner *Happy Couple,* the brig *Henry,* and others being prepared for long voyages.

Salem's fleet kept everyone employed. Its vessels—brigs, ships, and schooners, ranging in capacity from eighty to four hundred tons burthen[1]—were built by shipwrights and were outfitted and repaired by blacksmiths, painters, carpenters, and sailmakers. Most of Salem's townsmen were working-class, with large families in crowded apartments. The chief occupation was that of mariner: Salem boys looked forward to the seafaring life, full of adventure and camaraderie, taking them over the oceans into the endless summer of the tropics

MERCHANT'S ROW ON WASHINGTON SQUARE. *Salem's Republican elite—the Whites and their relatives—gave frequent parties and hosted the town's many distinguished visitors. The three Story sisters, Charlotte, Harriet, and Eliza, resided in these mansions with their children and husbands, John Forrester, Stephen White, and Joseph White Jr. Their brother, Judge Joseph Story, lived around the corner.*

and past the looming icebergs of the northern seas and off to places far more exotic and interesting than virtuous New England. Hundreds of mariners, young and old, toiled on their planetary voyages for low wages, heedless of terrible danger and long absences. Most of the sailors were from Salem or Marblehead, and most were white; but virtually every vessel sailed with a black cook, typically called "the doctor," often with a black steward to attend the officers. A Salem crew might include a European or two, usually Italian or Scandinavian, adopted Salemites; and at least one Sumatran sailor had settled in the East Parish to raise a family.[2]

White, black, or otherwise, almost every sailor went off into the world with an "adventure" for himself or a family member—barrels of salt fish, boxes of candy, puncheons of rum—to be exchanged in foreign ports for more valuable items or for "tea services and rich eastern stuffs and beautiful carvings of ivory" as gifts for sweethearts and family members. Sometimes a sailor or cook would honor his employer by returning with gifts for the girls of the mansion: "strange spices in daintily woven baskets," singular seashells, or "dresses from China of soft and lustrous white satin . . . with graceful borders woven into every breadth."[3]

If Salem was the richest place in America, it was also the least democratic, with a socioeconomic hierarchy as rigid as that of a medieval principality. At the top of its India-inflected civic culture were about one hundred merchant ship-owners, many of them related, most of them, like the Whites, members of the East India Marine Society. The society had been founded in 1799 by Captain Nathaniel Silsbee and others who had scientific and ethnographic interests and wished to create an enduring museum of the Orient. During the war, the society had served as a refuge of friendship for the feuding merchants.

Membership was limited to those who had sailed as captains or supercar-goes[4] beyond the capes of Africa or South America. Society members tended to marry the sisters and cousins of their fellows. Their dues went to an insurance fund for the benefit of the few members who died leaving their families in need. In a hall over a bank, the society's East India Museum displayed the treasures of the Orient: artifacts, artwork, clothing, natural specimens, weapons, tools, mannequins, paintings of ships, landscapes, and portraits of native traders.

The society also maintained a library of published works as well as mem-bers' charts and logbooks of scientific and navigational importance. In 1815, the librarian was Salem's favorite son, the insurance company president, Nathaniel Bowditch, forty-two.[5] When still a penniless boy-clerk in a store, he had taught himself navigation, higher mathematics, and physics. Entering manhood without hope of going to college, he had been hired by Hasket Derby to sail in Salem's merchant fleet—but as a special kind of sailor, sent out to the Orient in the 1790s to test his patron's suspicions about the accuracy of the time-honored British navigational tables that were standard guides on every ship.

Over the course of three year-long voyages, Bowditch had proved those calculations to be thoroughly and fatally flawed. At first he had revised the tables in editions of other men's books; then, in 1802, his *New American Practical*

Navigator had been published. Overnight, all other reference works became obsolete. Bowditch's correction of more than eight thousand errors had the direct effect of preventing scores of shipwrecks and preserving thousands of lives and millions in property. Bowditch's *Navigator* also served an intensely democratic purpose as the first guide to seamanship written not for officers but for ordinary sailors. Reading it, an ambitious American deckhand could master the knowledge needed to progress up the ranks to shipmaster.[6]

The intense, gnomish-looking Bowditch had since become a world-class mathematician and astronomer, a correspondent of the great scientists of Europe, a holder of honorary degrees and awards and memberships in learned and royal societies. In Salem, the Federalist merchants had made him the president of their Essex Fire and Marine Insurance Company; and he resided in the tony West End, one block from his patrons' ultimate stronghold, the many-mansioned Chestnut Street.

J oseph Jr. and Stephen White, princes of the realm, had arrived at their status unexpectedly. One day in 1795 they had been living in crowded quarters as two of the seven children of Phebe and Henry White, a hard-pressed mariner; the next day they had been carried off to a palace. Joseph was then fourteen, Stephen eight. Their new parents, Captain Joseph White and Elizabeth Stone White, uncle and aunt, welcomed them to a new home with a dozen rooms and a staff of servants. Without children of their own, Joseph and Elizabeth, twenty years before, had adopted two nieces, the cousins Mary Ramsdell and Eliza Cook, who by 1795 were supervising their own households as Mrs. John Beckford and Mrs. William Carlton.

In their new guise, the White boys had become the sons of a nearly illiterate former privateer who had pursued every means of making money in the Orient, Europe, the Caribbean, and even the African slave trade, forbidden to Massachusetts merchants by a law that was unenforceable over the horizon. His cousins the Graftons had recruited him to the nefarious "trade to Guinea," a profitable sideline in which Captain Joseph White had, for a few years in the 1790s, "no reluctance in selling any part of the human race."[7]

Joseph Jr. and Stephen were given beautiful clothes and excellent opportunities. Stephen, the younger, would truly become the couple's son, an eager, curious little boy raised in their home, to their expectations, absorbing their values, educated in the best of private schools. Joseph, already old enough to have been apprenticed to a tradesman or a sailor, had begun clerking in the countinghouse at White's Wharf. Both young Whites would be exempted from the perils of the sailor's life. Other boys, the sons of Salem's mariners, haunted "the wharves, swimming or climbing about the vessels at the docks, rowing around the harbor in the small boats or dories," playing at the grand life of a blue-water seaman. "What a treat for us boys," recalled one of them, when a brig or ship hauled into the wharf at the end of a foreign voyage; "how we youngsters swarmed on board, exploring every nook and cranny of her, climbing over the rigging, daring each other to mount higher and higher, until with a feeling of triumph I at last placed my cap upon the main royal truck, the highest point, and, looking down, saw the admiring, though envious, gaze of my young companions! Then again, to sit around the fo'c'sle . . . to see the sailors at their meals, and hear them spin their yarns, was happiness indeed. To go to sea, to become a sailor, visit foreign lands, and in due time to become the captain of a fine ship— this was the goal to be looked forward to, the great aim of our lives."[8]

Another sailor wrote that "though the hardships and privations of a seaman's life be greater than those of any other, there is a compensation in the very excitement of its dangers, in the opportunity it affords of visiting different countries, and viewing mankind in the various gradations between the most barbarous and the most refined; and in the ever-changing scenes which this occupation presents."[9] Their employers, the urbane, well-educated merchants, "being persons of great intelligence and shrewdness in business," could outbargain the sailors on wages and influence them when ashore at election time.[10] Many sailors were so superstitious that their own captains found it "strange that a class of men who were continually exposed to storms, hardships, and dangers, should be so powerfully affected by the traditions" concerning "omens, charms, predictions, and the agency of invisible spirits."[11]

Between the merchants and the mariners, there was a fatal conspiracy, time-honored and mutually acceptable. Terrible loss of life was the price paid for

Salem's splendid commerce with the world. Every month, without exception, men were lost overboard and died of tropical fevers and disease, and every year whole vessels and crews went down in hurricanes and gales; but no sailor ever left port thinking that this voyage would be his last. In the war with the sea, in the struggle with the world, the merchant employers usually made the crew's health and safety a priority by hiring sober, intelligent officers and outfitting seaworthy, well-supplied vessels. If something then went wrong, the merchant, at least, could not be blamed, although he could certainly blame himself. For a merchant of long standing, the town was made up of people whose sailor husbands, fathers, and sons had been lost from his ships. He would meet these people in church, in shops, in the street. It was important to be able to look them in the eye.

Although Joseph White Jr. was being bred as a merchant and was not among the seafaring boys who sang the chanteys and jumped aloft to take in sail, still he had his chance to go to sea. At seventeen in 1798, he went on a voyage to Europe and the Orient to learn how business was conducted in the markets of the world. That world had been at war for five years, as the French and the British and their allies fought on, leaving America at peace as a favored neutral—one whose ships carried the freight of all nations at a time when no others could do so. It was an incredibly lucrative business, at which the merchants and mariners of Salem prospered mightily.

Out in the Orient on his second voyage, in 1803, Joseph had observed Salem's freewheeling shipmasters in action. His travels were his higher education. At that time Salem merchants owned about 125 large vessels, of which 50 ships and brigs traded to the ports of the Indian Ocean and beyond. The rest went to Europe and to South America, to the Caribbean islands, and to southern seaports. They loaded up with valuable cargoes: one typical merchantman of three hundred tons burthen might carry away goods worth $50,000, or tens of millions of dollars in today's prices. So extensive was Salem's trade that the admirable Republican congressman, Jacob Crowninshield, could report to the secretary of state on the full extent of the nation's foreign commerce simply by describing that of Salem.[12]

India, said Crowninshield, was not the only place in which to make an immense profit in the Orient. The trade to Batavia, the great mart of Java, "under Dutch control but coveted by Britain," had grown to more than fifty American vessels annually, about twenty of them from Salem. They carried goods to and from Holland and France, too, and sometimes took away the entire supply of Batavia's sugar and coffee.[13] In most of the East, trading was conducted in the great seaports, dominated by the dispersed Chinese and the Europeans. Prices were set in the market, and deals were arranged by middlemen. It was an orderly and civilized process.

Not in Sumatra. And more than any other market, Sumatra was the special trading province of Salem.[14]

The northwest coast of the great island of Sumatra was the only district that had remained free of Dutch control. On that coast, the warrior people of the pepper ports and highlands were ruled by Muslim rajahs and sultans pledged to the king of Atjeh. The Atjehnese had developed a culture of ferocity and even treachery that kept them independent but also made them as willing to engage in tribal conflicts as they were to give battle to Western invaders. Pepper was exceedingly valuable, as both a spice and a preservative, but the Dutch and the British had forfeited most of their Atjeh trade through futile efforts at conquest. Salem men were recognized as a different breed of "white devil,"[15] and Salem's merchants took full advantage to corner the American pepper market while also shipping to Europe and the Caribbean. They insisted that their shipmasters show respect to the rajahs and exercise great restraint if provoked. Living up to their ideals, they found themselves winning friends and growing rich.

Among sea captains in trade with Sumatra, George Nichols, one of the best, wrote about a visit he had made while Joseph White Jr. was on his own tour of the Orient in 1802. At twenty-three, Nichols commanded the two-hundred-ton bark *Active,* a heavily armed privateer-fashion with cannon and swivel guns and muskets, as were all of Salem's East India trading vessels. After landfall at Hog Island, so called, a bull's-eye on a twelve-thousand-mile trajectory, he proceeded with "utmost caution" to the outport of Muki and came to anchor alongside the much larger Salem ship *America.*[16] Captain Briggs resented the intrusion, but Captain Nichols soon was weighing the rajah's bags of peppercorns as they came down from the hills to the beach.

Nichols moved easily among the natives, picking up their language and adopting their mode of dress in the tropical heat: a turban, a short, open jacket, and striped silk cutoffs, with a kris, or dagger, and a short sword tucked in the waistband. He respected their reputation for violence and never spent the night ashore, nor did any of his men. Atjehnese visitors to the *Active* had to lay aside their weapons before coming over the rail; still, some of the Yankee sailors feared them by appearance alone, with their eyes flashing and their lips and teeth blackened from chewing narcotic areca and betel nuts. Nichols's first mate, Slocum, utterly refused to leave the vessel, "he was so much afraid of the natives."[17]

Despite many precautions, Nichols had problems. One day a man from Briggs's ship antagonized a native, who tried to knife him. Missing his mark, he began chasing one of Nichols's own crewmen. Nichols hustled through the stirred-up crowd and caught up to the aggressor, clapping him on the back and demanding to know, in his own tongue, "what he meant by such doings." Then, following local customs, Nichols sent for the rajah, to whom he "complained of the man" and stated "that if ever anything of the kind occurred again I would immediately resort to my ship, fire upon the town, and destroy it, adding, 'You know I could do it.' "[18]

Nichols's threat was real enough. Salem captains were on their own when out in the world. To the islands of Java and Sumatra, they usually carried no outward cargo—New England produced nothing of value to the people of the Orient—so they took sea chests full of specie and enough cannon to outgun the local artillery. The whole point was not to use them.

George Nichols, fortunately, did not hold a grudge. That afternoon, upon returning to Muki from the *Active,* he encountered "the Malay who attempted to kill my man. He was seated upon some bags of pepper, and, being at leisure, I sat down by him. With his permission, I took his creese [knife] in my hand and found, upon examination, that it was poisoned, and the least wound with it would have caused instant death. This Malay was a very civil, pleasant fellow, and one of the smartest men I ever knew. We afterward became very good friends."

In showing respect to the locals by dressing in their attire and learning some of their language and spending time with them, Captain Nichols won a trading advantage: "Nothing pleased the natives more than to find me ready to conform to their customs. I often walked arm-in-arm with their leading men, went into their huts to light my cigars, and, offering them some, would sit down and smoke with them."

Friendship, improbably, would permanently mark the relations between Christian Salem and Muslim Sumatra, good partners across the waters separating a sophisticated Western capital and a scattering of bamboo villages. For all of their daunting reputation, the Atjehnese would not cause problems for the ships and sailors of Salem; and trade along the Pepper Coast would be preserved in unbroken peace over the course of hundreds of voyages and many millions of dollars in profit.

In Calcutta, Joseph White Jr. had negotiated for a fortune in cotton textiles, and then, after dropping down to Batavia[19] to acquire first-quality sugar, he had met Franz Bessell, the Prussia-born agent of the Dutch East India Company for both Java and Sumatra.[20] Bessell, a man who had been out in the islands too long, had recognized in White the very fellow to whom he might entrust his most prized possessions.

No supercargo of Salem had ever brought home boys from his travels, but Joseph White Jr. stepped onto White's Wharf holding the hands of little Charles and Mathias Bessell, who came complete with large trust funds. Joseph's adoptive parents helped the young bachelor in his new role as father, but they themselves had not finished with their own family. In 1805, in their mid-fifties, they took in an orphaned grandniece, six-year-old Elizabeth White Carlton, as their last child.

The sociable, handsome White brothers had become popular fellows, high-spirited and partygoing, devoted to their careers and to things military—both had been elected officers—and to the town's Republican politics, then dominated by the Crowninshields. Advised by the young lawyer Joseph Story, the five Crowninshield brothers, partners in a shipping firm, had adopted Jefferson's Republicanism, while their cousins the Derbys had carried the banner of Federalism. Between the Derbys and the Crowninshields there was constant civic warfare, forcing the townspeople to take sides, Federalists and Republicans, Anglophiles and Francophiles, evenly matched, with separate newspapers, banks, insurance companies, churches, and neighborhoods. The merchants of the divided city continued to wrest great fortunes from the world, and the money flowed in with the tides even as Salem grew more deeply riven.

In October 1805, Lord Nelson's ships had destroyed the French naval fleet at Trafalgar, a victory with global impact. At the outset of 1806, however, the reverberations of Trafalgar had not reached America, and Salem was thriving as never before. The world's wealth, channeled into the streets and countinghouses, raised up all classes in Salem. Artisans became contractors, hustling traders and astute mariners rose to become merchants, merchants became masters of global trade with a fleet of about two hundred tall ships in foreign trade. Their return cargoes were not luxuries: America had no sugar, salt, pepper, coffee, tea, or iron and very little of the cotton cloth that Salem imported by the hundreds of tons. A smaller fleet of coasters carried goods to and from other American ports.

Salem's riches, or a part of them, went into new architecture that was suitable for an imperial capital. Several mansions went up on Chestnut Street, the new boulevard for rich Federalists; but the finest house was built at the other end of town, on Essex Street, near the White mansion. It was designed by Salem's architect Samuel McIntire for John Gardner Jr., a merchant nephew of Hasket Derby.[21] Around the corner was the entrance to the town Common, recently redeveloped as Washington Square, a fourteen-acre greensward with lofty wooden arches at the corners and a perimeter path for promenading under young poplars.

During that same year, Stephen White had begun his own trip overseas. Although Napoleon's armies dominated the Continent, Britannia ruled the waves, which meant, post-Trafalgar, that English shipping was free to take back the worldwide trade that had been ceded to the neutral Americans. The British therefore began blockading much of Europe and all of the Caribbean, which forced American ships to light out for other markets. It was a dangerous world, but most American shippers were not dissuaded: they added armament and crewmen to their vessels and took their chances. There was too much money at stake not to try. In 1792, the total value of American export cargoes had been just $21 million; in 1806, American vessels would carry more than $100 million in exports, $60 million of it in goods that had been imported and were reshipped abroad.

A sudden upward spike in European prices irresistibly summoned Salem vessels and cargoes to the Continent. In May 1806, sailing as supercargo, Stephen White had shipped out on board the three-year-old *Mary & Eliza,* owned by his adoptive father and commanded by one of Stephen's older brothers, John White, twenty-three, on his first voyage as captain. The first leg of the trip took them to Leghorn, or Livorno, in Italy, a great mart of southern Europe, where Stephen used the services of Patrizio Fillichi, an experienced agent who would remain a lifelong correspondent. From Leghorn, Captain White navigated the *Mary & Eliza* ten thousand miles to Calcutta, the brilliant polyglot capital of Bengal. Stepping onto the dockhead, Stephen White entered another world, one for which all of the stories had not prepared him. The streets and squares of Calcutta were full of astonishing scenes, thronged by the naked, the bearded, and the turbaned, by veiled women and girls, snake charmers, dignified holy men and abject beggars, people of all races and colors speaking a babel that somehow was intelligible, amid a fantastic architecture, under the blazing Eastern sun.

In their free time, Stephen and John purchased mementos and sampled some of the local customs, including the charms of the hookah, or hubble-bubble, the ornate water pipes used for smoking tobacco, opium, and hashish. Stephen made many friends in his visits to the merchants and maharajas. One, Ram Chinder Miter, would still be writing letters to him a decade later, offering his services as an analyst of the markets. Americans took pride in the firm friendships formed with their Indian hosts. Many a Salem mansion had on its walls the portrait of a turbaned merchant of Calcutta or Bombay—honorable, wealthy, gracious, intelligent men whom the Salemites genuinely admired and sought to emulate.

Stephen White concluded his business by taking on a large cargo of colored and white cotton muslins, among other goods.[22] They began the homeward trip in early April, carrying two passengers who had come up from Batavia: Franz Bessell, fifty-two, and his third son, Frederick, looking forward to a reunion with his two Salem brothers. The *Mary & Eliza* made good time to the Cape of Good Hope and then to St. Helena, whence John White began a sprint across the Atlantic, with the crew piling on all sails to outrace any British or French predators. A few days from home, they were overtaken by a hurricane. More than equal to this final challenge, Captain White battled onward and broke into the clear of Massachusetts Bay. The *Mary & Eliza* arrived triumphant in Salem Harbor in August 1807. Captain and supercargo had made a good voyage for the house of White; and John posted over to Marblehead to claim his prize, Elizabeth Blackler, whom he married in a jubilant wedding ceremony. For his part, Stephen hastened to join his brothers as a member of the East India Marine Society.

Joseph White Jr., twenty-seven, and Stephen, twenty, began the next phase of their princely lives as Captain Joseph White bankrolled their new commercial house of Joseph Jr. & Stephen White, Merchants of Salem. Right away, the partnership would be tested by the worst maritime disaster in young America's history. It was neither storm nor naval assault, but an act of Congress: the Embargo Act, proposed by President Jefferson and passed in November in the belief that the belligerent Europeans would change their policies rather than forfeit access to American markets. The Embargo Act prohibited Americans from engaging in overseas commerce. In the seaports, it was a plague, stilling their fleets and putting their sailors out of work.

During the course of the year 1807, Joseph White Jr. had come to know Joseph Story, the Crowninshields' lawyer, and his large family of siblings across the harbor in Marblehead. Story, son of the local physician, was good company, with many amusing stories about his boyhood in the strange and superstitious old town, among them his job of driving cattle to and from the highlands overlooking Salem Harbor, pastures so remote that his mother would send him off with his jacket turned inside out to protect him from the pixies.[23] A romance had developed between White and a Story sister, and then an engagement, and on January 19, 1808, at the bride's home, Joseph White Jr., twenty-seven, had married Elizabeth Story, twenty-three. It may have been on that occasion that Stephen White and Harriet Story, both twenty, announced their own engagement. Through their double-sibling marriages, the Whites would become more than brothers.

In a matter of a few years, Joseph Story, still just twenty-eight, had risen to the head of the Essex bar, with a lucrative practice and political ambitions that had him serving alongside Joseph White Jr. as a representative in the state legislature. Story was a brilliant strategist and operative. Shortly after the wedding, he traveled to Washington to look after legal matters and to meet with Salem's congressman, Jacob Crowninshield. Story was stunned to find that the embargo, then a few months old, seemed to have become permanent. He wrote the Whites that maritime commerce was being extinguished—thanks to Jefferson, who had long seen it as the basis of Federalist power and had never thought it worth the risk of war.[24]

Story was ready to take action, and sudden death was the catalyst. In April, the stalwart representative Jacob Crowninshield, thirty-eight, a reluctant proponent of Jefferson's policy, spat up blood while speaking in Congress and soon died. Story, knowing that the rest of the family relied on Jacob's leadership, brought together the grieving Crowninshields and organized a Republican caucus to elevate Benjamin W. Crowninshield as successor to his deceased brother. But before anyone was quite aware of what was happening, Story, backed by the White brothers and a host of Marbleheaders, snatched away dead Jacob's crown.

The Whites had dared greatly and had triumphed. After their coup, nothing was the same. They had become the new power brokers, and Story was launched as a leader, free of Crowninshield influence, permanently allied with the brothers White. On August 8, 1808, the sixty-first birthday of Captain Joseph White, Stephen White and Harriet Story, both twenty-one, were wed in Marblehead. Thereafter, the White-Story faction would rule over Republican politics in Salem.

Salem's merchants, Federalists and Republicans, tore into each other over the embargo. Secretly, some of the High Federalists even plotted secession, while proud shipmasters and their crews became smugglers. Story watched and listened and feared the outcome: men were willing to risk civil war rather than live with government oppression. Up close, he was not impressed by his president and party chief, Jefferson, who was quite willing to keep the ships rotting in their docks.

This was unacceptable to Joseph Story and the White brothers, and together they decided to undo the embargo and restore America's commerce with the world. Representative Story visited with the powerful in their Washington hotel lobbies and boardinghouses, and he sketched out a clear picture of the impending calamity in New England. After priming influential men and lighting the fuse, Story confidently left the capital. A few weeks later, Congress blew up the Embargo Act and held a parade for the newly elected president Madison.[25]

Story had become a hero in New England. Although he would remain a Republican and hold the respect of most of his party's leaders, henceforth his greatest admirers would be the Federalists, who recognized in him a kindred soul.

Salem had roared back to life in the spring of 1809. Its population of 12,613 people made it the seventh-largest place in America. Its merchants spent lavishly on ships and within a year had expanded their fleet to 220 blue-water vessels of various types, owned by many firms and individuals. The Whites, sometimes together, sometimes with friends and family, owned ten merchantmen, from the small sloop *Julia* to the 260-ton ship *Alfred*. Most traded safely on the risky seas, but in 1810 the Whites were caught up in an incident at Naples, where a new French policy was invoked to confiscate forty American vessels and cargoes, including the White brothers' brigantine *Sukey & Betsey* and the brig *Romp*, of which Joseph White Jr. was a part owner with Joseph J. Knapp, Richard Crowninshield, Nathaniel Silsbee, and others.

The French and British were still at war, and neutral commerce could still make profits, especially if one was willing to purchase European licenses, send out vessels under various flags, smuggle when necessary, and endow captains and crews with the sovereignty of gunpowder and heavy cannon. Joseph Jr. & Stephen White, Merchants of Salem, pursued these courses for two years with mixed results, but their adoptive father's loans and gifts made all things possible. In 1811, on adjoining lots overlooking the town Common, Stephen and Joseph Jr. put up splendid three-story brick mansions; and their wives' brother, the lawyer Joseph Story, put up a third nearby. Among them they formed the core of the Friday Evening Club, ten friends and relatives meeting weekly to discuss the news and manage the affairs of banks, insurance companies, and the local Republican Party.

The year 1811 closed in triumph with the appointment of Joseph Story, thirty-two, to the Supreme Court of the United States. Story, the youngest man ever so chosen, would remain in Salem, happy in his deep friendships with the Whites and able to spend most of the year in New England as chief of the federal district court. Still, he had to spend a couple of months in Washington. On his first visit to the nation's capital as a Supreme Court judge, Story once again found things far worse than he had thought. He reported to the White brothers that their shipping was in grave danger, for the president had been listening to the men of the West.

In the spring of 1812, Madison and Congress declared war on Great Britain.

Post-war, the Salem merchants loaded their vessels and sent them out, hoping for a resumption of imperial commerce, knowing that they would not have good answers for a year or two. Once the fleet was gone, the Whites and other younger Republican merchants made a point of indulging in long-deferred enjoyments. Joseph and Eliza White threw parties for the Republican gentry, most of whom resided in the east end of town. Their soirees ended with several hours of reels and square dances, interspersed with intricate minuets and other "fancy dances."[26] A black fiddler typically played the music, but formal assemblies called for small orchestras brought in from Boston and a stag line of Harvard students from Cambridge.

The Whites decorated their Washington Square mansion with ostentatious Boston-style furnishings: alabaster statues of nymphs and naiads, mahogany furniture, and impressive paintings and prints (*Aurora* and *Rum* were favorites). Joseph had 175 leather-bound volumes on his own shelves and membership in an old-line private library. His success as a wine importer and his fame as a host were reflected in his collection of French and German crystal decanters, several sets of wineglasses, and a silver bucket and six silver tumblers. For fun, he kept a small yacht; and he got around town in an elegant four-wheeled convertible.

When visitors came to town, he drove them over the bridge to South Salem to enjoy the view from the green hilltop of Mount Pleasant. Steeples and masts gave vertical strokes to the picture of the low-lying seaport of Salem proper, a peninsula running from the Great Pasture cliffs about two miles eastwardly to the sea, backed by the North River and fronted by the South River's inner harbor, where the streets ended in short wharves, big warehouses, and many vessels, with sailors calling and teamsters shouting and small boats and barges moving busily along.

To the right, one saw the broad waters of Salem Bay, streaked and dotted by islands. Along the eastern waterfront, crowded with the sailors' houses and thick with masts and spars, were the lengths of four great wharves and their warehouses and lofts. In the distance were the low hills of Salem Neck and the ramparts of its forts. Across the South Bridge was Salem's downtown, with the steeples of seven churches and the big business blocks and the stores and shops and, close in, a noisy shipyard. Along Essex Street were the two hotels, many brick mansions interspersed among older wooden houses and stables, and the roofline of the grand Derby house.

To the west, distant highland farms flanked the Boston Turnpike, which entered Salem at Mumford's village, a cluster of cottages. The still millpond waters shone in the sun, and the roofs of Knocker's Hole crowded up the slope from the wharfed-out head of the inner harbor. Beyond were the big houses and deep gardens and lofty elms of Chestnut Street in the Federalist West End. Beyond them, across the North River, rose the green hills of the rural section called Paradise.

Some people thought that Colonel White enjoyed himself a little too much for a merchant and a military leader. It was true that he was often ill; and his former minister William Bentley saw him as "a young man of high relish for social life who has long been paying for the freedom of his pleasures." But if Joseph lacked the stuffiness expected of his rank, most people liked him better for it. Few in Salem had put more into the war effort, yet Joseph White Jr. was preeminently a man of peace, a bon vivant, a lover of people and of ships, wines, food, trade, and adventure. He looked forward, with high hopes, to the arrival of profitable cargoes.

Politically, things were improving: the Republicans seemed capable of taking back Salem's seat in Congress, held by old Timothy Pickering. As their candidate, they drafted Nathaniel Silsbee, a busy merchant and Crowninshield in-law; and Silsbee, to his surprise and regret, won. In Washington, Judge Story had become the favorite of Chief Justice John Marshall and had just set off a bombshell with his majority opinion in *Martin v. Hunter's Lessee,* holding that federal courts overruled state courts in all constitutional cases. Few had made such large claims for the authority of the national government or gone so far to weaken the power of the states—a power jealously guarded by the slave states especially. Marshall had an ambitious agenda: for the upcoming Court session, Story had also prepared opinions in favor of a strong navy, an activist judiciary, a shipping and navigation act, and a merchant-friendly national bankruptcy system. For all of his influence, Story was not well paid as a judge, and he wrote to Stephen White that he might quit and take up a lucrative law practice in Baltimore. He asked that Stephen talk this over with Joseph Jr. and their brother-in-law William Fettyplace.

Joseph White Jr., however, was not feeling up to a discussion. He had been fighting a sickness of some sort—it was hard to know what it might be; the doctors could not agree. Within weeks the illness turned serious, much worse than his big bout in 1813. Matters of trade and politics, for which he had lived and worked his whole life, now began to slip away. As he lost his strength, he had to let go of that world and refocus on the smaller world of his family—his wife, Eliza, and three little girls—and on his own life, and the fight against whatever was trying to kill him, and he not knowing what to do, not believing that it was happening, and certainly not ready to die.

Through the cruel weeks of April, the colonel struggled on, with much of Salem praying for him. In early May, as flowers bloomed in the dooryard of his five-year-old mansion on Washington Square, he succumbed. People were stunned. It hardly seemed possible: Joseph White Jr. had been the life force itself. In the newspaper, his passing was treated as a public calamity, and he was remembered as "liberal in his views and principles" and "ever ready to extend the hand of charity, or to promote any objects of public utility; and his mansion was the abode of hospitality and friendship."

Eliza Story White, thirty-one, and her children—Elizabeth, six, Mary, five, and Charlotte, one—inherited a homestead valued at $7,000 and other property worth $30,000, plus the partnership with Stephen, which was to be divided with Eliza. In fact, it was not. They agreed that she would be a full partner in the firm and that he would manage it for the benefit of both families. Captain Joseph White volunteered to act as trustee and referee in any matter that might threaten the stability of the arrangement, which enabled Eliza and her little daughters to stay on in their lovely house on Washington Square.

Joseph's death fell very hard on many people—his wife and children, his parents, his foster parents, his siblings, and his many friends. None, perhaps, was as affected as Stephen White, twenty-eight, for whom life without Joseph seemed impossible. Since boyhood, Stephen had idolized his older brother, and for years they had been best friends and confidants. They had done everything together, had married sisters, had built their houses side by side, had fought political battles and won honors, had built ships and sent them into the world. For Stephen, things could never be the same. Only Joseph knew what it was to have been transformed, with the wave of a wand, into a prince—and to have struggled to be worthy of a crown.

3.

WHITE HEAT

After his brother's death, Stephen White stepped up: he had many new responsibilities, as a Republican politician, principal of an international merchant house, head of two families of young children, and guardian to the three teenage Bessell brothers. Thirty, happily married, and in the prime of life, Stephen was considered handsome, with a high forehead, long thin nose, and dark hair stylishly brushed up in front and forward at the temples. He had the face of a Roman philosopher, and indeed he had a taste for literature and the law and a streak of idealism. In his new role he was not alone, for he was supported by the members of the Friday Evening Club and his foster father, Captain Joseph White, grown old and wise and quite partial to Stephen.

The difficulties that lay ahead were prefigured in the summer of 1816, as Salem's mariners returned from their global voyages with bad news: America's carrying trade was extinct; ships under all flags now competed for freight; South American colonies were in revolt; pirates ran wild in the Caribbean; and the shipping lanes of the Orient were jammed. These changes were epochal.

Worldwide, the British had emerged far stronger than before. On every sea the Royal Navy held sway, not least in the Indian Ocean. Liberated by London's new antimonopoly policies, the merchants of Liverpool alone had sent dozens of vessels into markets formerly dominated by Americans.[1] Most crucial was the transformation of India, from which Salem had been absent for three years. There, the beautiful handwoven textiles of the pre-war years had all but vanished as the British had forced the Indian weavers to go work in the fields of new

THE BRIG NANCY ANN *OFF MOUNT VESUVIUS. Brigs, not ships, made up most of Salem's overseas fleet. Two-masted with square sails set from cross-yards, the typical brig was 80 feet in length and 200 cubic tons in capacity, manned by nine seamen, two officers, a boy, a carpenter, a cook, and a steward, and was commanded by a shipmaster (in this case, Richard J. Cleveland of Salem, bound from Naples for London with a cargo of wine, raw silk, and licorice).*

English-owned cotton plantations. In a total reversal of the earlier trade, most cotton textiles in the Orient now came from Great Britain.[2]

India's raw cotton fed Britain's huge manufacturing capacity, formerly dependent on the cotton of the American South, which had been inaccessible during the war. In the English and Scottish industrial cities, steam-powered looms produced millions of yards of muslins in imitation of the colors and textures of the best in India. High-quality knockoffs—calicoes and paisleys and ginghams—flowed out of the factories of Liverpool and Manchester at a price so low that both India and America became prime markets.

The British had supplanted Americans as the freighters of choice in the Orient. British entrepreneurs conducted a robust trade throughout the region using Salem-sized vessels based permanently in the East. The British had never had much access to specie, but now they had something just as good: opium.

Produced in Bengal poppy fields, opium was auctioned to East India Company licensees and carried to China in country vessels. Bengal-based British merchants traded into the southern archipelago as well, exchanging cloth and opium for gold, pepper, sugar, coffee, and tin.

All of this had its impact on Salem, whose pre-war trade in Oriental textiles had been its most profitable. But the worst was yet to come, in the form of a proposed tariff. The British pushed thousands of tons of their wonderful factory textiles into American seaports, thrilling consumers but infuriating politicians. In Congress, House Speaker Henry Clay thundered against the British onslaught and praised American manufacturers as patriots. He proposed a protective tariff—something never before attempted—with duties so high as to exclude most imports. Clay, more than anyone, had been responsible for pushing the country into war; and he reigned as the most powerful man in America. Nowhere in his formula for a revitalized economy was there a place for foreign trade, especially as practiced by treasonous Federalists.

Fearing the prospect of this huge barrier, the East India merchants of Salem, Republicans included, petitioned Congress to prevent "the ruin which impends over their trade from the adoption of the proposed tariff on imports."[3] But President Madison and his cabinet deferred to Speaker Clay, whose pet Society for the Encouragement of Domestic Manufacturers considered maritime enterprise as an un-American activity: "We cannot help regretting that not only the objects of our commerce, but our moral and political opinions, have been too long of foreign manufacture. Shall we manufacture for ourselves, or shall Britain manufacture for us?"[4]

The Tariff Act of 1816 passed easily. It hit Salem hard, effectively killing off the faltering trade in cotton textiles, with only two out of fifteen Calcutta ships able to continue—and those two had to sell their cargoes abroad.[5]

Turning from the problems of world commerce, Salemites, on a post-war high, focused on making over their home port as a modern city. The cheerleaders, Stephen White and Joseph Story, persuaded their townsmen to authorize public works of all sorts: tree plantings, sidewalk curbs, paved roads, new schools, a new Town Hall and marketplace, and a new charity house for the poor and sick. When some grumbled about emptying the treasury, Story replied with a new concept: deficit spending. Take out bonds for important projects and let the prosperous citizens of the future help pay for the ongoing benefits created in 1816. Everyone had seen the great work going forward at Boston; if the Bostonians could tear down hills and fill in ponds and coves to create whole neighborhoods, surely Salem could pave its streets and put up some new public buildings.

Few people doubted Salem's destiny. For forty years, it had been a place where good things happened, with rewards for those who abided by the strict rules of local society. Those rewards included freedom from crime. In Essex County, of which Salem was the seat of government, major crime did not exist; and Salem had long been so peaceable and secure that it did not even have a prison. Its jail was occupied mainly by hard drinkers and by jaunty debtors, singing songs, always about to be released. Those guilty of more serious charges were kept locked up in the rooms of the jailer's large house.

Salem did have its social problems, alcoholism foremost. Alcohol constituted a very big business: Salem had six distilleries, a brewery, and warehouses full of imported liquor and wine. In every setting in the seaport, from merchant to laborer, the men drank their way steadily through the day. The distilleries made rum, the drink of choice: sweet, thick, dark New England rum, transformed from Caribbean molasses and lubricating the seaport from morning till dark and much of the night. Those worst afflicted found themselves lolling in the town charity house or working in the ropewalks, where the line spinners spent their days trudging back and forth along the twisting skeins of hemp. Salem females steered clear of their smoky doorways.

Salem's so-called vicious people—the vice-addicted—were connected with a few bordellos and the unlicensed tavern of John "King" Mumford, an African American who trafficked in prostitution and stolen goods at the edge of town. These were generally tolerated and even protected, for the community's high standards had slipped somewhat in wartime. Early in 1816, the minister William Bentley found that "the habits of war and privateering have sensibly injured the public morals," reflected by a few store break-ins and minor looting during fires. Still, most property was left "uncovered through the night."[6]

Salem's leaders expected a full recovery of the traditional social virtues that came with full employment and abounding prosperity. They relied on a powerful male hierarchy, with ministers in the pulpit, rich people in front pews, blacks in the back, and everyone else knowing their places in between. In addition to the class structure, all levels of society were bound by deference and obligation, including long-running barter accounts among neighbors. The basic unit of this society was, of course, the family, with the breadwinner providing for his oft pregnant wife and big family of children and for live-in apprentices, serving girls, and older parents and grandparents. The men were often absent at sea, so certain women played the role of shopkeeper and head of household—and many were widows. The Bible was read every day, along with the newspaper, the poets, and a few English essayists and novelists, for it was a time entirely lacking in pop culture, in spectator sports, and (except at Boston) in theater, opera, or shows. Childhood was short-lived. Many children died of simple diseases, and those who survived were educated through the age of thirteen, after which boys were apprenticed into trades and girls were bound out to work in other peoples' homes. Only a handful went to college, at the age of fourteen, often to be trained as ministers, in graduating classes of about fifty.

Rituals and calendars had great importance. People worked from dawn to dusk six days a week and kept the Sabbath on the seventh. Gambling was illegal, vacations were unknown except among the wealthy, and women, deprived of education and jobs in the workforce, were forced into very narrow channels, with most girls working as housemaids until the day they escaped into the constraints of their own marriages. Ministers' sermons and church activities had high social and spiritual importance, with certain churches reflecting the interests of the wealthy and well-read—in Salem, these were the three Unitarian congregations—or the conservatism of the orthodox post-Puritans.[7] It was no wonder that women were attracted to the new sects—Baptists, Methodists, Universalists, and evangelicals—which de-emphasized male domination and offered the excitement of ranting ministers, fervent hymn singing, and torchlit night meetings.

In all of this, there was no room for crime or criminals. The sensational Major Goodridge case—a violent crime of the Kentucky sort, in which a traveling up-country merchant had been attacked near Salem early in 1817—had everyone worried about the existence of local brigands; but the criminal, as it happened, was the major himself. He had staged a robbery and framed two brothers in order to win damages.[8] The general lack of criminality is indicated by the fact that this incident reverberated for years.

Other portents impinged on Salem's innocence. Although Salem had no history of manufacturing, its people had concerns about the impact of European-style industrial culture in which crowds of poor factory workers were reported to be unable to earn a decent wage. In nearby South Danvers, Richard Crowninshield still had no functioning factory, but he did have imported Irish and Welsh workers residing with his family in their magnificent brick house, like a displaced Chestnut Street mansion, standing alongside the unfinished factory. Growing up at Buxton Hill, Richard and Ann's half-Irish offspring had found themselves as unwelcome as their parents' workers, and eldest son Dick had taken to lapsing into trances and staring into flames, some of his own making: he had been caught setting fire to the local schoolhouse.

As the head of Stephen White & Co., White was determined to do all in his power to restore Salem's high standing in the world, and to do it through a new sort of commerce, one that avoided high-duty retail goods and instead provided raw materials for the manufacturers. He had no interest in the coasting business, sea trucking to other American ports; but he did see the potential of voyages to South America. His brig *Henry* ventured into the South Atlantic and opened trade with Maranhão, on the Brazilian coast, in August 1816. White's men were the first from Salem to go there, and they found cattle hides of very good quality, in vast amounts, brought down from the pampas and heaped up on the shore. A cargo of stinking hides was worth a lot to the Salem tanners, who produced leather for the makers of shoes, trunks, saddles, and other items. While Maranhão did not have the cachet of the Orient, it did create profitable opportunities for Salemites in their own hemisphere.

White continued to send his tall ships to ports all over the world, although specie was scarce. Now he turned to the Mediterranean, where he did a large business in wine and fruits and marble; and he pushed his vessels farther east to Smyrna, in Turkey, to enter the opium trade. Turkish opium was better than that of Bengal, but London had forbidden British carriers to take it to the Orient. Since 1800, however, Boston vessels had been shipping opium to Europe and America, where apothecary shops sold the drug mixed with alcohol as a sedative known as laudanum. When introduced in the East Indies in 1815, Turkish opium was unpopular with skeptical Chinese merchants, who had since revised their opinion and accorded it top prices in Java and Sumatra as well as China.[9] For White and others trading with the East and hard-pressed to find specie, Smyrna opium was the cure.[10]

White and his colleagues also discovered that they could sell British cotton textiles profitably in China at a price lower than that of the East India Company. Paying with checks ("bills of credit") issued by London merchants, Yankees conducted a trade from Europe to the Orient quite apart from their trade from America. Shipmasters bribed the officials at Whampoa and increased the America-China opium trade from $7 million in 1815 to double that in two years. Whatever could not be smuggled into China was sent into the southern archipelago, mainly through the Dutch-held Javanese port of Batavia. The Malay and Indo-Chinese people in general were already addicted to mildly narcotic betel and areca nuts and leaves; the opium supplied by Western shipmasters created another population of addicts.[11] Salem's richest merchant, Joseph Peabody, led the way in his direct trade with China, and opium now began to arrive regularly on the Pepper Coast of Sumatra. In their role as major international drug suppliers, White, Peabody, and other Salem merchants had found a new way to invigorate Salem's commerce.

At the center of that commerce—fixing values, organizing pools, selling policies, assessing the perils of routes and destinations—stood Nathaniel Bowditch. No one had a better idea of the extent and profitability of Salem's worldwide enterprise than the actuarial genius of the Essex Fire and Marine Insurance Company.

Famous for his *Navigator,* Bowditch had pursued his researches widely and deeply and had written for learned journals on both sides of the Atlantic. In the mornings, after a night at the telescope or among his many notebooks and journals, he would rise at dawn, get his exercise, then dress for work. In a big coat and high hat, the small, slender Bowditch had only a short walk to the office for one of his five-hour days, nodding to one and all as he came and went. In his simplicity and courtesy, in his modest street-level celebrity, he was one of them still, a true son of Salem, with preternatural insight into the risks and rewards of its perilous business.

Bowditch was deeply engaged in his own mental voyaging in the year 1817. Shut up in a chamber of his mansion by midafternoon, Bowditch the scientist would be poring over thick tomes filled with numbers and charts, furiously taking notes and scribbling out long pages of ink-stained manuscript. Several years of steady labor ended in the strange summer of 1817, as he completed his journey to the farthest reaches of human comprehension: translated, revised, annotated, and explicated, Bowditch's version of Laplace's magisterial new work on astronomy, the *Mécanique Céleste,* was complete.

In writing the last paragraphs, he smiled his elfin smile; then he locked up the manuscript in a secret place, to stay safe until the moment when the world might call for it. Affluent as he had become, not even Dr. Bowditch cared to pay for the publication of a four-volume set of books that no one else could understand.

Home from Java, Salem's Odysseus, Captain Richard Cleveland, forty-three, rested from his voyaging. No other shipmaster had made so many voyages to so many places over so many seas. Yet even he, the ultimate independent trader, found it hard to prosper in post-war foreign trade. "The general peace of the civilized world," he wrote, "by producing great commercial competition, made it difficult for the most experienced merchant to project a voyage in which the chance of loss would not be equal to that of gain." Early in 1817, on a visit to New York City, he heard of the revolution in Chile, where he had traded with great success in years past. Cleveland welcomed the news of war: war was the founding of Salem's fortune, and war had sustained it; and he planned a bold, dangerous voyage into this new war zone. Now that the people "had emancipated themselves from royal government, it occurred to me that I might profit by it."

The captain needed a proper sponsor. No one in Salem or Boston, he thought, had the courage to hear his proposal, no matter how large the potential profits. Cleveland of Salem, daring citizen of the world, had a reputation that opened all doors. When he called on the richest man in America, John Jacob Astor asked him right in and gave him all that he wanted: an open-ended voyage to the rebel west coast of South America, with freight of $140,000 in European goods and command of Astor's grand ship *Beaver*, 490 tons burthen, straight out of Washington Irving's book *Astoria*. Sustained by "hope, ever buoyant hope,"[12] with a brave heart and a wild plan, Cleveland and his men cleared Sandy Hook bound for the Pacific.

Cleveland was headed for waters that were beginning to interest Stephen White. Having pioneered at Maranhão, White now became Salem's pioneer in the sealing trade of the South Sea, near the Antarctic Circle. This difficult but lucrative business was dominated by the British and the hardy crews of Connecticut and Boston, whose merchants had a specialty in the oil of walruses and elephant seals and the pelts of seals and sea lions, highly valued in China. White's brig *Albatross* sailed in June 1817 under Captain Joseph Phippen, with orders to make camp in the Falkland Islands and set his men to seal bashing.

As one vessel left, another arrived. Whatever else might change, White could count on the profitability of trade with Sumatra and the on-time return of his brig *Mary & Eliza*, commanded by Captain Joseph Beadle, forty, a man who had sailed for the White family for thirteen years. Constantly at sea since clearing Java Head, 125 days from the spice-scented winds of the archipelago and thirteen thousand miles across the rolling ocean, master and crew at last came upon their own coast in early June 1817, entering Salem Bay and passing the rocky shores of Marblehead. In the fishyards the old men, like natives of some savage village, waved their straw hats and shook their spears of dried codfish and shouted curses of welcome. The deckhands laughed and made as if to fire their guns and instead let fly with a volley of their own happy profanities.[13]

The vessel's three officers and ten young crewmen, along with seventeen-year-old supercargo Mathias Bessell, had sailed in August 1816 for East India. Now, as she came into the wind and let go her anchors, and her men jumped into the ratlines and went running into the rigging to wrestle in her angry sails, the people of Salem gave thanks for the deliverance of this fortunate one of their many prodigal vessels out in the world. The crowd murmured the names of her crew, all suddenly among them again; and family members grabbed their children and headed down to the end of the quarter mile of Derby Wharf to make a little party of welcome.

Captain Beadle arrived in the ship's boat, and the federal revenue officers in their uniforms escorted him, a hero, up the length of the wharf's dirt road and its high-walled warehouses and piles of lumber and freight, to the cobbled street where the yellow Crowninshield mansion surveyed the waterfront. On its roof was a glassed-in cupola; on top of the cupola stood the painted statue of a merchant, looking toward the horizon.

Stephen White was determined to bring the benefits of modernity to Salem, even if Salem was not ready to accept them. The world, which resembled the Middle Ages in its reliance on men and horses to make things go, was suddenly changing, and new enormities were on the way, replacing muscle power and even wind and water. In certain factories, automated looms did the work, tended by humans who had become parts of the larger production process. The new scientists and the men called engineers were the cultural transformers, achieving mastery over nature, channeling the rivers and now harnessing the new power of steam, used in only a few factories stateside but widespread in industrialized Great Britain. Steam also powered the famous new American steamboats, plying freshwater seas and rivers in a new commerce that was already greater than Salem's. Someday such vessels might churn across the oceans, seaworthy and powerful enough to leave the fastest sailing ships astern.

White summoned a harbinger of the maritime future from New York. Arriving one day in June 1817, the steamboat *Massachusetts* came off the horizon, smoldering in the distance, a stripped-down hull with a foremast stump.[14] Out in the bay, she stopped and dropped anchor. People stared at her through telescopes. If she had been a sea serpent, they could not have been more perplexed.[15] Marblehead fishing pinkies sailed past on their way after mackerel, and home-trending trading vessels tacked over to get a better look. Up close, there was power in her repose, as if she were gathering strength, and there was something daunting in her crewless deck and elaborately alien features: rows of huge, poised outboard oars like the legs of a giant centipede, and a big black funnel amidships, raked back and finished in a sculpted dragon's head, with wild eyes and mouth agape, ready to breathe fire. Boys in their moses boats jibed around her, fascinated, listening to the banging in her bowels and wondering what strange things would happen when she woke.

Late the next day, the hull gave a roar and came to life. With a thick cloud of smoke and a racket like a factory, she surged onward, propelled by the brute force of a steam boiler and an engine that drove her straight into the wind, where no sailing ship could go. *Massachusetts* came slouching toward Salem under her own ominous power, frightening and portentous as she entered the harbor. She drew closer and grew larger, and then, sliding past the crowd, she went roaring and smoking into the dock at White's Lower Wharf. For the next few months Stephen White, with the help of Franklin Story, ran *Massachusetts* on excursions from Salem to various places—Boston, Portsmouth, Gloucester— in an effort to educate his townspeople in the ways of modernity.

The Manning family, stagecoach operators, certainly responded. They put up shares in their company at a discount, fearing that stages would be replaced by steamboats. Such confrontations with the future had driven some of the Mannings out of Salem and into the semi-wilds. Richard Manning, the new squire of Raymond, Maine, had built a house there for his sister, the widow Elizabeth Hathorne, and her children. Elizabeth's husband, a Salem shipmaster who had sailed for the Whites, had died of yellow fever in the Caribbean at the outset of 1808—an incident that had turned her permanently against the seafaring culture of her hometown. Another brother, Robert, split his time among a Salem brokerage, the stage line, and up-country fruit orchards. Elizabeth's young son Nathaniel, a semi-invalid in Salem, became an athlete in Raymond, hiking, gunning, fishing, and riding, far from the waterfront to which his father had never returned.

As fall set in, the Mannings found that their stage line was safe. White's steamboat had proved unprofitable and would not be tested against the rigors of the winter. She steamed away toward the South, leaving many questions and much discomfort in her wake.

Early in October 1817, Salem beheld another sensation: the return of George Crowninshield Jr. in his oversize yacht. Here was something they could applaud: a beautiful sailing vessel and a flamboyant Crowninshield. In contrast with the alien utility of the *Massachusetts, Cleopatra's Barge* was a privateer-sized fantasy, built at great expense in Salem and regarded as the finest vessel of her type ever seen. She was also a monument to the ego of the stumpy fifty-year-old rich boy George, a bachelor who drove around town in a bright yellow chariot. His miraculous yacht had sailed in April for the ports of southern Europe, where he hoped to attract royals and come away with a princess. This bizarre quest had struck a nerve, and Salem approved. What would Europeans think when they saw George Crowninshield's imperial vessel and its uniformed crew? How could they resist his energetic charm and his wonderful stories?

Cleopatra's Barge now came gliding back into Salem Harbor, a harlequin with tales to tell. In George's stirring fictions, the Old World had paid homage to the New; but his crewmen said otherwise. On some Mediterranean coasts, the multicolored vessel had been mistaken for a pirate ship. At stop after stop, Crowninshield had been snubbed by the gentry but overrun by armies of freeloaders feasting on huge spreads of food and drink. He had kept repainting and remodeling, hoping to bag his princess in the next port. Napoleon's sister had played him for a fool; his "scribe," Curwen Ward, had stayed drunk the whole time; and the sailors tended to agree with Crowninshield's cousin and passenger, Philosopher Ben, disgusted by the misadventures of "the greatest lump of deception in the whole world."[16]

One quiet Salem evening about two months later, George Crowninshield was relaxing in the saloon of *Cleopatra's Barge,* perhaps lost in a reverie of the blonde ports of the Baltic, when he pitched out of his chair and died. At that very hour, in a house not far away, Curwen Ward, wasted by drink, passed out in his four-poster bed, never to awake, never to know that their cruising was done.

In December 1817, the grand redbrick Crowninshield factory, three years in the making, stood in industrial splendor on Buxton Hill, about to begin production upon Richard's return from a brief trip to Boston. Early-morning passersby noticed something moving inside the great building. Looking closely, they saw that it was smoke, swirling, and then fire rolling through its big open spaces and bursting out of its windows. Nothing could be done to save it. The conflagration gathered force over the course of hours, and the high walls wavered and then crashed into the cellar.

Richard's neighbors came by to stare, and fancy carriages wheeled up from Salem. The devastation was impressive, and the silent visitors were satisfied. But they did not know Richard Crowninshield, a man who thrived on chaos. In the days that followed, he cheerfully directed the cleanup of the blackened rubble and moved his workers and salvaged machines into his own great house, where he threw a party to celebrate the resilience of a modern manufacturer. For a second time, he had lost everything just as his factory was finished; but he stayed upbeat, with a visionary's confidence. New opportunities presented themselves, and he seized them. Swooping down on his dead brother George's famous yacht, he sold *Cleopatra's Barge* in Boston by fraudulent conveyance. The courts reacted harshly.

In the months following the fire, Parson Bentley, Richard's admirer, made several visits to South Danvers to check out scurrilous rumors. He began in bewilderment and ended in outrage. All of the stories were true. Richard and Ann fought in the streets, and woke up drunk, and held revels with the foreigners. One of their young daughters had run off with a pair of Irishmen. In the Crowninshield mansion, as grand and handsome as any in Salem, wanton immorality, if not criminality, had found a home in Essex County. "The tales of this family," fumed Bentley, "exhibit something yet unknown in this part of the country, for want of domestic economy, education of children, management of affairs, and conduct among their servants and neighbors."[17]

The master of Buxton Hill paid no heed to the parson. He had got the prize he really coveted, his dead brother's chariot, blazing yellow and built for speed. Cross-eyed Richard would hitch it to his fastest stallion and take it thundering through South Danvers, descending without warning into the sedate streets of Salem, forcing people to the curb as he cracked his whip and shouted his commands, another Nero.

In post-tariff commerce with the East, Salem's merchants struck on the idea of keeping their vessels out in the world for years at a time, trading in various foreign ports, carrying goods from region to region, and selling freight without having to pay high American duties. The risks of disaster, by storm or accident, were greatly increased, as was the level of danger to the long-suffering mariners.[18] After multiple cargo turnovers abroad, real profitability usually hinged on the value of the final return cargo. What did Americans want?

A few years before, they had depended on the merchants for most of their staples: iron, medicines, porcelains, textiles. Now, protected by the tariff, brand-new factories were producing these same things, to be distributed in bulk directly into the interior by means of new roads and new canals and steamboats puffing up the rivers. The increased availability of goods helped to create a national consumer culture and a preference for cash rather than barter.

In this way, a market economy took over in much of America, from the seaports to the mountain valley villages. The merchants augmented large shipments of viable imports—sugar, salt, pepper, wines, fruit, dyestuff, coffee—with raw materials for their new best customers, the manufacturers: animal hides for tanners, molasses for distillers, shellac and mahogany for furniture makers, hemp for rope makers, dyes for textile mills, ores and minerals for painters and chemists. In addition to the cargoes imported into America, the astute merchant could compete in the world markets as both a shipper of others' freight and a purchaser of foreign goods to be sold overseas. Amid all of these permutations and complexities were good opportunities, but Salem itself had no manufacturers and no canals or highways leading westward. This meant that Salem, as an emporium, was shrinking and that its merchants were more likely to profit by selling in New York City, Baltimore, Charleston, or New Orleans than by landing their hundred-ton cargoes in Salem, Massachusetts.

Accepting the challenges of the new commerce, Stephen White imbibed the spirit of the Medicis: the merchant as nation builder, employer, art patron, and world citizen.[19] Ships sailing under his tricolor house flag represented America in its relations with the world. He savored the moment, in which foreign trade had at last recovered, thanks to lucrative coffee and pepper voyages; and White's successes were multiplied throughout the town. America had a hunger for these commodities, as did Europe, and somehow, despite many competitors, the demand still exceeded the supply.

When he sought a new partner, he turned to his brother-in-law Franklin H. Story, now twenty-one, who had entered the White brothers' employ in 1809 or so, alongside the Bessell brothers. By the age of eighteen, in 1813, he had been signing company documents and serving as a member of Stephen's militia company. In 1817, Stephen had made him a co-owner of a brand-new brig, christened with his name, *Franklin*.

Toward year's end, the partners made plans for White's largest ship, the 343-ton *Wallace*. She would make an old-fashioned point-to-point voyage, given the high retail prices of pepper and coffee. Her master, Joseph Lee, and his large crew were to come straight home. Captain Lee, who harbored his own hopes of joining the White firm, was much admired as a first-rate navigator and an even better teller of ribald tales and surprising stories of his worldwide encounters. It was said that Salem always knew when Joe Lee was back in town from the roars of laughter coming out of the custom house.

Late in 1817, Lee set sail as master of the *Wallace* and co-owner with Stephen White and White's political lieutenant, Dr. Gideon Barstow. After bidding farewell to his new bride, Lee sailed for Sumatra. With him went fifteen crewmen, two officers, and a passenger, George A. Hodges, twenty-six, a Boston merchant and new husband of Stephen White's sister Elizabeth.

Old Captain Joseph White was more than ordinarily interested in the voyage of the *Wallace*. Frank Story had been staked to an ownership interest in honor of his new status as fiancé of Elizabeth White Carlton, nineteen. Just as Stephen had married Frank's sister Harriet, so now Frank, Stephen's protégé, would marry his adoptive sister Elizabeth. Overcoming their reluctance at parting with a beloved last child, Captain Joseph White and wife Elizabeth proudly announced the engagement by which the White and Story families would be drawn more deeply together, in a bond that was keenly resented by another of the captain's foster daughters, the widow Mary Beckford.

Mary's affluent husband, Captain John Beckford, had been murdered years before while blockaded at Montevideo. Beckford had left his family a large estate, and Mary had not remarried. Her eldest, the highly capable John Beckford Jr., was now a teenage sailor, on track to become a shipmaster and not a merchant; and the difference was felt sharply by his mother. Mary had riches but no spouse, and neither she nor her children moved in the upper reaches of the society dominated by her cousin and foster brother Stephen and his friends and Story relations.

Captain Joseph White knew that his vast wealth had the power to plunge his family into conflict. He dreaded the prospect of the feuding that had racked other Salem families, and he did all that he could to promote harmony, if not equality, among his prospective heirs. Mary Ramsdell Beckford was the first of five adopted children. The second, Mary's contemporary, the celebrated beauty Mrs. Elizabeth Cook Carlton, was long dead, as was her husband, of tuberculosis. Stephen's older brother, Joseph, had been the third, and Stephen was fourth. The fifth, Elizabeth White Carlton, was the surviving child of the first Elizabeth. The solace and joy of the senior Whites' declining years, young Elizabeth had blossomed into a rare person, intelligent, attractive, accomplished, and kind. None of that meant much to Mary, whose own four fatherless children had not been as favored as her dead sister's one, Elizabeth, elevated to Mary's own status as a daughter of the house of White.

Frank Story had great prospects as Stephen White's partner and as Elizabeth Carlton's intended husband. Through both, he stood to become immensely wealthy, not a typical Story condition. In this summer of 1818, Franklin and Elizabeth enjoyed each other's company and waited for their future to arrive. Although it would come in various ways, none, they thought, was so dramatic as the return of the *Wallace*, back from the Orient with a cargo that ought to make Frank rich enough to marry his true love.

But the long, withering shadow of "consumption," the tuberculosis that had killed her parents thirteen years before, now fell on Elizabeth Carlton. Anxiety gripped the household. Elizabeth, confined to bed in her beautiful chamber, surrounded by the cheerful keepsakes of her girlhood, suffered through the end of summer and into the early days of October. She seemed equal to the fight.

The autumnal drama played out amid the hopes and sorrows of her lover and visits from several physicians, the attendance of nurses and friends, the prayers of ministers, the constancy of her distraught old parents, and the comings and goings of the Story-Whites.

Red and yellow leaves began falling from the trees, and Elizabeth battled on against the gravity of fate. On Wednesday, October 21, 1818, she died. It was not supposed to happen, according to William Bentley: "The hopes of life were strong until the last," he wrote. Elizabeth could not be resigned easily by those who loved her; and her funeral, from the White mansion, was an occasion of the most oppressive grief. On that very day, the *Wallace* appeared from the other side of the world, arrived with a valuable cargo, just in time for Captain Lee to join the procession to the new White sepulcher, in company with Elizabeth's desolated step-parents and heartbroken husband-to-be.

The world kept calling and Stephen White replied, sending out four brigs and a ship in a period of three months at the end of 1818. Bentley was crowing about the resurgence of overseas trade and the new fortunes being made from shiploads of coffee from Java, India, Mocha, and even South America. Salem had finally mastered the difficulties of post-war commerce—the ferocious competition, the tariff, the falling prices, the changeover from goods to raw materials, the search for friends and partners overseas. Young mariners, caught up in the adventure and profitability of global voyaging, were advancing from their jobs as mates to positions of command, just as shipmasters were retiring with a stake to invest as merchant shipowners. The old promise of Salem was being met.

Building and repairing in the shipyards, prospering from active commerce and good voyages, the waterfront was buzzing. Salem had never been "in greater motion than at the present in fitting vessels for foreign markets."[20] And those vessels now constituted a fleet—and a level of capital investment—that matched the pre-war years. Inspired by Salem's healthy economy and the launching of a "beautiful copper-bottom brig," Bentley wrote an article about the importance of ships and their owners: "We cannot too freely express our obligations to those active merchants, who are the soul and strength of business and who give generous energy to the arts and employments of society."[21] Old Joseph Peabody, owner of the new *Cambrian* riding proudly in Salem Harbor, enjoyed Bentley's praise, but he wondered about his brig *Canton,* sent out for China by the Pacific route and not "spoken" for months. Although no one in Salem knew it, she was caught up in the plotting of Richard Cleveland and the fate of nations.

At Talcahuano, a port in war-torn Chile, the *Canton,* with other American vessels, had been captured by royalist forces. Cleveland entered the harbor, spotted the *Canton,* grasped the situation, and allowed himself to be made a prisoner on board the *Beaver* even as he devised a grandiose scheme to trigger the liberation of all of Peru and Chile. However, on the eve of the uprising he fell desperately ill, and when he recovered he found that the royalists had impounded Astor's *Beaver* and her cargo, worth $220,000. "O miserable man!" he wrote. "You have a prospect of reaping only disgrace and ruin." However, the ship had not yet been sold, nor had half the cargo. He and the *Canton*'s supercargo, Francis Coffin, went to Lima to demand justice for their owners. There, Americans had the protection of the naval frigate *Macedonian,* commanded by Captain John Downes, who was helping himself to a fortune in trade.[22]

The viceroy summoned Cleveland and Coffin to his royal palace and berated them as rebel-rousers, smugglers, and arms dealers. Still, he said, they could expect a fair trial. Cleveland's respectful demeanor won him further audiences. Downes sent a lawyer to assist in recovering damages of $200,000, with $100,000 in cargo still vendible. When he agreed to carry out a mission to Lima as the viceroy's secret agent, Cleveland was handsomely rewarded with restored command of the *Beaver,* an official obligation for repayment of all claims, and an exclusive privilege to trade duty-free.

Cleveland needed manpower, so Downes detached a naval midshipman, Alex Pinkham, to serve as mate over the *Beaver*'s small crew of deserters and jailbirds. They had to navigate between the royalists and the Chilean rebel navy, led by a British mercenary, Lord Cochrane, nephew of the man who in 1807 had robbed Cleveland of his vessel and cargo in the Caribbean. This Cochrane now proclaimed a blockade and ordered neutrals to clear out. All of them did—except for one. Flying the Stars and Stripes, a defiant Richard Cleveland would stay on the coast, hiding in the fogs, visiting in the ports, making friends among governors and merchants, charging exorbitant rates, and ghosting his way past navies and armies, Chileans, Peruvians, rebel Creoles, royalist Spaniards, and always the arrogant British.

Adjusting to the combined effects of British colonial policy and the American tariff, Stephen White was conducting a trade with the Orient in which chests of specie and bales of Turkish opium were exchanged for pepper, indigo, sugar, spices, gums, ivory, hides, coffee, and other things not produced in America. White refitted his old brig *Mary & Eliza,* arrived after a profitable voyage to the Orient. During the summer, worn-out rigging and a topmast were replaced, and new copper sheathing was installed below the waterline. In mid-October 1818, she sailed for Sumatra.[23] A smaller White brig, *Eliza & Mary,* 132 tons, had already sailed for Sumatra via Charleston.[24] Sumatra pepper was still reliably profitable, but trade with Sumatra was not the basis for a worldwide commerce. Other markets had to be developed.

Just as the *Mary & Eliza* cleared for the Orient, White learned of the disaster that had befallen his sealer, the brig *Albatross,* homeward bound under Joseph Phippen with a full cargo of oil and pelts from a year's work at the Falkland Islands. Within a few days of Salem, in the mid-Atlantic, the *Albatross* and her ten men had been overtaken by a hurricane and she had gone down, with only the mate and three sailors surviving.[25]

White's brig *Britannia,* 197 tons, was set to sail in December under Samuel Tucker, twenty-five, a Marbleheader, for the same freezing Falklands.[26] The voyage required some disregard of maritime superstition, but Captain Tucker prepared to go with his men, one of whom, Daniel Bliss, twenty-five, had survived the wreck of the *Albatross.* Some of the sailors grumbled, given the loss of that vessel and the fate of a fishing schooner, also improbably named *Britannia,* which had just wrecked on Baker's Island in Salem Bay. Perhaps these omens accounted for the general drunkenness of Tucker's men when they sailed late on a dark, blustery afternoon. That evening, they ran into a blizzard. Turning back, Captain Tucker was groping along blindly under short sail when the *Britannia* suddenly struck a ledge just north of Baker's Island. All of the men, Daniel Bliss included, escaped in the boats, except for one who was evidently too drunk to realize the danger. Some would later claim they saw him that night, by the glare of the lighthouse beacon, riding the jibboom of the wreck, roaring at the storm.

To Stephen White, the *Britannia*'s mishap, resulting in the shortest trip ever made out of Salem, was but one more difficulty to be overcome in the great game of commerce. He had insurance coverage on both vessels, so he focused on his ship *Wallace,* poised for an ambitious voyage under the brisk, bold, cheerful Joseph Lee. Coming home from Sumatra, Lee had battled his way through a long spell of heavy weather off the Cape of Good Hope, in which the *Wallace* had sprung her bowsprit, foremast, and foretop yard; but he had driven her in overdue in late October.

With murmurs and promises to his wife, Kitty, very pregnant with their first child, Joseph Lee spent the last two months of 1818 overseeing repairs for the next voyage. With a treasure chest of specie for his outbound cargo, he was to hustle from place to place in the Indian archipelago, then head northwesterly to Arabia, then double the southern tip of Africa, dispose of the cargo in Europe, take on another, and set sail for Massachusetts Bay. During the next year and more, Captain Lee was to be assisted by Frederick Story, twenty-one, just returned from Europe and now signed on as his boon companion and captain's clerk. Frederick was the brother of four of the most important people in Stephen White's life: his wife, Harriet, his partner, Eliza Story White, his associate Franklin Story, and his best friend, Judge Joseph Story.

On December 8, repaired, armed, and provisioned, the *Wallace* fired a salute to her home port and cleared away for the Orient. On the passage down the shipping roads, her men could see the wreck aground near Baker's. Three weeks later, as the *Britannia,* salvaged, lay dockside in Salem, the missing sailor's body was found floating in the hold among the barrels. His fellow mariners gathered to see the corpse lifted out, stiff and bluish white, a terrible omen.

Stephen White completed the outfitting of his fifth vessel, the 251-ton brig *Franklin,* with new rigging and several additional heavy cannon, to use on the pirates of the eastern seas. She would be commanded by Stephen's older brother, the gallant Captain John White, forty, assisted by captain's clerk Frederick Bessell, twenty, bound beyond Sumatra to Vietnam in Cochin China, a place not visited by a Salem vessel in sixteen years. John's wife, Elizabeth Blackler White, had resigned herself to another year of husbandless housekeeping with their daughters, Elizabeth and Phebe.

Captain John White was still hoping to make it big. After three years of service in the navy, long past the usual age of retirement from the quarterdeck, he pursued the fortune that had come so easily to the chosen ones, his two brothers. On New Year's Day 1819, the men of the *Franklin* shook out her foretopsails at White's Wharf. Slowly at first, then gathering speed as more canvas caught the breeze, she made her stately way down the harbor, firing her long guns, bound for fabled ports of the rich Indies.[27]

THE NEW CUSTOM HOUSE. Finished in 1819, the imposing Custom House overlooked the warehouses, distilleries, vessels, and traffic of White's Wharf and Derby Wharf. The grand edifice was something of a boondoggle, built just as a worldwide economic depression caused a sharp falloff in commerce and in the revenues collected from foreign-trade merchants.

4.

PANIC

As the vessels of the East India fleet were making their slow way homeward across the vast waters in 1818 and into 1819, Salem and all of New England began to feel rumblings and tremors from distant regions of the country. Then, with a cataclysmic noise, the overheated financial structure of America came crashing down. The Panic had begun.

The American economy, seemingly destined to roll on forever with the course of empire, had seized up and prostrated large sections of the South and West. Worldwide, the prices of commodities plummeted. in Great Britain, the Liverpool cotton market, which set Atlantic prices, collapsed; and the total value of American staple exports fell by half.

According to the eastern seaports, the West had caused the disaster. For a decade, the nation's main business had been to colonize its own vast interior: clearing out Indians, raising cotton, extending slavery, the hard-driving westerners had funded their activities through wildcat banks that printed paper money and made unsecured loans. Alarmed at the rising levels of inflation, the chairman of the Bank of the United States took drastic action in August 1818 by calling in his bank's many loans to state banks. This set off a disastrous chain reaction, which ended with huge amounts of money being demanded where it could not be found, among western banks and their overextended customers. Foreclosures, bankruptcies, dispossessions, and violent resistance were the results.

While the first waves of the Panic smashed most of America, New England sailed on, buoyed by high levels of equity and banks with specie-backed currency. The newer states were not the only disaster areas. In many towns and cities, manufacturers stopped producing, and thousands of people were thrown out of work. In the face of economic crisis, the nation did not unite. Instead, the various regions split apart as the leaders of the South, the West, the Northeast, and the middle states looked for their own solutions. To western men like Henry Clay, Speaker of the House of Representatives, for whom the Tariff of 1816 had been a good first step toward much wider reforms, the Panic was an opportunity to get rid of Hamilton's old financial and economic system, based largely on foreign trade. It was time for a new one, to balance out the interests of each section.

In the country as a whole, commerce was in a shambles. Customs revenues, $37 million in 1815, were down to $19 million in 1819. The other main source of revenue, the sale of federal land in the West, was negligible, for no one could pay the balances on their loans.

In the privileged seaport of Salem, the delayed effects of the Panic struck home by the summer of 1819. Shipyards fell silent and long-planned voyages were canceled. Salemites fretted about their prospects and lined up for the funerals of an alarming number of staunch old citizens: Enos Briggs, the great shipwright; postmaster John Dabney, the dean of booksellers; Dr. William Stearns, apothecary and builder of the Salem–Boston Turnpike; and Colonel Benjamin Pickman Sr., the Tory prodigal who had redeemed himself as town treasurer, merchant, antiquarian, and raconteur. These men were among the last to connect Salem to its revolutionary past and the glory years of empire building that had followed.

Salem's biggest losers in 1819 were, of course, the poor. However defined—as the sick, the lame, the aged, the addicted, the disabled, the fatherless—they had no savings and no jobs to keep them afloat. Many were old sailors, too feeble to labor for a living; many more were the widows and children of men who had been lost at sea.

As the weight of the depression came down on Salem's marginal workers, some turned to crime: forgery, prostitution, theft, fencing of stolen goods, and counterfeiting. Although Salem had never been as innocent as it liked to think, the illusion of virtue was becoming harder to sustain, despite exhortations from the pulpits and redoubled efforts at charity. A new group, the middle-class Moral Society, focused on alleviating poverty and started its campaign by assailing the elected Overseers of the Poor, old-line merchants whom the Society accused of ignoring the needs of families "addicted to those vices," leading to "poverty, ignorance, and absence of religious principle."[1]

Salem itself was to blame, said the Moralists—the seaport culture itself had created the absence of fathers, the poverty of the sailors and their families, the large number of deaths at sea, the indifference of the merchants. The neediest children were those "whose parents are deceased, or abroad on the ocean, or in foreign climes. There are in this town many children whose fathers have perished abroad by the casualties incident to a sea-faring life." The rich had their own moral problems: "Surely they who enjoy the wealth, luxuries, and conveniences of an *extended commerce* should have a heart to relieve the wants of those whose fathers have died a premature death in *its prosecution*." The Moral Society's criticism hit home. By the end of 1819, the rich men underwrote a brand-new organization, the Salem Dispensary, with free medicine and medical services for the very poor.

Economic darkness spread, and the merchants grew concerned about more than the town's poor: for the first time, they questioned their own business judgment. Clearly, they had plunged too quickly and too deeply into post-war commerce, missing the signs, disregarding the likelihood that war-inflated prices would keep falling until they found a new, solid, sunken level in the world.

The year before, Salem's enterprise had been in "great motion"; now, William Bentley told his diary, the markets abroad were overstocked and "the stagnation of commerce everywhere has given occasion to the endless complaints of the people" gathering in the grogshops and lamenting their lack of work. Bentley saw the problem as epochal. He had never accepted Salem's myth of itself as a superior place destined to harvest the wealth of the globe; instead, he had seen that the world war had created special conditions for Salem's prosperity. The absence of that war now changed everything. Salemites, he thought, had been spoiled by their success and were not prepared "for the slow gains of a general peace," without any of the war-related "rich prizes, irregular markets, and opportunities from public miseries in foreign nations."[2] In a tragic end to the disastrous year of 1819, Reverend William Bentley, sixty, died of angina on the evening of December 29.

From his insurance office, Nathaniel Bowditch had an unmatched view of the Panic's impact on foreign trade. In just one year, Salem had lost about one-quarter of the value of its commerce. In the taverns, the shipmasters compared notes on a whole world of dull markets and paralyzed seaports. Vessels did not go back out to sea but tied up alongside the wharves and rode at anchor in the harbor. Rich men could afford to outlast it, but the younger and more marginal merchants had loans to repay. They bought insurance policies and sent forth their vessels, but most voyages ended in losses large enough to put them out of business.

Nathaniel Silsbee, Salem's congressman and an active merchant, described the faltering Oriental trade, shorn of the textiles of India. Chinese silk and nankeens, he said, were "almost the only manufactured articles now imported from beyond the Cape of Good Hope. Our cargos from thence are principally of sugar, coffee, tea, pepper, and other spices." Specie paid for most of it, but some cargoes were "paid for in skins, copper, sandal wood, and other articles from the Pacific Ocean, in wines and other liquors, quick-silver, opium, and other articles from this and other countries; and by drafts on Europe and the United States."[3]

Even well-established merchants were feeling the strain. Joseph J. Knapp, a strong Republican long connected to the White family, operated West Indies freight packets from Union Wharf and had stock-in-trade worth $5,500 in 1818; but his assets had fallen by $1,000 in a year and would fall again in 1820. Beyond financial losses, he had suffered the worst outcome possible for a merchant shipowner: in December 1818, his brother-in-law Captain John Phippen, commanding Knapp's brig *General Jackson* on a voyage to the Caribbean, had been lost with all hands.[4]

Late in 1819, bad news arrived from Washington: Speaker Clay had an economic stimulus plan, but it did not include Salem. In the bruising sectional politics of the country, Clay took dead aim at the seaports. He proposed a new tariff with higher duties on more types of imported goods. In addressing the crisis, Clay saw his chance to break the back of Federalism, to pillage its remaining strongholds in the port cities. Clay could strike at the heart of their interests—at the shipowners themselves—by passing a tariff and smashing up the Customs mechanisms that helped them stay in business.

When the merchants saw that Clay's solution was another prohibitive tariff, they bitterly protested: bashing commerce was not the cure. Self-discipline and sane fiscal policies, including a strong national banking system, a uniform currency, equity-based lending, and closure of irresponsible banks—these were the necessary measures. But the merchants were only talking to themselves, for the Speaker was the voice of power; and he was a man of the West, perilously overextended in his own finances. What had worked in 1816 would work in 1820. Wrapped in a manufactured flag, Clay made support for industry a test of patriotism. A new tariff had the virtue of simplicity. The merchants, dealing with the complexities of a global depression into which they were sending their ships, realized that America's problems were part of that depression; but Americans did not want to hear that. Speaker Clay had a plan for ending the crisis.

Remarkably, many of the citizens of Salem were not listening to the merchants, either; they had found a different cause, more stirring than international economics. On a bright December morning in 1819, the voters gathered at their Town Hall to instruct Congress on the issue of extending slavery into Missouri. Judge Story, out of his robes, was the main speaker.

Story saw the protracted Missouri debate in Congress as the best chance to begin the discussion of how to end slavery in America. Some hoped that there would be no compromise, forcing a constitutional convention and the withdrawal of perhaps thirteen states to form a new nation without slavery. As John Quincy Adams expressed it in his diary, "if the union must be dissolved, slavery is precisely the question upon which it ought to break."

A great advance had been made that spring with the passage of a federal law declaring the maritime slave trade to be a form of piracy, punishable by death. Since then, Story had already presided at a slave-trade case in which he alluded to the evils of slavery.[5] On this chilly morning, looking out at the crowd of his townsmen, black and white, he assailed the laws under which some Americans were born as the property of others. He decried the rule by which the southern states' white voting power in Congress was tied to the number of slaves they owned. He blasted the extension of slavery as unconstitutional— The needs of the nation outweighed the desires of the various states, and one policy should apply to all people: freedom.

Salem's antislavery rally, one of the first ever held in America, concluded with a demand for civil and property rights for Native Americans, too. In their dealings with the world, most Salem merchants did not believe in imposing white Christian values on others, nor did they support missionary efforts. Regarding Native Americans, most in Salem thought that the tribes had a right to preserve their cultures and homelands, safe from the rapacious agents of manifest destiny who wanted to divest them of territory they had held for thousands of years.

It was an impressive civic statement, but some wondered what Salem hoped to accomplish with its righteous indignation, far from the Capitol and farther still from the frontier.

On New Year's Eve, Stephen White and Joseph Peabody presided at a meeting of merchants. It was a matter of life and death: the goal of their rivals in Washington was not just to curb overseas trade, but to extinguish it. White and his colleagues came together as a band of brothers at last. As chairman they chose the Federalist Benjamin Pickman and as secretary the Republican Franklin Story, and they designated a committee to work with Judge Story to draft a memorial to Congress.[6]

Stephen White was one of the few merchants who continued to send his vessels out into the world with profitable results. He was trading to Europe, South America, and the Caribbean, and two of his Sumatra brigs had returned in the summer of 1819. The *Mary & Eliza,* Captain John Beckford, arrived at Salem with twenty-six tons of pepper for White and seventeen tons for his cousin John White Treadwell. Two months later, when the *Eliza & Mary* arrived from Sumatra, White sent her pepper to New York to be sold. The pepper from a third White vessel, the ship *Adaline*—co-owned by Captain Joseph White and Thomas Gwinn—also was sold into non-Salem markets.[7] In January 1820, Stephen White dispatched the *Eliza & Mary* to Sumatra for more pepper. He had not received recent reports from the *Franklin* or the *Wallace,* his two largest vessels, both making complex voyages fraught with more than ordinary peril.

The last sighting of the *Wallace* had put Captain Lee at Mauritius, the island east of Africa. This meant that he had already made his tour of the dangerous coasts of Java and Sumatra, taking on a cargo of coffee and pepper. According to their plan, Lee was to shape his course for the Cape of Good Hope and make another long trip northward to Europe, where he would inform himself about the state of the markets and proceed to Hamburg, or Ostend, or Elsinore, or sail on to Kronstadt to trade with the czar.

Finally, in mid-February, news of the *Wallace* came to Salem. Sailing in September from Padang, Sumatra, with three hundred tons of rice and nearly forty tons of coffee, she had touched at Mauritius for supplies, then had worked northward to Europe, arriving in the English Channel in mid-December 1819. Having decided to make for the North Sea port of Hamburg, Captain Lee took on a pilot and entered the narrow Strait of Dover in a thick fog and heavy seas, with winds freshening from the southwest into a gale. As night fell on December 19, Lee consulted the pilot, not wanting to come up with the treacherous Goodwin Sands till daylight. Reassured that they were in the clear, he close-reefed the topsails, hauled up the courses, and drove east by south along the coast near Boulogne-sur-Mer. Captain Lee was a cool head and had fought his way through many a hard blow, but he greatly preferred the perils of the open ocean to the darkness and chaos of a coastal storm and reliance on a pilot's advice. A little after eight o'clock, with a massive, ship-long shudder, the mighty *Wallace* crashed into the shore. There was only a minute to act; to fail was to lose everything. Great roaring swells came rolling over her deck as Lee ordered the sails laid all a-back to move her off. Shouting and swearing, the frightened men did their duty, scrambling into the rigging and wrestling the stays into place. But the rudder was gone, and a hard current pinned her down, and the *Wallace* soon bilged.

The ship carried a pinnace and a longboat, and the men on the afterdeck— Joseph Lee, second mate Joseph Cheever, Frederick Story, and seaman Joseph Perkins—took to the pinnace and pushed off into the howling blackness, unaware of how far offshore they might be. First mate James Brown, forty-six, rallied his sailors at the foredeck to launch the longboat, but it slid away and broke up when the *Wallace* slumped over. Brown and his men scrambled to stay alive as the ship's hulk was buried under tons of water with each convulsion of the sea. Her bell kept ringing through the long hours of the night, and she fell farther over until finally the whole length of her deck burst open and the cargo tumbled out. Still Brown held on, realizing that they were in close on an ebb tide; and at three thirty in the morning, he jumped into the surf and got his footing and led his men to the safety of the beach. They stumbled shouting along the strand, but the others did not answer.

Brown had his crew start making a raft to head back out in search of Captain Lee and his party, but suddenly some figures loomed out of the night. A company of soldiers made them captive and marched them over the dunes to the village of Comyea and held them there, forbidden to return to the wreck. In the afternoon the Americans were released, and as Brown came over the top of the dunes, he was treated to the sight of the wreck the *Wallace* being plundered by hundreds of men, women, and children. There was no sign of the pinnace or its ill-fated crew until December 22, when the body of Captain Lee came ashore, and then Cheever and Perkins, washing up among the broken barrels and the scattered boxes, remnants of a cargo carried thirteen thousand miles from Java to the killing coast of France.[8]

Brown stayed on a while longer, out of respect, but the sea had taken Frederick Story for its own.

The beleaguered lords of Salem gathered in the taverns for long, subdued, alcoholic evenings. Their empire was in jeopardy, they were losing the policy war for the future of commerce, and their seaport seemed to be fading—its population had not grown at all in ten years. In Washington, Congress warily approached the explosive issue of the economy. Never before had it dared to intrude directly in the private sector. The Constitution instructed Congress to oversee foreign trade because of its revenue implications, but Clay's tariff was aimed less at raising revenue than at creating an economic system that favored manufacturing. Salem applauded when Representative Ezekiel Whitman of Massachusetts challenged the right of government to interfere in economic matters. Shipping had created prosperity, he said; commerce, "which pushed the Constitution into existence," had always paid the nation's bills. How would the economy be improved by crippling its main source of revenue?

President Monroe deferred to Speaker Clay. The tariff, said Clay, was necessary: the tariff would save the day. America had once been a nation of agriculture and commerce; now it was a nation of manufacturing, too. Behind a new tariff's protective barrier, America would rise again. Bankrupt mill owners would put the factories back onstream, and farmers and ranchers would get back to clearing the forests of the frontier. The seaports were irrelevant to the future of his America.

In the seaports, though, many people had already encountered the industrial future by visiting cities like Pawtucket, Rhode Island. Women and children, the preferred workers, were pale ghosts working in noisy, dark, dusty factories six days a week, dawn to dusk. The Massachusetts Legislature realized that modern life had arrived in their state, too, in growing urban populations and new levels of crime and poverty requiring large expenditures on prisons, hospitals, and public relief. Unprepared for this brave new world, the legislature ordered that the towns be canvassed to see how they conducted relief of the poor. Josiah Quincy, a former Federalist congressman, headed the survey and found that the "desperate and malignant" poverty of industrialized England had arrived in Massachusetts, now the home of seven thousand paupers.[9]

Sure of his footing in Congress, convinced of the triumph of manufacturing, Clay smiled broadly when his man Representative Henry Baldwin resorted to sarcasm: "Commerce has presented herself as the Atlas which supports the government, the country, and all its great interests. Now, it seems, she cannot support herself."[10] There was no reply, yet, but Joseph Story was busy in Salem drafting his argument for free trade and against a high tariff. On this work depended the future of a whole world: the well-being of the seafaring population, the profits and political fortunes of the merchant class, the trading fleet of America, and the nation's connections overseas.

One former merchant who was getting richer was Richard Crowninshield of South Danvers. To the surprise of many, his rebuilt factory was producing popular woolens. His eldest son, Dick, a moody fifteen, could take apart and reassemble any of the patented machines, but Dick was not just a budding machinist. He had a defiant attitude and a predilection for costumes and for fire starting; he liked to affect a Byronic pose and to write poems and songs, and to get drunk with his father's Irish workers, long his best friends, countrymen of his mother. Richard solved the problem of Dick's eccentricities by sending him and his younger brother George to New Hampshire to be civilized in boarding school and prepared for Harvard.[11] No one knew all that Dick had been up to—the fires started, the nasty tricks played, the minor crimes committed. His Salem connections, and even his cousins, avoided him; but Dick found social gratification in other ways.

One summer evening, he convinced himself to go incognito to a South Danvers barn dance, where the locals did the high-stepping contras and breakdowns of their sturdy forebears. The barn was bright with lantern light as the fiddler dropped in the first droning notes of the dance, summoning males and females in opposition, two lines slowly advancing, slowly withdrawing, wary and poised, then colliding as the tune kicked in and the men and boys were swinging their partners over the floor. Dick watched as they flew around the room, forming and breaking ranks in time to the music, then pairing off with a woman or a girl for a hard rush around the hay bales of the periphery. The villagers danced with all the energy and skill that the hard-driving fiddler could unleash.

Among the pretty girls, one was the star: a teenage stranger who had something of the gypsy about her, with a flashing eye and a teasing smile. Typically, a barn dance did not attract girls from beyond the neighborhood, let alone one so striking. Tall and beautifully outfitted in bright silks and ribbons, she danced with a rare strength and freedom and soon became the center of attention. Her partners—a different one for every dance—found her cool and pliant and self-possessed, with no betrayal of a hard-pounding heart that felt as if it would burst. Veering in and out of the familiar country figures, she kept moving and smiling and swirling, thrilled and terrified. Before the end of the last reel, the gypsy skipped out of the barn into the darkness. A few men followed, too late, stopping to watch as their fantasy disappeared out of the barnyard and down the street. The panting teens and grinning men would not see her again, but the dancer would see them, look them right in the eye, as the brash boy Dick Crowninshield, and they would never know—just as they would never once in their dreary lives feel the pure exhilaration of such a night: the wild rush of otherness, the crazy thrill of risking everything, pointlessly, and coming away triumphant.

Away from home, Dick thrived, in his fashion. By threats and violence, he led his fellow students into secret sadomasochistic games and manipulated them to act out his contempt for adult authority. Once he locked a terrified, bellowing, shitting cow in the library of the headmaster's house; another time he ruined a formal presentation ceremony by substituting moldy leather patches for shiny medals. Dick saw the absurdity of everything, and the futility. Adults were pompous frauds; teachers were sadists who would hit boys with a stick, as hard as they could, to enforce the rote performance of pointless lessons and tasks. To Dick, it was all a ridiculous waste of time, to be subverted whenever possible. He was good at his work, and so sarcastic and casually violent that other boys willingly took the fall for imputed crimes. Over time, Dick had not shone as a scholar, but he had learned a great deal in school. And in later years, none of his classmates ever forgot the strangeness of their days under the spell of Dick Crowninshield.

In his *Memorial of the Merchants & Others Interested in Commerce in Salem & Its Vicinity, Addressed to the Congress of the United States,* Judge Story delivered a strong brief for commerce. The contest, however, was not in a court but in the House of Representatives, where the rich and generous manufacturers had made impressive converts to their cause. Commerce with East India, Story advised, was a "trade in which Salem has been long and deeply and successfully engaged; a trade, too, which . . . has largely contributed to the revenue of the United States." He noted that the Tariff of 1816 had badly damaged Salem and its commerce with India, forcing "ship owners, and seamen, and commercial artisans" to make painful sacrifices that they "had borne in silence."

Story and the Salem merchants closed by asking Congress to uphold a "system conceived in political wisdom, justified by experience, and approved by the soundest maxims of national economy." The *Memorial* was a strong effort, but on the floor of Congress, which was the final battleground, it would not be heard. Something else, some act of heroism, was needed to prevent disaster.

In the light rain of an April afternoon, Stephen White and the Bessell brothers, his former wards and current associates, walked from Washington Square down to Derby Street, past the big distillery and the warehouses and workshops and out to the dock of White's Lower Wharf. One block from the shipyard where she had been built, Stephen's brig *Mary & Eliza* waited, refitted and ready to begin her twelfth voyage to the Orient. Mathias Bessell, twenty-two, was supercargo, and Charles, twenty-three, was captain's clerk. Their brother, Frederick, was still at sea as clerk to Captain John White in the *Franklin*. The *Mary & Eliza* would be making its second voyage under stubby Captain John Beckford, twenty-eight, with two mates and a crew of ten.[12] The White family went to the harbor to wish them all a good voyage and a safe return.

Coming into the family when Stephen was sixteen, Charles and Mathias were more like his younger brothers, essential members of the clan. White affection, confidence, and privilege had produced a pair of tall, smart young American gentlemen. Mathias, in particular, consciously aimed for a life of personal virtue and of honor and integrity in his dealings as a merchant.

As the *Mary & Eliza* began moving away from White's Wharf, the brig *Washington* arrived from Matanzas, Cuba, carrying molasses and sugar for the merchant Joseph J. Knapp, with Knapp's cousin Isaac as master and with second mate Joe Knapp Jr., sixteen, making his third voyage and his first as an officer. The *Washington,* with extra armament, had avoided attack by the pirates now operating in the Caribbean. At about the same time, Captain Charles Forbes and the crew of the old brig *Beulah* came surging into Salem Harbor, overdue from Mocha in the Gulf of Arabia. On reaching shore, Forbes, twenty-seven, was surprised to find a new landmark at the head of Derby Wharf. Gone was the foursquare Crowninshield house from which old Captain George had bossed the Lower End; in its place stood a big building with a broad set of stone steps. It was, they told him, the new federal custom house, looking like a redbrick temple.[13]

For his first command, Forbes had been given the trusty *Beulah* and a good set of cannon. On arrival at Mocha, he had laid out some of his specie on coffee and then had sailed off westward to the torrid desert coast of Africa. For hundreds of miles he had seen nothing but long stretches of empty beach, scrubby vegetation, and a few straggling fishing villages. At last, in the Mozambique Channel, he had entered a gulf, unvisited by Americans, and had made his way to Mahajanga, Madagascar, impressive, if not opulent. There he had found a sultan eager to trade. Forbes loaded up on tallow, gum copal, and hides, with the promise of ivory, palm oil, cloves, gold dust, and salt beef, the stuff of a brandnew commerce. Forbes's breakthrough was a triumph for the new firm of J. W. & R. S. Rogers, protégés of the Crowninshields. As with Salem's first incredibly profitable voyages to the Pepper Coast, the secret of Mahajanga would be kept as long as possible, against the inevitable day that others would flock to Madagascar, laden with gunpowder and the output of the rum distilleries. In the meantime, Charles Forbes was a hero.

And William Rogers, twenty-nine, was jealous. He and Charles had grown up together, and now Forbes was having the life that William wanted for himself.

Back from his second India voyage as a supercargo, he had been playing at the law and politics, trying to make himself fall in love and settle down when he knew that he had a bad case of wanderlust. Rogers, a Harvard graduate, was a handsome fellow, with brown eyes, thick dark hair, and a somewhat sultry expression. A firm Republican who had spent time in the American legation at Paris in 1812, William had read the law under the lawyer and litterateur John Pickering and had been admitted to the bar and elected to the state legislature. Intelligent and facile, he should have been a success; but a young lawyer needed patience to build a practice, whereas a shrewd and lucky overseas trader might strike it rich in one voyage. His three older brothers were all former shipmasters turned successful merchants, and William wished to join them.

In his first voyage to the Orient, as supercargo, he had been entranced by the polyglot city of Bombay. It was better than Paris. In two weeks ashore, he had explored the various districts of the metropolis and visited the wilds of Elephanta Island, where he found torchlit caves of "imposing grandeur" filled with gigantic figures carved into the high walls: "as numerous a collection of gods and goddesses, he- and she-devils, saints and heroes, as ever existed in heathen mythology." Rogers had the usual Republican reaction against the British: he felt that their tyranny had struck deep into the soul of Bombay, and he resented it bitterly. On the inevitable day that the United States became the great power in the world, the British would see "their scepters broken, their thrones and palaces converted to the purposes of liberty and justice, and their long and boasted dynasties sinking into oblivion." Rogers thought that Christian missionaries, even Americans, were no better than the British. Up close, he saw them as weak, adulterous agents of cultural imperialism and financial exploitation.[14]

He much preferred the company of his agents, the native Parsees, speakers of Sanskrit, the holy and literary language, and practitioners of Zoroastrianism. The Hindus he considered "degraded" idol worshippers, an opinion highly colored by his presence at the citywide Holi festival, a sort of Mardi Gras in which "everything gives way to debauchery and drunkenness." It was not exactly Thanksgiving in good old Salem.

On the voyage home, Rogers filled his journal with impressions. Everything he wrote reminded him of how different America was and how excellent were its laws, customs, and freedoms; yet he could not deny the power of this exotic culture and the fascination of its otherness. Like so many others from Salem, he had discovered that the world's peoples were just as successful and civilized as Westerners, and as deserving of respect. At home, William had taken his pay, profited from selling some "adventures"—goods that he had bought on speculation—and restarted his law practice. But he was not like his friend Franklin Story: he did not fall in love with a rich Salem girl or with his profession.

The Orient, and its lure of wealth and exotica, kept calling to him, as it had to Charles Forbes and so many others, with an irresistible song.

The Committee on Manufactures pushed Congress toward a tariff vote. Salem's *Memorial* was distributed widely, with a tract from Virginia agricultural societies that explained the depression as part of the world's transition from war to peace. American manufacturers, they said, already had a big advantage over foreign competition. Not every manufacturer had a right to prosper, and a turning inward was dangerous. Were Americans afraid to trade with the world? If so, consider China, sealed off and backward, "the timid slave creeping through the shallows in his clumsy junk," versus the hardy American shipmaster and his men charging over every ocean in their great ships, "penetrating to the antipodes."

Speaker Clay said that the interests of foreign traders did not override the needs of manufacturers, the great hope for the future, who asked only for a few years of better protection to make America self-sufficient. On April 21, the tariff bill was presented for final debate, and the Speaker overruled Salem's representative Nathaniel Silsbee three times on proposed amendments. When Silsbee got back to his boardinghouse he felt ill, and he swore to himself that he would never accept renomination to Congress.

At the outset of the final week of debate, Representative Henry Baldwin of the Committee on Manufactures, ironically self-described as one of "the Goths and Vandals of the West," argued that the merchants had used the commerce-based revenue system to get rich while sticking the consumer with the costs of the duties. They were tools of the English and unworthy of credit and support.

Baldwin ended his speech by blasting commercial men from Savannah to Boston for fleecing the federal government. Only one seaport escaped his wrath: Salem, the model of honorable American commerce, even by the cynical standards of Henry Baldwin.[15]

Nathaniel Silsbee was understood to be too unwell to reply. Sick and dismayed, feeling betrayed by manufacturing-oriented Massachusetts colleagues, Silsbee rose to be recognized and went to the well of the House chamber. He thought of his late brother-in-law, the admirable Jacob Crowninshield, who, in the midst of addressing Congress in 1808, had spat up blood prior to an untimely death.

Silsbee began modestly, not as a Salemite but as an American. "Being an inhabitant of a commercial district of the United States," he said, "I feel compelled by a sense of duty to my constituents to make a few remarks upon the bill now under consideration." Then the former shipmaster straightened up and let fly. "It seems to be generally admitted, sir, that every interest of the country is depressed at this time; and what does this bill propose—measures for the relief and benefit of all? No, sir; its object seems to be to impose new restrictions and additional burdens upon that interest which, at this moment, is more depressed than any other: I mean the commercial and navigating interest. In the course of the past year a loss has been sustained by the merchants of this country, *of at least twenty five percent of the whole capital employed in foreign trade,* and the prospects of the present year are not more flattering than those of the past. There will not be so much capital employed this year as there was last, because there is not so much *to* employ; but, in that which *is* employed, the loss, judging from present appearances, will be as great or greater than it was last year."

In a few short blasts, Silsbee had reduced the issue to one of fairness and justice toward commerce and all who depended on it. The House realized that here, at last, was the authentic voice of foreign trade, and the speaker was not a sleek, polished, downtown lawyer, but a tall, rawboned, somewhat haggard man of Roman dignity. Silsbee spoke as one who even now was keeping many families afloat and many vessels at sea under the Stars and Stripes. He acknowledged the manufacturers' statements that "our ships are rotting at the wharves;

that they are not worth half their cost; that a large portion of the merchants are already bankrupts; and that others are almost daily added to the list. If this be true—and no one who has recently visited our seaports will be inclined to doubt it—if this be true, I say, is it wise, or is it just, further to depress this interest at this time?"

Silsbee had seen the deadening hand of the depression on the waterfront of Salem and other seaports and the large losses of the merchants. The real sufferers, however, were the seafaring families. The sailors, who in wartime had made up the crews of America's privateers and victorious navy, had already had their wages cut in half, without benefit of the new tariff. "Shall we, Mr. Chairman," asked Silsbee, "deprive of their daily bread, shall we drive to our poor-houses, those brave men whose recent and, I may add, renowned achievements have given such imperishable fame to our country? I hope not."

In this last scene of a long fight in the House, Silsbee played to the Senate, too, which would soon be taking up its own debate. He gave a masterful exposition, with good balance between detailed data and personal reflections. Silsbee gently corrected those who "seem to think that importations from [the Orient] are principally manufactured articles, which is not the case. It is true that large importations of coarse cottons were formerly made; but the present duty from 1816 has operated as a prohibitory one. . . ." Maritime commerce, he argued, was an essential part of the American scene. The country's economic problems were not connected to commerce, nor were they solvable by destroying it.

While he knew he would lose in the House, Silsbee hoped that he might sway a few senators; but he was fading, and he decided to close. At the end, he tried to make his audience understand what commerce was really about: thousands of men employed, the navy supplied with splendid sailors, and the sciences of navigation and naval architecture advanced. But it was all up to Congress: "If it is wished to paralyze the commerce and commercial enterprise of the country, it cannot so effectually be done, in any other way, as by restraints upon the India trade." With one last plea for removing the high duty on India textiles, he was finished.[16]

Most in the House put their faith in Speaker Clay, whose plan, they thought, really was the nation's only hope of overcoming the sectional divisions caused by the economic crash and the slavery extension crisis. Many other issues awaited them. Tired of hearing about auctions and drawbacks and ad valorem duties and other complicated seaboard matters, the men of the West called for a vote. Their opponents could not stop them, and the Speaker's tariff package passed by twenty-one votes, 90 to 69.

The House had spoken. The future of Salem's empire now lay with the Senate.

Silsbee did not spit blood. He felt well enough to stay on for a few days to see what would happen. The Senate was not the House. In the small, courtly, forty-four-man club of the Senate, the members had a respect for one another and a fellow feeling that dated back to the founding of the nation. Like the House, the Senate had one merchant among its members. The imperious Federalist Harrison Gray Otis of Boston wore a gold-laced hat and breakfasted on pâté de fois gras,[17] and he, like many friends and associates, had shifted shipping money into mills. However, while others now called themselves manufacturers and capitalists, Harrison Gray Otis still considered himself a merchant. Unlike Silsbee, a seafaring man, Otis was a blue-blooded Boston Brahmin, born into wealth, educated at Harvard, honored as a peer of the Federalist realm, vilified for the same.

The Senate allotted only a few days for the matter. On May 4, the debate's final speaker was recognized. Otis declared that the intent of this bill was not to advance manufacturing through boosting some tariff duties; no, "this was not the simple aim" of the bill's authors and backers. They in fact intended nothing less than a coup: to effect "a radical change in the long established policy of the commercial and financial system of the nation," to impose a tariff that would leave America "chained to the manufacturing systems," like Europeans.

America, he said, had encountered a terrible storm, but its leaders must not overreact. Acknowledging "a great uneasiness pervading the whole country—a sickening swell of the waves after a long tempest," he believed that soon "the violence of the undulation would cease; that the waters would subside, and the ark rest in safety on Ararat." The tariff bill, he urged, must not pass.

The contest was as close as it could be. Of the forty-three senators present, the vote was split evenly in the West and the middle states, while the South was wholly anti-tariff. In the North, all but one man supported Speaker Clay's tariff package. The final tally, which would end the session and send the legislators back to their homes, came in at twenty-one in favor of the tariff, twenty-two opposed. By the margin of a single senator—and it would always be Harrison Gray Otis's boast that it was he—the merchants of Salem and the other seaports could continue to send out their ships.

5.

LOST AT SEA

Like the clouds of a massive coastal storm, the forces of liberation gathered in the Andes, threatening all that lay below. With a fragile license from the viceroy of Peru and protection from the U.S. frigate *Macedonian* under Captain John Downes, Captain Richard Cleveland sent the *Beaver* on a four-month charter voyage at a guaranteed $40,000.

After nearly three years of hard usage the *Beaver* was wearing out, and so was her master. At the end of the charter, he loaded her with cocoa worth $100,000 in Europe, and he placed $15,000 with the merchant house of Arismendi & Abadia to be invested in goods sent to China. Cleveland navigated the *Beaver* around the Horn without ever seeing the sun and made Rio by August 1820. He wrote his wife, "I doubt whether my voyage has any parallel in the annals of navigation. It presents not the brilliancy of victory, but it is a retreat which ought to be equally creditable to the ability of the commander." On October 6, he came ashore at New York City, done with the sea, rich enough to educate his sons and live in comfort. He was in his forty-eighth year, the thirtieth since he had first set out from Salem with Captain Nathaniel Silsbee on a voyage for Hasket Derby.

In the summer of 1820, Captain John White, thirty-eight, finally arrived in the *Franklin,* home from Vietnam. He filed his logbook with the East India Marine Society, whose new president, Nathaniel Bowditch, took an interest—it

ON THE BEACH. Salem men often found themselves in strange settings far from home, loading commodities in the tropics or stacking hides on a frozen beach. Stephen White, the pioneer in bringing a steamboat to Massachusetts Bay, was also the first Massachusetts merchant to challenge the English trade in oil and hides, conducted from sealing stations on the remote islands of the South Atlantic.

was the longest journal ever submitted. The great navigator showed it around, and John Pickering offered to consult on a manuscript. Flattered, John White began to seek subscribers—a new career as an author might get him the fortune that he had never made.

White's admirers included William Rogers, twenty-eight, now a member of the East India Marine Society. Rogers, studying the *Franklin*'s logbook, concluded that he might be just the man to make Cochin China truly profitable—a new market for Salem, with a new hero. The Rogers brothers agreed and gave him co-ownership and command of his own vessel, the sleek brig *Texel,* four years old and 275 tons burthen; and in November 1820, with a crew of fifteen, Captain Rogers gave the order to clear away for the East Indies.

At the same time, Charles Forbes, that other young shipmaster for the house of Rogers, received his reward. The newly combined firm of N. L. Rogers &

Brothers gave him command and part ownership of a brand-new vessel, quite different from the pokey old *Beulah:* the brig *Thetis,* 182 tons burthen, was a racehorse. Just after Christmas, Forbes, with his namesake nephew as cabin boy, cleared for Majunga to trade with the sultan. Already his owners had sent out another brig, *Nereus,* to Madagascar and then to Zanzibar, the first of scores of such voyages, following in the *Beulah*'s golden wake.

Not all of Salem's sons washed in from the sea: Nathaniel Hathorne, sixteen, arrived from Maine on one of the family stagecoaches.[1] The youth was tall and lean in build, with broad shoulders and a fine Manning head with dark curly hair, arched brows, blue gray eyes, and a jutting chin. He could not escape Salem, much as he wished to. His summer vacation in Maine was over, and once again he was preparing for college at the Archer school in Salem. He moved back into the Manning house in the Lower End with his grandmother and seven unmarried aunts and uncles.

He entertained his younger sister Maria with a hand-lettered mock newspaper full of jokes, letters, stray news, and fake ads. A "great sea serpent" cruised in Salem Bay, but editor Hathorne knew of "no news, either domestic or foreign" and so hoped that "our readers will excuse our not inserting any." Nor did he write reviews, although a Boston theater company had begun a season of local performances, the first in Salem "after a lapse of 15 or 20 years."[2] At the street level—and the horsey streets were not very clean—Hathorne observed that public charity was motivated by "pride, envy, and ostentation" rather than "pure, disinterested benevolence"—the "wealthy man" was likely "to throw a few cents haughtily to a beggar, accompanied with a reproof, and a threat of being sent to the Alms House." Already a resentful Republican, Nat proudly snubbed rich relatives but still could be moved spiritually, as by a guest preacher, Reverend Henry Colman of Boston: "We have never before heard a sermon which so perfectly coincided with our own sentiments."

Nat Hathorne dutifully attended class, read books and magazines, went dancing, wrote his articles and squibs, and took long walks in the evening, down to the Juniper, over to the hills of Paradise, out into the countryside by way of

Dark Lane. When school ended, he did not return to Maine but stayed on in Salem as a Manning clerk, making a dollar a week in the stagecoach office and prepping for college. His uncle Robert would be sending him to Bowdoin, north of Portland, Trinitarian and reasonable in price, and not to expensive Unitarian Harvard. With no interest in pursuing a traditional profession—minister, doctor, lawyer, schoolmaster—Hathorne thought of becoming a writer, "but authors are always poor devils," he wrote to his mother, "therefore the Devil may take them."[3]

A t the local Republican convention in October, postmaster Joseph E. Sprague, a White-Story protégé, engineered the unanimous nomination of Stephen White, Esq., thirty-three, as Silsbee's successor in Congress. "His whole views, interests, and livelihood are dependent on the prosperity of commerce," declaimed Sprague. "No merchant has been more active or enterprising, and none better understands the commercial interests of this district."[4]

White did not attend the meeting, so they waited upon him at his mansion. There, they found that their enthusiasm was not shared by the nominee himself. Stephen White turned them down, stating that "the most serious personal objections" had "induced him to decline the honor of the nomination." Sprague was very unhappy.[5] To walk away from this high office was the act of a man who was quite sure of his priorities. No doubt White had thought about Silsbee's retreat into private life and had decided to remain at home among friends, attending to the needs of his large extended family and his shipping business.[6]

Unwilling to go to Washington, Stephen White yet had large political ambitions. In November, Boston hosted a convention to revise the state constitution, to which Salem sent a bipartisan group of eleven, including Joseph Story and Stephen White. They saw it as nothing less than a chance to start a national movement. American politics were confused as the two parties became one, and various regions contended for dominance. Out of the chaos, something new would emerge; some group holding certain values and principles would guide the next phase of the nation's development. The Massachusetts convention, called by those who sought to make democratic revisions, afforded Story and White a chance to assert their own conservative brand of Federalist-influenced Republicanism. Their movement would be led by a young Federalist former congressman from New Hampshire, Daniel Webster, who had been pursuing a lucrative law practice in Boston but now sought to resume his national political career.

At the close of the three-month convention, Story and White were celebrating. The constitution remained intact in all major aspects, and Daniel Webster was famous[7] for his speeches in the convention and for two orations given outside of it: one in Plymouth for the bicentennial of the landing of the Pilgrims, and one in October in Boston, in which he addressed the tariff bill that had been revived in the House. The tariff, he said, would hurt consumers and require the unprecedented imposition of federal taxes; it would promote the moral and societal ills of manufacturing, as in the industrial ghettos of Great Britain and their poverty and rioting. America had opportunities for all in agriculture and commerce—why create a large, volatile underclass? No sane man, said Webster, would advise his sons to become factory workers, "taking the chance of the ignorance and the vice, the profligacy and the poverty, of that condition, although it were in the best manufactory in the richest city in the world."

His concern for social stability in the aftershocks of the Panic and his powerful pro-commerce views were exactly what the rich men of Boston had wanted to hear, and they came away convinced that they had found the man to serve them in Washington. That Webster, as a lawyer and investor, could also speak eloquently in favor of manufacturing made him all the more useful to men whose portfolios included stock in textile mills alongside titles to brigantines and deeds to wharves and warehouses. These old Federalists had been abused and discredited in the nation's politics, but they had always believed in themselves. Now, in rising statesmen like Joseph Story and Daniel Webster, they saw that their principles lived on.

In Salem, Captain John White told a long, twisting, fascinating tale. After arriving at Batavia in the *Franklin*, he had shaped his course northerly across the Java Sea toward the fabled river city of Saigon. On May 24, 1819, entering the Straits of Banca, near the mouth of the great river Donnai, the brig was attacked by three large Malay proa canoes, pennants flying blue and green, paddles flashing in the sun. Each had a large cannon and dozens of opium-stoned warriors and their poison-tipped spears. Captain White would not run. He warned them off and then gave them a lethal broadside of "grape, langrage, and double round." Two weeks later, cruising the Cambodian coast, the *Franklin* entered a small bay where the locals told White to go seven miles upriver and await permission to proceed to Saigon.[8]

At the village of Canjeo, Captain White and his clerk, Frederick Bessell, had to stay and trade for several days in a place that rippled with "vast swarms of vermin" while voracious tigers roared in the hinterlands. When the local mayor, an old man, came out to the *Franklin*, he grabbed at everything in sight, from mirrors to bottles of brandy to Captain White himself, who described him as "hugging me round the neck, attempting to thrust his dirty betel nut into my mouth from his own, and leaping upon me like a dog, by which I was near suffocated." White had just resisted the ritualized greeting expected between men of high caste.

At dawn on September 7, the *Franklin* of Salem became the first American vessel to reach Saigon. The crew dropped anchor a mile below the city and admired a wide river filled with "boats of light and airy construction, each, in many cases, managed by a single woman, in picturesque costume," while "great numbers of the native vessels, of different sizes, plying in various directions upon the stream, gave a busy and lively interest to the scene." That first night, White and Bessell stayed in a typical riverbank house, standing on pilings two feet above the mud, sided with boards and roofed with enormous palm leaves. Inside were teenage girls, big jars of fish-pickle, pigs, ducks, and fowls, a "blear-eyed old woman, furrowed and smoke-dried," and, asleep in a hammock, "a miserable child, covered with filth and vermin, and emaciated with disease." The morning tide brought the *Marmion*, a Boston ship that White had encountered at Manila. Captain Brown and his supercargo, Mr. Putnam, came ashore, and they and White and Bessell were "surrounded by a bevy of old women, soliciting employments as merchandise brokers and offering us assistance in purchasing our cargoes." He did not realize that they were eunuchs, designated as their culture's trader caste. The Yankees demurred and went on to Saigon, where their appearance caused a sensation. At the "great bazaar or market-place," an "immense concourse of the wondering natives" manhandled these improbable *don-ong-olan,* strangers from the West, with their unreal faces like pale masks.

When he had a chance to observe the workings of the city, White regretted his error in rejecting the female traders' offers back at the house. Women ran Saigon! Everywhere he looked, in every job, women—or those who seemed to be women—did the work. The Americans were also surprised by performances of wonderful six-day "dramatic entertainments" in the crowded marketplace. Equally remarkable were Saigon's exotic animals. Huge elephants served as fire engines. A few "royal tigers" were caged in public and fed on fat puppies. Rhinos, revered, roamed the countryside; Chinese hogs and packs of dogs ran in the streets. The people were "foul feeders," fond of "rats, mice, worms, frogs, and other vermin and reptiles," wrote White, who described most of them as prematurely aged and disfigured by poor diet, bad water, illnesses, and addictions. He himself contracted water-borne elephantiasis, causing violent fever and terrible swelling of the legs and racking pain that would plague him for the rest of his life.

The *Franklin* and the *Marmion* swung at their anchors for almost four months as their masters endured insult, illness, indifference, and occasional rock peltings as they laid siege to the traders of Saigon. Through it all, the Yankees kept smiling, trying gamely to break through. Finally, the two captains understood: the king controlled everything; women were forbidden to make bulk deals; and Western armament was wanted, not goods. Giving up their dream of starting a new commerce, the two captains paid Spanish gold for half cargoes of sugar, promised to return with guns, and sailed away in their tall ships. Each had been given a parting gift of a young royal tiger and a pen full of squirming puppies.

At Batavia, Brown sold White his sugar and the *Franklin* sailed for home on April 29. Soon after, one of his seamen died of fever. White's tiger, "a beautiful female," died, too, when bad weather finished off her food supply and the captain was "obliged to shoot her." He saved the pelt for the East India Museum in Salem. On June 17, in a gale off the Cape of Good Hope, all hands tumbled aloft; horribly, the ship's boy, Nathan Brown, fourteen, lost his grip while furling the main topsail and fell to his death on the deck. At last, a few days from home, on peaceful seas, seaman James Pearson died of dropsy, followed by "a most violent hurricane" that had the men cutting away the spars to keep from capsizing. Diseased and death haunted after two years at sea, *Franklin* staggered into Salem with an unprofitable cargo and three stumps where the masts had been.

The *Marmion* fared worse. Carrying coffee from Java, she had made the English Channel by January 1821; but when Captain Brown tried to force the passage into Rotterdam, ice floes blocked the way and a gale descended from the north. Brown ran his crippled vessel aground to save the cargo. Some of the coffee was removed before a ferocious blizzard set in. Captain and crew escaped, but the four-hundred-ton *Marmion* did not, and pieces of her wreckage washed up all along the stormy coast of England.

John White, like Richard Cleveland, would go no more a-roving. After nearly twenty years in command of Salem vessels, he was done with the sea, except for the writing. He had hoped to end in triumph, but, like Captain Brown, shipless and stranded in Holland, John White had been completely defeated by his misadventure in Vietnam.

Joseph Jenkins Knapp, merchant, did his best to turn a profit in these lean years. America's economy was in recovery, but Salem's bravery and boldness did not count for much in the absence of war; and competitors appeared in every gulf and sea. Some merchants had decided to run their vessels out of the big markets of Boston or New York, but Salem sufficed for more modest shippers like Knapp. He had three[9] older vessels plying a busy trade to the West Indies, each making two or three voyages per year: the 178-ton brig *Washington*,[10] the 149-ton brig *Betsey*, and the 95-ton schooner *Fame*.[11] Captain Knapp was still well patronized in the freighting business and carried assorted goods for his friends among the big-time merchants. He and his wife, Abigail, had the typical large family of

eight, ranging from a newborn, Ellen, to a twenty-year-old, Nabby, and five sons
and a daughter in between. The oldest boy, Joe, now served as second mate on
board the *Washington*. All of Joe's Knapp relatives were seafaring men, as were
the ill-starred Phippens—of his mother's three brothers, two had been lost at
the sea and the other had never returned from a British prison.

While Joe's talents ran toward seafaring and socializing, his younger
brother Nathaniel Phippen Knapp was a different sort: though just twelve, Nat
had been vouchsafed to Harvard. None of the other Knapp boys appeared to
have Nathaniel's studious nature, so it would be the parents' job eventually to
find berths for their sons and give them the same advantages toward a nautical
career that they were giving Joe.

Every day Captain Knapp, a rugged-looking man of fifty with a shock of
still-dark hair, made the same pilgrimage along three blocks of Essex Street. After
passing by his store in the front yard—it was run by his wife and children—he
would go to the barber to get a shave and chew the fat, then visit the 'Change to
listen to the burble and bluster of deal making, then reverse his course and drop
in at the Union Insurance office to pick up Republican scuttlebutt, and then
amble down Union Street, past the old Derby house where he had once lived,
and on to Union Wharf and his warehouse on the pier, with a view of the comings and goings of vessels on the South River.

Union Wharf, once a small island, had many warehouses and piers like
Knapp's, owned by similar self-made merchants who had offices there, with room
in the docks for a couple of vessels at a time and space on the piers for firewood
to be unloaded and passageways for teamsters to get their wagons down. The
warehouses were not as large as those on the long wharves—Derby, India, Orne's,
or Stephen White's—but they served well enough. Knapp had a ground-floor
counting room and a store for retail as well as bulk items; he used the upper floor
for storage of barrels, bales, and boxes of whatever his vessels might bring home—
usually sugar, molasses, cocoa, and coffee.

Knapp's trade, though limited, was brisk, for 1821 had been a better year at
Union Wharf. The merchants and freighters there were not exactly competitors.
They tended to specialize in certain markets and commodities, without much
overlap; and when they did overlap, there was usually enough local demand for

their goods or enough knowledge about submarkets to transship them some-where else for a profit. Joseph Howard, perhaps the busiest merchant at Union Wharf, specialized in freighting to Baltimore and the Chesapeake and dealt ex-tensively in the various grades of flour, beef, and hides from that area. Robert Upton had a preternatural talent for profitable trade with emerging markets in the new nations of South America. Michael Shepard traded to Cayenne and other Caribbean markets, dealing in cocoa and coffee, and he also sent his schooner *Tatler* on regular trips to Baltimore and Philadelphia. John Dike ran vessels to the peninsular and Potomac ports of Virginia, as well as to New Orleans, and he dealt extensively in many different products, from good wine to cheap shoes.

Far out at sea, on board the Salem brig *Mary & Eliza*, the Bessell brothers were thriving. They had cleared Marseilles in April 1821, having gone first to Genoa and then back across the Atlantic to Rio de Janeiro, the capital of Brazil and the home of Portugal's king, João VI. Flanked by mountains, Rio was a huge city of 110,000 people, many European but most enslaved blacks—20,000 Africans were imported in 1817 alone. Ashore, Rio looked like Lisbon, with narrow stone houses and red-tile roofs, many churches, and fountains in the city squares. At night, illuminated by "lamps placed before the images of the Virgin Mary,"[12] its streets were melodious with African songs and the music of guitar-ists, bands, and vocalists. Along the waterfront were the king's palace, the public promenade, warehouses, and crowds of people, white, brown, and black, and the firing of the guns of the fort and of vessels arriving from all parts of the world, and "the crackling of the rockets, with which the inhabitants celebrate religious festivals, almost daily, from an early hour in the morning." The Salem men noted with interest that Rio had begun direct trade with India and China, only a seven-month round-trip.[13]

The *Mary & Eliza* sailed once again for the Mediterranean. As supercargo, Mathias Bessell turned over their cargo at Marseilles, perhaps taking on cases of opium as well as a treasure chest of specie. By 1820, American opium exports from Smyrna to the Orient had outstripped those of the British at Bengal. Batavia was the mart for the trade of Java; in Sumatra, especially along the Pepper Coast, each outport now expected American vessels to bring Turkey opium as well as specie. Specie made the rajahs rich, and opium helped them consolidate power, for the rajahs and their favored lieutenants were the only suppliers for a growing population of addicts.

Well into the Indian Ocean by the end of May 1821, near the lonely volcanic island of Saint Paul, the *Mary & Eliza* ran into a violent gale from the north. Captain Beckford and the crew held their own, shortening sail and keeping their vessel pointing into the wind and waves as much as possible. The storm grew monstrous, with deafening winds and raging seas. Higher and higher, the brig climbed each terrible wave to its breaking crest, then scudded down the huge slope to face the next great mass of rising water. Long at sea without repairs, the old vessel weakened in the face of the onslaught; her topmasts threatened to part, her masts groaned, stanchions and rigging broke loose. An immense wave appeared in the distance, different from the others, a steep white wall already breaking as it charged headlong. Captain Beckford held course; his men cringed and prayed; and the collision staggered their vessel. Tons of rushing water drove her under, and she came up slowly, shuddering. Beckford and the crew had survived, and they got her driving once again into the endless typhoon. The *Mary & Eliza* was grievously wounded. The oceanic blow had smashed her in her strongest places,[14] but she fought on, with men in the hold pumping furiously and men on the yardarms wrestling the sails. Two days later, William Maxwell, a seaman formerly of Salem, fell overboard and drowned.[15]

In early June, Captain Beckford finally brought the battered *Mary & Eliza* up the channel to Padang. Beckford and the Bessells conferred. The vessel needed more repairs than they could get there, but they had come all the way around the world to see their old home, and they had a keen desire to set foot on land, any land, after their terrifying experiences. It could not hurt to go ashore briefly, to assess the market and see if they might take on some of the fading season's pepper crop. The *Mary & Eliza*'s men stayed just long enough to get water and supplies and to make some emergency repairs. It was a fatal mistake, for cholera morbus was rampant ashore, and Charles Bessell fell ill and died within days. He had gone home to be buried.

The crippled *Mary & Eliza* moved on eastward, toward the Strait of Sunda. Captain Beckford sailed on to Batavia, where Governor Franz Bessell had worked for the old Dutch East India Company. Here, too, they found great sickness, as was so often the case; but they had to stay. They came to anchor, and the surveyors inspected her. After hundreds of thousands of miles, eighteen years since her launch at the Magoun shipyard—at a point about as far away from Salem as one could get on the planet—the *Mary & Eliza* was finished.

The men sought out John Shillaber, the expatriate Salem merchant who served as American consul at Batavia. Better than anyone, he would know what to do. He met them at the dock and led them up into the hills. Shillaber had news about Salem vessels on the coast that spring, looking for pepper and coffee, impatient for a lading. Captain William Rogers, the former lawyer and politician, full of interesting talk about Salem and Cochin China, had been there with the *Texel,* and Samuel Hodgdon with the *Perseverance,* and together they had decided to try their luck at Siam.[16] Rogers had borne the bad news of Charles Forbes's death at Mahajanga—a reminder of the terrible power of disease in the tropics.

From the heights near Shillaber's estate, the visitors looked back at the roofs and glittering canals of the feverish city, and the fleet of ships anchored offshore, and the grandeur of the turquoise ocean beyond, running out to the edge of the world. Upon arriving at the house, they found that Shillaber's younger brother, Jonathan, nineteen, lately come out from Salem to make his fortune, had just contracted the plague.

At Thanksgiving 1821, Joseph J. Knapp's brig *Betsey,* under Captain Symonds, arrived home with a ghastly tale. Having sailed in June with Knapp's brig *Washington,* Symonds had made his usual tour of the tropical islands. He had a crew of nine, including second mate Joseph Knapp Jr., sixteen. At Havana, they found the port in the grip of an epidemic, but they entered anyway, for there were pirates in the offing. They unloaded and sailed away quickly without picking up a cargo and dropped down to Cap Haitien. By then, nearly all of the crew had the fever. Four young men died, and their bodies were thrown overboard. Nineteen days later, the *Betsey* was back in late autumn Salem as if the tropical nightmare had never been. Captain Knapp was horrified at the deaths and dismayed at the lack of a cargo; but as the family gathered around the table for New England's holiday, he gave thanks to the Lord for their blessings and for preserving the life of his eldest son, Joe.

During that same Thanksgiving season, the White family learned about the *Mary & Eliza*. Stephen White was especially anxious—losing Charles was a bitter blow, and he could not rest until Mathias was home. He opened Captain Beckford's letter, and it was not good news. The *Mary & Eliza* had been condemned at Batavia. As passengers on another vessel, Captain Beckford and the crew were on their way, but not the supercargo: Mathias Bessell had died on July 17, aged twenty-three, a month after his brother. The sudden loss of Charles had been a fatal blow, leaving Matthias deeply depressed and unable to fight off the effects of the Batavia epidemic.

It seemed impossible that the two brothers had been lost on their voyage of adventure and homecoming. Stephen White and Captain Joseph White experienced terrible grief in the deaths of these young men and in the brutal finish to the old story of Joseph White Jr. and the two little boys whom he had promised to raise into gentlemen.

Stephen composed an elegy for the *Register,* recounting the arrival of the boys and how, in "a family of strangers they were cherished with all the interest and care which the nearest ties could have claimed or created." Mathias himself—suave, generous, friendly, talented—was "truly, a virtuous man. He valued virtue for its intrinsic excellence, scanning and regulating his actions by its most rigid precepts. Integrity and honor were stamped upon all his transactions with mankind—it was not, however, that appearance of honesty, which circumstances and occasions and interest exact of us for effect, but an habitual and indelible principle upon the mind."[17]

William Rogers and the crew of the *Texel* left Shillaber's Batavia in April in company with Captain Samuel Hodgdon and *Perseverance,* two Salem vessels on the same course up the Gulf of Siam. At Bangkok, he hoped to get access to some of the goods of Cochin China that had been denied to John White. It was thrilling to be moving through parts of the world that few Americans had ever seen. Rogers had once written that the spectacle of first encountering an Indian city was unlike any other; and he hoped for splendor at Bangkok. What would he see? What of the people? What were their customs, their architecture, their mode of dress?

At the mouth of the river Menam, he was allowed to ascend to Paknam, the first station on the way. There, Captain Rogers went ashore with a few of his well-dressed men, who attracted the usual curiosity of the natives, themselves nearly naked, dressed only in loincloths, men and women.[18] The Americans went through "mean lanes crowded with huts" and came out at the governor's modest bamboo house, where, after several days of pleasant meetings, meals, and gift exchanges, Rogers was given a pass for the *Texel* to go on to Bangkok.

After sailing up the wide river for two hours, they passed a thick jungle noisy with the cries of birds and monkeys and saw a few huts overhanging the shore, then an old Dutch redoubt crumbling into sand. Beyond it, they slipped between two stout masonry forts and were serenaded by a band. Rogers went ashore to exchange gifts, then proceeded another twelve miles to a point where the river widened and the *Texel* came upon a paradise of miles of rice paddies and villages with orchards of palm and fruit trees and people waving from the fields and birds winging by and water buffalo grazing.

Beyond lay the great city. Rising from both banks of the Menam, Bangkok presented a busy waterfront filled with houseboats and, "conspicuous among the mean huts and hovels of the natives," the gilded, tall-spired temples of Buddha. The houseboats turned out to be both dwellings and Chinese shops, sturdily set on rafts of bamboo, riding above the swift current of the river. Close by were anchored scores of native vessels and many junks of great size, just arrived from China. As at Saigon, many of the sailboats were handled by women, flitting over the waters with their wares of crockery and prepared foods: shrimp plates, dried fish, fresh pork. Other sailboats were filled with "priests of Buddha," shaven-headed and saffron-robed, singing as they came looking for alms.

Tropical Bangkok, with its golden *wat* temples and its tall trees and its friendly half-dressed people, its strange music and its abundant food and hospitality, was the largest native center of trade in all of Asia outside of China. Even the royal officials were reasonable; and there were many Europeans, Portuguese especially, with whom to converse and learn the ways of the city. Bangkok's warehouses bulged with native pepper, sugar, salt, oil, and rice, along with imported ivory, eagle-wood, dyewood, and barks, all destined for the Chinese markets.[19] Huge junks carried a thousand passengers, eager to resettle, with teas, silks, porcelains, and silver ingots. This was no Saigon: Captain Rogers could congratulate himself on having come around the world to the perfect place for trade.

Early in his dealings, William Rogers struck up the acquaintance of an English supercargo. In the mid-June days of monsoon season, it was blazing hot or it poured sheets of rain; and at night the sweltering shipboard air whined with mosquitoes. The Englishman invited Rogers to come by his houseboat for a meal and a couple of bottles of burgundy. He did so, had a grand time, and decided to stay the night. In the terrible heat he went outdoors and lay on a platform, perhaps trying to conjure an image of relief: the cool, echoing caves of Elephanta and their great stone statues; the jingling horse-drawn sleighs in the snowy streets of Salem. He was far, very far, from home. He closed his eyes and felt the swaying of the river, and heard the whisperings of the seaport, distant syllables in a strange tongue, a burst of birdsong, the faint splashings and creakings of boats in the night wind, the murmur of the wavelets alongside; and at last he was asleep.

Jostled by the tide, the platform gave a lurch and William rolled off with hardly a sound and was carried by the current into the blackness under the hull; and if he awoke, he could not find his way to the surface.

NATHANIEL BOWDITCH. The genius offspring of a hard-luck shipmaster, he clerked throughout his boyhood in a Salem ship chandlery until Hasket Derby sent him out on an East Indiaman to begin an extraordinary career as navigator, astronomer, physicist, actuary, and business executive. Bowditch (1773–1838), Salem's favorite son, had the gift of second sight.

6.

THE PROPHET

Dick Crowninshield heard the rumors about the terrors of Coy's Pond, north of Danvers, in the far reaches of Wenham Woods: bonfires blazing by the hellish cave mouth, men and women in drunken revels and demon dances, celebrating their predations and the freedom of their lives as outlaws. Dick could hardly wait to join them.

Early in 1821, Salem was hit with a crime wave, from highway robberies to urban break-ins, usually without the harming of persons, always with clockwork precision and clean getaways. Nothing short of murder was beyond the reach of the invisible gang. They had even gone into the "resurrection" business, digging up fresh corpses in graveyards for sale to physicians and students.[1] With no real police department and no effective means of detecting criminals, the townspeople were jittery and a little desperate. In an act that had no precedent, a Salem jury lashed out at a deranged boy: for setting fire to a barn, they sentenced him to hang.[2]

Crime became a business and a threat to the community. Dick Crowninshield was having great fun as a criminal mastermind. Resorting to the charismatic persona of his school days, he soon had his new friends organized as a strike force to carry out military-style raids on Salem and environs, with clean-outs of barns and mass pilfering from orchards. He kept his cool and expected loyalty and efficiency from his followers; most of all, he demanded anonymity. He did not exist: his name was not known, his voice came out of the shadows, in a whisper. Materializing at the bonfires in the forest, he had a gun and a knife, and he would hurt anyone on a whim.

After the 1822 burglary of a store in downtown Salem, 159 men responded to a notice to meet at the Essex Coffee House hotel. Stephen White volunteered to lead the new Society for the Detection of Thieves and Robbers, with William Mansfield, a deputy sheriff, as president and White and his merchant neighbor John Andrew as two of the three trustees. And so the citizens became quasi vigilantes, offering rewards to informers and paying for identification of thugs.[3] Their actions did not go unnoticed, and the break-in artists cooled off and took their skills on the road and out to sea.

That summer, Dick Crowninshield found a berth on the brig *Persia*, commanded by Captain Moses Endicott. As a companion he had the captain's teenage brother, Lewis; Dick himself was a pale eighteen-year-old, five feet eight inches tall and ready for adventure in the world.[4] The *Persia* made a good passage to Sumatra, where Captain Endicott began charting the treacherous waters of the Pepper Coast and trading with the rajahs, who were happy to receive his specie and happier to get his Smyrna opium.

Coming west early in 1823 from Sumatra, the *Persia* breasted heavy seas off the Cape of Good Hope and closed out the summer in Italy at Leghorn.[5] In July, Dick toured the countryside and lounged on deck, reading his copy of Byron's *Don Juan* and practicing his own defiant verses. The English poet's scandals and stylishness, his gutsy defiance of convention, his love of Oriental exotica, his self-infatuation, and his grand passions—all held a deep fascination for Crowninshield. Dick found that he had just missed his hero, who had stopped there in June, headed east to help in the fight for Greek independence.[6]

Behind them in Salem, the men of the *Persia* had left a seaport that was struggling to find its place in the economic landscape. Salem had long been at the center of an imperial commerce, lucrative and expansive, run by merchants who had seldom failed to find new markets and create new opportunities. At home, however, the impact of industrial manufacturing was transforming everything, in America at large and in Massachusetts in particular. It was impossible not to feel the tremors of a new world coming into existence, terrifying and exhilarating as it began to take form.

Far out in the countryside, twenty miles north of Salem, where the fields were planted in corn and the herds of cattle drifted like clouds, a springtime traveler might come to the final knoll, overlooking the waters of the mighty Merrimack, and behold a true vision: a brand-new industrial city in the middle of the rural landscape, with huge brick buildings bright red against the intense grass green and sky blue, like a dream set down by the river. It was in fact the dream of the Boston Associates, shipping merchants turned industrial capitalists, builders of the Waltham factory ten years before, now creators of an entire city at East Chelmsford.[7] The city was still taking shape—streets, parks, boardinghouses, stores, city squares, and churches, fit for fifty thousand workers—but it was finished as to the first factories. A huge dam pushed the side of the river into a canal, and the canal waters turned the great wheels beneath six-story buildings filled with hundreds of power jennies and power looms and people to tend them.

The industrial chimera was producing large quantities of midgrade cotton textiles every week. One factory employed two hundred young women, another one hundred, and another was being built for more than a thousand. Every day, about twenty-five hundred yards of cotton goods were placed on barges and floated on the Middlesex Canal to downtown Boston,[8] where the teamsters loaded the bales and trundled them over to the waiting stores and to the ships at the docks. In less than a year, several massive mill buildings had risen on the banks of the Merrimack. East Chelmsford, soon to be renamed Lowell, was recognized everywhere as the apotheosis of the American industrial imagination; and its long shadow fell across the wharves and warehouses of Salem.

Throughout the period of the depression, Salem's poor had grown poorer and more numerous. Fewer vessels were sailing, less freight was being moved and stored, and the tide of overall maritime enterprise was ebbing. People needed jobs, and manufacturing held the best promise of employment. While the seaport's modest chemical plant, tanneries, and distilleries were good employers of the poor, none was conducted on a large scale. In terms of high-output manufacturing, Salem, which lacked falling water for hydropower, could not compete with even the poorest country town that had a modest stream of rapids—South

Danvers, for example, where Richard Crowninshield was partying with his Irish employees and producing tons of high-quality woolen broadcloth.

Ironically, Salem's rich men owned majority interests in three out-of-town manufacturing plants: the Amesbury Nail Factory in the northern part of the county; the New Hampshire Iron Factory, a maker of bar iron and stoves;[9] and the Salem Iron Factory, on the Danvers River, producing everything metal from anchors to nails, and good dividends, too.[10] Salem merchants were not alone in putting their money into the new manufacturing sector that was leading the way out of the depression. Harrison G. Otis, once the champion of commerce in Congress, was now heavily invested in industrial projects at Amesbury and other water-powered sites, especially in the cotton, woolen, and rolling mills of Taunton, in southeastern Massachusetts. Only the year before, "manufacturing stock, with its liabilities," he wrote, was "considered so much minus. All is now reversed and the stocks as well as spirits have risen *inordinately*. I have never known an impression so deep and general in favor of the prospects as well as actual prosperity of the business people. It is amazing to see what is done by the puff on one hand and the panic on the other."[11]

As a sophisticated investor, Stephen White placed money in textile enterprises on the Merrimack and many other rivers, deep into the backcountry of New Hampshire and Maine, all of them producing the cloth that had once been imported by Salem's East Indiamen. He was happy to diversify a portfolio that had been heavy on bank and insurance stocks and shares in turnpike companies as well as in ships and cargoes. Yet his commitment to foreign trade remained strong, and he was able to buy up the shipping assets of the less fortunate. He was satisfied that his vessels were engaged in remunerative markets, trading, by the hundreds of tons, in the opium, wine, fruit, marble, spices, pepper, ivory, hides, pelts, drugs, coffee, mahogany, essences, and luxury goods that would find profitable markets somewhere.

In 1822, White joined his Salem colleagues in purchasing a mill site in southern New Hampshire. At Newmarket, in 1823, they erected a large stone textile factory, six stories high, in which they installed the latest in English-style power looms, driven by crankshafts and outsize undershot wheels. It was not a modest creation: the Newmarket Manufacturing Company mill, looming over the village and its rapids, had more spindles under one roof than any other textile plant in the nation. The Salemites built spacious boardinghouses and hired five hundred nimble children and bright young women to tend the mill's machinery. The owners had designed the work spaces to be sunny and well ventilated; they had been careful not to replicate the industrial prisons of Europe or Rhode Island.

Salem's rich men believed that anything was possible with brains and money. They had built Newmarket out in the countryside, and they might do no less for their own people, who still depended on them for their livelihoods. Looking at a large wharf that had recently been built for the handsome Salem Neck Charity House, the merchants listened to the superintendent there, Paul Upton, who had the idea of extending it to make a dam at Collins Cove,[12] an inlet of the sea that might provide tidal power for a textile mill. In 1822, the editor of the *Essex Register* publicly endorsed the idea, and even the *New England Farmer* praised Upton and the possibility of creating "sites for mills of various kinds."

On the town meeting warrant for March 1823 was a proposal for determining the costs "of erecting a dam at the expense of the town, from the poorhouse farm to Bridge Street, for the purpose of erecting a mill or mills thereon." In the upstairs meeting room of the Town Hall, men crowded around a plan of the proposed dam.

At the meeting, the proponents asked their fellow taxpayers to authorize the costing-out of the mill dam—a modest request, requiring a small outlay for a consultant. But no orator came forth and said that a new era had opened, that the days of maritime commerce were numbered, that Salem was sinking fast, and that its best chance was to reinvent itself by building dams and factories. Everyone was aware of the national onslaught of manufacturing and the mania for machinery and improvements. However, these things loomed in the offing, ominous and expensive, freighted with unknown consequences. It did not seem that they belonged to Salem. Challenged to take the first step toward industrial development, the voters declined.[13]

The plan of Collins Cove was rolled up but not tossed out. Rich men liked the idea; and if the voters did not think it suitable as public works project, still it might be good for private investment.

A s Salem stalled, Boston accelerated toward becoming a metropolis. Frequent visitors to Boston, three of Salem's most distinguished sons—Joseph Story, John Pickering, and Stephen White—found themselves facing an overwhelming challenge. What had once seemed instructive about Boston's metamorphosis, offering models for Salem to consider, had come to seem frightening. Boston was insatiably pulling money and talent into its vortex, fed by the mass energies of the resurgent economy.

The burgeoning consumer culture in Boston called to young people to join the middle class. Without any advantages other than hustle and intelligence, they could become prosperous brokers, managers, clerks, factors, and agents amid the great flow of people, goods, and money—and the oyster parlors, busy wharves, crowded streets, and theaters and shows, all concentrated in a small space and packed with explosive urban energy. Newly incorporated as a city, Boston embodied the principles of innovation and transformation. Salem, quiet and orderly, with most of its assets at sea, was not convincing as a center of modernity.

Boston merchants were now reinventing themselves as capitalists and repositioning Boston and its forty-five thousand people for success in the region's economy, competitive with the American megaports of New York, Philadelphia, Baltimore, and New Orleans. Boston's leaders understood the new outsize scale of things in America. Like John Quincy Adams, their candidate in the upcoming presidential election, they envisaged an ever-growing nation that would eventually extend to the Pacific. They foresaw endless innovations in transportation and manufacturing, and they supported the controversial idea of federal funding for projects to connect the huge spaces of the American interior.

Salem, however, was permanently connected to the world overseas, and it could not benefit from an economy whose main growth was in America, stretching westward and coastwise. Salem's magnificent fleet of ships might, in fact, become more valuable as Boston coasters. Boston had already made a dependency of Newburyport, the once active shipping center to the north. If that happened to Salem—if it were unable to maintain profitability in its own lines of special-ized trade—its best citizens would follow the money to Boston and New York, and its day would be done.

This was the prospect that haunted the three men, Story, Pickering, and White, each the head of a family of bright children, as they contemplated the disaster that lay before them.

Judge Joseph Story, forty-four, lord of the law in New England, had to handle this case with extreme delicacy. It was no easy matter, for Nathaniel Bowditch, fifty, loathed the public events that Story loved. When they finally met face-to-face, Story prevailed, impressing on the little genius the need for the ceremony and its importance to Salem. The Navigator was trapped: rich men had encir-cled him, and Story left him no means of escape. Bowditch acceded, but on the condition that he not give a speech of any kind, even a very short one—no speech, or no supper! Story smiled. Dr. Bowditch would accept their accolades in silence; but of course many would speak for him. Foremost was Story him-self, no particular friend but a splendid master of ceremonies, always plausible in front of a crowd, never at a loss for fine words or correct sentiments.

Much more than Story and White, John Pickering had a personal stake in the upcoming event. The tall, slender Pickering, a forty-six-year-old lawyer, was a dear friend of Bowditch, with whom he shared frequent conversation and many secrets. The two men were bookish, modest, and shy. John was musical and lin-guistic, areas in which Nathaniel was notably deficient; Nathaniel's talents in physics were astronomically greater than John's. Pickering, eldest son of the arch-Federalist Timothy Pickering, was less intense and vehement than his father, having been raised by his kindly uncle and namesake, a bachelor lawyer and politician who had resided in the old house on Broad Street built by a John Pick-ering in 1664. John Pickering, nephew, had grown up with all the advantages of wealth and taste. Classical languages—the dreaded Latin and ancient Greek of prep school—were John's passion. With a superb private education, the honors of Harvard College, years in Europe serving in American legations, a thorough exposure to the art, culture, and languages of the Old World, and devotion to the purest forms of the King's English, John Pickering had returned to Salem in 1801 to take up legal studies under his cousin Judge Samuel Putnam, Story's mentor, too. Bowditch, meanwhile, had been working as a grocery clerk and a sailor. Raised so differently, the two men had arrived at the same place; and they agreed on all things cultural and political, even to an aversion to public speaking.

Bowditch and Pickering, Salem's Harvard overseers, served as a refuge for each other, in which unguarded musings could safely be shared. Both contributed to learned journals and belonged to the American Academy of Arts & Sciences and wrote for the *North American Review,* in which an article might end in a Latin paragraph or an apostrophe in Pickering's ancient Greek. They got together every day. Pickering loved his wife, Sarah White, who was his second cousin, and their three gnomish, big-nosed children, two boys and a girl. But he was going bald and mad in the repetitious boredom of his legal duties, and Bowditch was his only companion in a mental life whose other consolations were the flute and violin, linguistic essays, rehearsals of the Oratorio and Mozart Societies, and the compiling of his lexicon.

Every morning at four thirty Pickering rose and put on his skullcap and slippers, wrapped himself in his robe, lit his lamps, pulled down the leaf of his desk, spread out his papers and notebooks, and devoted a few hours to his lexicon of ancient Greek. In it, he was building the temple of his intellect, word by word. However, even as Pickering compiled his masterwork, modern America was challenging the need for it. Prep schools and colleges, Harvard with the rest, were dropping the classics from their curricula. Their students were far more interested in modern science than dead languages. The times were changing, but John Pickering fought back from his position on the Harvard board, pushing for a restoration of the classical education that justified all of his work. The laborious productions of genius, it turned out, might only have an audience of geniuses.

Pickering had great respect for Judge Story, also a very hard scholar, once his rival at the bar. Story had moved so far toward Federalist principles that even John's father, the fierce old colonel, had come to admire him. Of Stephen White, the Pickerings held no such high opinion: White had not attended college and had not cultivated scholarly pastimes. He was a merchant and a gentleman, but a man of business, who shared with his late brother a reputation for the high life and an unseemly love of the grape. In his day, Stephen had been a deep-dyed saltwater Republican partisan, an enforcer and a power broker, a preening militia captain and something of a bully-boy, typical of the young bucks of the Lower End. Things had changed, it was true. White had joined his brother-in-law Story in developing a conservative wing of the Republican Party. One could admire his energy and his willingness to take leadership of committees and societies, now made up of men from both sides. But White remained a bit rough-hewn, quick to laugh and quick to quip, with the swagger of a man—like so many in Salem and like so many of his fellow merchants—who sent others to their deaths in pursuit of cattle hides and who had himself haunted the exotic bazaars and back streets of foreign ports, unhampered by scholarly thinking or puritanical scruples.

Bowditch had been fated to see things that others did not, and to be correct about their meanings. As the actuary of Salem commerce, as the rate setter for insurance and the hardest-headed of all bottom-liners, he had long studied the algorithms of supply and demand, profit and loss. The old markets had changed profoundly in the past ten years. Tariffs had been imposed, national policies had been set, and the flow of money and the currents of profit had been disrupted, not least with regard to Salem's major trading partners. India's enormous output of beautiful cloths had dwindled to scraps as a result of the Tariff of 1816 and of British industrial policy, and Sumatra's pepper remained a volatile commodity, subject to prices set at large in the world. London continued to rule the global economy and had recently closed all of its West Indies ports to American vessels.

Bowditch regarded this dispassionately, not as one who owned ships, in love with a trade that had made him wealthy, but as one who cast a cold eye and who calculated unerringly. He was not sentimental about vessels and voyages. Salem's predicament was clear, but not even he could solve the problem—there was no *Practical Navigator* by which to plot a better course. And while Salem was slipping, the future of New England was gloriously unfurling in Boston. He had received a handsome proposal from Boston, and he had made trips to New York and Philadelphia, too. Boston had won out. The capital city's urban power—its mass market, its muscle and money, its manufacturing, its financial and educational institutions, its political influence, its cultural attractions, its tone and style—appealed greatly to a modern man who was still evolving. Long courted by Boston financiers in love with his brains, Bowditch was, at last, ready to be seduced.

Salem had given him a salary of $1,300, the honors of the town, and a pleasant and comfortable lifestyle. Boston would pay him $5,000 per year to run its largest insurance company. What could he say to Salem? Bowditch had risen high, but he had no inheritance and no treasure store from the golden days of the Oriental trade—then, he had been a nobody, clerking and shipping out. Now, as an expert in the field of managing risk, he had cast the numbers and followed the logic. Boston offered his many children, still young, a metropolis of opportunities. It was clearly a powerhouse in young America, a place with limitless vistas of prosperity. Salem loved Bowditch, but Boston would make him rich.

He had informed his closest friends, and he had hoped to leave quietly. But in springtime, as he was called to sit on boards and serve as president of societies, he had had to declare himself. Salem, of course, had been stunned at the news. Bowditch was its greatest asset, and his loss, everyone recognized, was a terrible liability. Someone was to blame: it could not be Salem or the immortal Bowditch, so it must be the jealous thieves of Boston. Salem's rich old rival had prevailed in the contest for the great man's soul, if not his heart. It was an act of infamy.

Bowditch dutifully had continued his work at the insurance company and enjoyed the last months with old companions. Each day, as before, he had conversed with his dear friend the talented Mr. John Pickering. Pickering envied Dr. Bowditch's great opportunity: at the age of fifty, he could start over.

The Bowditch celebrants convened on the steamy evening of August 1 at Hamilton Hall, the Federalist clubhouse on Chestnut Street, to render tribute to "their instructor, their oracle." Bostonians were not invited. President Kirkland and

Professor Farrar came up from Cambridge, and a merchant from Havana drifted in, but otherwise it was an all-Salem gathering of major merchants and professional men professing "their affectionate regard of his private virtues and of their high admiration of his extraordinary scientific acquirements."

Speaker after speaker praised him as the Salem lad who had educated himself to a mastery of physics and astronomy, as the Salem mariner who had gained fame as an author and navigator, as the businessman who had applied his unmatched talents to benefit Salem's commerce. During the drawn-out toasting ritual, the first glasses were lifted "to the town of Salem: She may boast of the honorable but painful distinction of producing men whom her neighbors will not permit her to retain." Other toasts were offered, some quite pointed. J. Augustus Peabody, the young merchant prince, toasted "the good people of Boston: not content with their own capital, they avail themselves of their neighbors' funds. This last *draft* on our *stock* of science had been *duly honored*." "The Astronomer of Salem" was informed that his townsmen "would rejoice if this luminary were a fixed star."

In the face of tribute, the guest of honor sat with his demure drawn-in smile, the smile of a rather strange little boy, enduring their praise until finally rising to offer his own toast "to Salem: distinguished for its commercial information, activity, and enterprise—ornamented by its literary and scientific society—honored by the general purity of the public morals—may this fair character of our town remain unimpaired to the latest time." Having spoken, Bowditch left the hall. The celebration continued with more toasts and a long talk by the always voluble Judge Story on the character and scientific pursuits of Dr. Bowditch. Judge Samuel Putnam affirmed all that Story had said and raised his glass to "Nathaniel Bowditch, our most distinguished citizen, first of his countrymen in the walks of science, second to no man on earth for purity and honor."

Imbibing copiously, the guests offered a few last brave toasts. One was made to the excellence of John Quincy Adams. Dr. Abel Peirson toasted Salem, "from which have sprung numbers of New England worthies—although stars of the first magnitude occasionally quit their orbit, may the light which remains prove that many a bright constellation is left to us." The Cuban raised his glass to "the commerce of Salem: may its prosperity be proportionate to the distinguished enterprise, intelligence, and honor of its merchants." Then the celebration was over, and Hamilton Hall was empty.

Two months later, Bowditch and family completed the move, and in their new home in Boston they were taken up by all the best people.

In Salem, the east winds of autumn came in heavy and wet from the North Atlantic, and the proud vessels arrived from their voyages, and the merchants met at the taverns to make their deals. Seafaring men, sailors and shipmasters, coming ashore after a year in the world, received the news with a shock, as at the death of a loved one. It seemed incredible, impossible, that their idol, the immortal Bowditch, the very essence of Salem's greatness, was gone.

COMMERCE AND INDUSTRY. *Salem's leaders, pursuing the power of the Industrial Revolution, envisioned their world-class seaport augmented by factories rising along the canals of the Salem Mill Dam project, their solution to the growing problem of unemployment. The smaller riverbank port of Saco, Maine, pursued a similar goal and achieved it; Salem's grandiose vision was harder to realize.*

PART TWO

VISIONS & DELUSIONS

What is this life? A storm at sea!

Let us help each other, for he that lives the longest

must sink at last, and return no more!

—REVEREND WILLIAM BENTLEY OF SALEM

A FATEFUL VOYAGE. Stephen White's stout bark Eliza *sailed for the Javanese coffee and sugar port of Batavia, now Jakarta, in the fall of 1824. Most Salem merchants offered the top spots on board to young relatives and friends; on this voyage, for example, the captain, first mate, and a seaman were all nephews of the owner.*

7.

WHITE HOPE

I n 1823, Stephen White became the new president of the East India Marine Society, succeeding Bowditch at the head of the seaport's elite group of merchant shipowners. White's business activities were backed by the vast fortune of his foster father, Captain Joseph White. He belonged to the Friday Evening Club and Saint Peter's Church, Episcopal, and he sat on the boards of the Merchants Bank and the historical society and the Society for the Detection of Thieves and Robbers. White and Story controlled federal patronage in Salem and Essex County, and they had made room for Federalists in their own version of Republicanism.

White admired the Massachusetts Republican John Quincy Adams and was putting a lot of money into his candidacy for the White House—some said that Adams's national campaign had been launched from Stephen's parents' home at Cherry Hill Farm in nearby Beverly.[1] Adams had done more for commerce than any other government figure since Alexander Hamilton. Recognizing the importance of the emerging nations' continuing republican development and of safe commerce between them and Americans, Secretary of State Adams had arranged with Great Britain and Russia for a hands-off policy; and in December 1823, President Monroe promulgated Adams's precepts as the Monroe Doctrine, declaring that colonialism was "an abuse of government" that "should come to an end." Regions already under foreign control could remain as such, but no others would be "subjects for future colonization by any European power," at the peril of war with the United States. Without firing a shot or dispatching a vessel, Adams had defied the rest of the world to prove that America did not dominate the western hemisphere.

Despite hopes for an Adams presidency and the reality of a fleet of merchant vessels and the barrels of money in its bank vaults, Salem was in trouble. In the past few years, the value of Salem imports had diminished by almost $200,000 to about $1.8 million, with exports falling steeply by $1 million to just $1.9 million. During the same years, the value of Boston's commerce had increased to a total of $19.5 million in 1824, compared with Salem's $3.7 million. And New York did about triple the business of Boston.[2]

Stephen White remained committed to maritime enterprise. For the maiden voyage of his new Salem-built bark *Eliza,* he hired three young relatives among the crew: William Story Jr., twenty-one, first mate, and the brothers Joseph White Beckford, seventeen, seaman, and Captain John Beckford Jr., twenty-three, on his first voyage in command. Story was Stephen White's nephew, just returned as second mate from Sumatra; the Beckfords were the sons of White's adoptive sister Mary. John had been first mate on White vessels for the past two years, and Joseph had made his first voyage on a White brig earlier that year.[3] Mary's daughter Elizabeth had just married John Davis, a young man of good family, evidently with the blessing of old Captain White.

Settled in as the captain's housekeeper, Mary had few responsibilities, for he had two able servants. But it gave her something to do, and he enjoyed her company and that of her youngest child, pretty Mary White Beckford, then fifteen. In the White mansion on Essex Street, Mrs. Beckford had her sitting room and command post in the eastern back parlor, overlooking the garden. She counted on her son John to rise high as a shipmaster and lift the whole family. He was indeed his father's son, a proud and capable fellow, well suited to command. Captain Beckford and his men, navigating the *Eliza,* had made the trip to South America and gone on to Russia. If all went well, they would be back in summertime, and then perhaps John would have his chance to command a voyage to the Orient.

Increasingly, South America was a favorite destination for Salem shippers. Colombia, Mexico, Chile, and Argentina, newly independent, had opened their ports for trade. Ports also opened in Brazil, where rebels battled the forces of

Emperor Pedro. For years, theft and piracy had plagued the West Indies as the Spanish colonial empire disintegrated. Privateers licensed by the combatants would prey on merchant shipping, a practice that took some into outright piracy against Americans, who were constantly threatened and sometimes attacked while making their trading trips to the Caribbean markets. The merchants' insurance rates went up, and their men were killed, and their cargoes and vessels were lost. From Salem, most vessels sailed heavily armed and were not as vulnerable; still, protection was needed. After years of losses and complaints, the Monroe administration authorized construction of steam-powered launches and other mobile warships in a naval war against the pirates. At the outset of 1824, Commodore David Porter and the Caribbean squadron proceeded to hunt down the pirates at sea and in the swamps, capturing their vessels, blowing up their hideouts, and shooting them down like animals, sometimes in groups of fifty and sixty, in a bloodthirsty campaign to make the Caribbean safe for American commerce.

It was not, however, the pirates that were the main threat to that commerce. It was the Congress of the United States and the proponents of a new tariff.

With me it is a fundamental axiom, it is interwoven with all my opinions, that the great interests of the country are united and inseparable; that agriculture, commerce, and manufactures will prosper together or languish together; and that all legislation is dangerous which proposes to benefit one of these without looking to consequences which may fall to the others." On April 1, 1824, Representative Daniel Webster of Boston offered the House of Representatives a surprising national perspective—the battle cry of the new political movement coming out of New England—hoping somehow to turn Congress against Speaker Clay's new tariff bill.

National politics had changed dramatically. With the Federalists gone and the Republicans unopposed in most regions, the new politics were marked by personal rivalry, sectional differences, and factions battling for party control and for promotion of favorite sons as presidential contenders. Clay himself, a Kentuckian, was running for the White House, as were William H. Crawford of

Georgia, John C. Calhoun of South Carolina, and John Quincy Adams of Massachusetts; and each one of them endorsed a pro-tariff, pro-industry policy.

With commerce badly weakened by the depression, Webster believed that a high tariff might send it to the bottom. "As to our foreign trade," he declaimed, "Mr. Speaker has stated that there has been a considerable falling-off in the tonnage employed in that trade. This is true, lamentably true! In my opinion, it is one of those occurrences that ought to arrest our immediate, our deep, our most earnest attention. What does this bill propose for its relief? It proposes nothing but new burdens!" Webster said that freighting rates had fallen so low that many shipowners could not afford to carry cargoes overseas. Far from seeking riches, they and their sailors were only trying to survive. Britain, he declared, understood the value of the maritime sector: shipwrights were considered the most important manufacturers, and Parliament strongly supported its commerce, as opposed to Clay's evident willingness to sink the American merchant fleet.

In too-quiet Salem, Stephen White formed an anti-tariff group and published their resolutions.[4] The merchants knew what they were up against, and they were dismayed but not surprised when, in May, Congress gave Speaker Clay the vote he had wanted.

By enacting the Tariff of 1824, the government blew the merchants out of the water. All but the most affluent or confident cut back on commerce, and some withdrew altogether, preferring to invest in the newly protected industries that offered safety with their profits. Vessels were sold at bargain prices, and the big shipowners increased their fleets and lowered the sailors' wages. In Salem, increasingly, those sailors came from other places as local men "swallowed the anchor" and found more remunerative jobs ashore, often requiring a move out of town.[5] Salem owners still dispatched more than 140 vessels: 31 ships, 1 bark, and 76 brigs were engaged in foreign trade, and 34 schooners coasted to United States ports and to the Caribbean.[6] Despite the numbers, Stephen White was haunted by the anxiety of his colleagues and the weight of economic depression that had not lifted in Salem. Smaller merchant houses were struggling for survival; younger merchants could not stay in the game; and Salem, as a warehousing and distribution center, was slipping. Many merchants sent their vessels to Boston and New York for outward cargoes with orders to land their return cargoes at those same ports before coming to Salem "in ballast," with empty holds.

As a politician and as president of the East India Marine Society, White meant to turn things around. His first task was to convince the doubters that Salem was seaworthy, but he encountered much resistance. Bowditch's departure still reverberated, and the high wall of the tariff seemed to cut off the port from its former horizons. Some Salem artisans and seafarers now argued, for the first time, that the merchants were unfit to lead. Greedy and shortsighted, the rich men, they said, could not be entrusted with the well-being of the public.[7] But others said that inciting class conflict was not helpful: "Strike out the class of merchants . . . and this district would become a desert. All the thousand trades now in active operation, of ship-building, rope-making, iron-work, sail-making, block-making, coopering, etc., would be annihilated with the fall of commerce; and their place would be ill-supplied with cotton and woolen factories."[8]

With its tall ships and its high society, Salem was an impressive place, as judged by the Alabaman travel writer Anne Royall: "The citizens of Salem are stout, able-bodied men, more so than any I have seen this side of the Blue Ridge, and their ladies excel in beauty and personal charms. . . . Their manners are still more improved than the people of Boston. Besides the affability and ease of the Bostonians, they have a dignity and stateliness peculiar to them. In short, the gentlemen of Salem may be said to have arrived at a maturity in all those perfections which are derived from education and a knowledge of the world. Most of them are largely engaged in commerce and, from their great wealth, have it in their power to gratify an inclination to improve by traveling. You find few gentlemen in Salem who have not visited almost every part of the world and who do not possess more general knowledge than those of any other town in the union."[9]

White strived to make Salem capable of maintaining its high place in the world. He loved his clubs and his friends, and he was appreciated for his energy and judgment. In his public persona, he was positive and inspiring; in business, he took great pride in his stable of nine merchantmen. Two of the brigs were large, new, and built in Salem—a true sign of his commitment, for a ship was a very expensive item and not many had been built since the Panic started. From his boyhood, he had loved the process of design and construction and had daily accompanied his adoptive father to the shipyard whenever a White vessel had been on the blocks, to inspect the work of the shipwrights and caulkers, the blacksmiths and joiners, the tar-handed riggers at their cordage, and the sailmakers up in their billowing lofts. He had visited the other shipyards as well, to watch the progress of their vessels-to-be and to think about how to make improvements and to scheme out the sparring and rigging and sail plans for the best combination of speed and capacity.

Two vessels he owned outright, and one he owned with his father, old Captain Henry White, seventy-four, of Cherry Hill farm. Stephen had other partners in his holdings, most notably his steady merchant brother-in-law William Fettyplace. White employed another brother-in-law, Captain William Story, as commander of the beautiful new brig *Cygnet,* and another, John Story, as master of the brig *Elizabeth.* Captain Joseph White, now seventy-seven, joined him in a half-interest in the brig *Nancy.* In very visible and public fashion, Stephen White boosted Salem's maritime commerce. He was doing his best to become the leader that the troubled seaport required, the personification of all that was special about Salem.

But Salem was not, perhaps, special enough for Stephen White. In amenities and opportunities, it could hardly compare with the vibrant scene in Boston, where White spent much of his time as a legislator and a businessman. Although incorporated under a city charter in 1822, Boston had retained most of its town characteristics under its first mayor, John Phillips. In 1823, Josiah Quincy was elected mayor, and from that moment the city had sped forward.

Quincy, an authority on pauper laws, had earned his insights the hard way, as judge of the Municipal Court of Boston, a low-level position, like that of Ezekiel Savage in Salem, with no prestige but great value in placing "a good man among whores and rogues" to deal with the consequences of poverty, vice, and crime.[10]

As mayor, he understood the real problems of the city—not the glamorous, high-end concerns that private enterprise would address, but the street-level issues of safety, health, and cleanliness. Every one of Boston's cobble streets stank of horse manure; and two thousand prostitutes turned their tricks, with four hundred in the brothels of Mount Whoredom behind the statehouse. Diseases were rampant, and children died by the hundreds each year.

With "Efficiency" as his motto, Quincy was wise enough not to try to scour away all traces of lowlife. However, "out of a sense of duty and respect for the character of the city," he demanded that vice be made "secret, like other filth, in drains and in darkness," and "not obtrusive, not powerful, not prowling publicly in the streets for the innocent and unwary."[11] He created a municipal fire department, erected a large workhouse for the poor, filled in old docks and built a grand waterfront marketplace, and named a single police-health chief to clean the waste out of the streets and the pimps and whores out of their hives. Brooking no opposition, Mayor Quincy made Boston into a model city, better and handsomer than any other, irresistibly attractive to real estate developers and to hopeful people from all corners of New England.

Salem's quality of life, at the highest levels, was hostage to the defections of its most ambitious people; and talented young men moved away continuously—a matter of real concern to White, who was raising six teenage girls. Rumors swirled, and insolvency and bankruptcy affected even the affluent; piracy and disease and ill fortune plagued the merchant fleet worldwide;[12] insurance rates escalated along with losses; the new textile factories attracted the investment money of merchants. Salem's poor, growing poorer, looked to the merchants for their well-being. The rest looked for new homes elsewhere.

At the parish meeting of the First Church, in which the people discussed choosing an assistant minister for their aged pastor John Prince, old Timothy Pickering surprised everyone by proposing Charles W. Upham, a recent Harvard graduate. Henry Colman, the leading candidate, was a forty-year-old Boston minister widely admired for his books of sermons. But Pickering claimed[13] that he had recently learned that Colman was unfit for the job, for reasons ranging from bad health and nervous excitability to his abandonment of his Hingham congregation, mismanagement of his girls' school, tampering with the North Church hiring process, and ignorance of "the modern improvements in theological science." Pickering's onslaught and young Upham's attractiveness had their impact. After a final effort to rescue Colman's candidacy, five wealthy men, all former Federalists and Pickering adherents—Stephen Phillips, Willard Peele, Hersey Derby, George Nichols, and Nathaniel West Jr.—pledged to pay for the building of a new church and a salary of up to $1,500 for Henry Colman.[14] Many in Salem were appalled at Pickering's attack on an earnest man of God, for it reminded them of their disgraceful civic past and the old, mad days of feuding and virulence.

The five First Church apostates were soon joined by defectors from other congregations, equally drawn to the Boston minister Colman and the possibilities of a brand-new Unitarian society in Salem. The other three such societies had all evolved within existing churches, but this one would make its own history, starting fresh. The founders were not young turks or cranks; they were wealthy merchants who wanted a sophisticated Boston-style spiritual life, and they had purchased a handsome lot very close to the First Church, right across Town House Square. Their church would be something new in Salem, symbolic of the triumph of an enlightened future, wrested from the grasp of a worn-out past.

In the battle of the First Church, Henry Colman was the victor. Timothy Pickering forfeited the respect of former admirers, and old John Prince traded some of his best members for Charles W. Upham. Colman, the inspiring persuader, would soon be a well-paid Salem personage, suddenly promoted from would-be assistant at the oldest church in Massachusetts to full-time pastor at the very newest—and one of the richest.

Stephen White was energized and inspired. With the tariff enacted and nothing more to fear, the president of the East India Marine Society and prince of merchants commenced a campaign of new building and new business. He started with the society: the most important institution in Salem had no permanent home. A large new downtown museum building, handsome and modern, would make the right statement about the society and what it represented in Salem, and what Salem represented in the world. To handle liability issues, White created the East India Marine Hall Corporation, in which the society itself became the largest investor. In May 1824, the corporation purchased a lot on Essex Street, nearly opposite White's boyhood home, as the site of its grand new museum.[15]

White was on a roll. To some of his corporation partners, he proposed the founding of two more companies: the Asiatic Bank and the Oriental Insurance Company. These were major undertakings, involving very large amounts of capital in a crowded field. Salem had three insurance companies and four banks, which, unlike commerce, yielded predictably high returns. Some rich people agreed: Joseph Ropes and Tucker Daland resigned from the Merchants Bank to join the board of the Asiatic Bank, and Stephen's uncle Robert Stone came over from the Commercial Bank. Altogether they raised $200,000 in capital and elected Stephen White as president. The Asiatic Bank symbol, painted on a large signboard, was the head of an Indian elephant holding up a large golden key in the tip of its trunk. At the Oriental Insurance Company, another $200,000 was raised to cover policies for loss of personal and real property and for "insurance on vessels, freight, money, goods and effects, and against captivity of persons and on the life of any person during his absence at sea. . . ."[16] The Oriental, run by Stephen's brother-in-law William Fettyplace, may have been the first company in Salem to offer life insurance to ordinary seamen.

In a matter of about a month, Stephen White had set in motion three major enterprises in Salem, involving massive amounts of money, much public benefit, and the creation of a new imperial monument.

By Independence Day, progress was evident. A new marine railway had been built, new vessels were under construction in the shipyards, a lead mill was in the works, and steam engines were being demonstrated.[17] Outsiders were again paying attention to Salem. White's friends were congratulating him. He was now both a state representative and a member of the Governor's Council. In recognition of his work in science and public education, he was elected as the only Salem member of the prestigious Lyceum of Natural History of New York City.[18] These triumphs were not lost on a citizenry happy to have a progressive leader committed to their well-being. Many wished to make Salem a Boston-style city, with Stephen White as mayor; and they hoped to see Salem follow Boston into the development of mill dams and factories. That idea, the one most important to working-class families, had been laid aside since being defeated at the town meeting in 1823. The people depended on the merchants to introduce such things, and the merchants still looked to the sea.

On July Fourth, the whole town turned out for a grand parade and an oration from the young teacher Henry K. Oliver, who spoke of the coming visit of the Marquis de Lafayette, the fight for independence in Greece, the deplorable slave trade, and the rights of American Indians. No longer divided by party and faction, the citizens cheered his oratory. But there was much that he did not say. Commerce was faltering, with dark consequences. The charity house remained full, and the Salem Female Charitable Society was never more challenged to provide financial and moral support to needy women and children. The town's prostitutes had become more brazen, and some of the "gentlemen" of the town had gone out of their way to have three of them arrested. While Justice Ezekiel Savage was sentencing them for their crimes and their "complete depravity of the human heart," the mother of one spoke out against a political system in which women had no rights and a town in which the poor could not find honest work.[19]

Such concerns did not trouble the rest of the country, in which prosperity abounded and the presidential campaign was heating up. The race had changed markedly with the rumors of William Crawford's ill health and the surprise entry of Andrew Jackson, famous for his victory at New Orleans and for his Indian massacres and invasion of Spanish Florida. He had often acted without authority and against the wishes of Presidents Madison and Monroe and their cabinet members, who saw him as a bloodthirsty guerrilla. Only one of them had been his defender: Secretary of State Adams, to whom diplomats from other nations had to make concessions or risk facing Jackson's troops.[20] Throughout the South and West, Jackson's love of combat and of dueling—he had shot many honorable men who had crossed him—added to his popularity as The Hero, a

rough-hewn democrat representing their smash-and-grab values. It had not occurred to Secretary Adams, his longtime patron and apologist, that Jackson
might do to him what he had done to everyone else: invade his turf and try to
beat him down.

The noblest old warrior of the War of Independence, the last of the fighting
generals of the Revolutionary Army, was making a tour of the United States, the
nation that had grown up since his departure forty years before. In the summer
of 1824, the Marquis de Lafayette, sixty-seven, accompanied by his son Georges
Washington de La Fayette, arrived from France and was welcomed as a symbol
of the heroic age of virtue and idealism. Salem, having read of extravagant re-
ceptions in New York, Providence, and Boston, prepared a celebration led by
Judge Story.

Captain John White, forty-two, Stephen's older brother, would be making
the oration at Lynn, just south of Salem, upon the arrival of Lafayette, whom
White had met while trading in France in 1812. Retired from the sea, left un-
employed by a navy at peace, White was living on his uncle's farm and trying to
advance the literary career that had begun with his *A History of a Voyage to
the China Sea* in 1823, the first American book about Vietnam. Now White had
proposed *The Mercantile Lexicon and Factor's Oracle,* a four-hundred-page work
intended for merchants and their agents. It would catalog the world's commercial resources "with the places of their production, the modes of obtaining them,
their characteristic marks of excellence, and directions how to choose them."
But maritime commerce had gone flat, and John's idea did not attract enough
subscribers to turn it into a book.[21]

On the last day of August, John White expressed "the deep, intense, and
indelible feelings of this free and happy republic" as the marquis passed through
Lynn. After a brief visit to fishy Marblehead, Lafayette was met at the Salem
line by Judge Story in Stephen White's handsome barouche drawn by four white
horses, and in it they drove through the beautiful outlying farms until coming to
"Mount Pleasant," just above the South Bridge at the inner harbor. Below them
were the pennants and banners of companies of cavalry, infantry, and artillery,

a large phalanx of mariners, the ships flying their colors, and a huge crowd of cheering Salemites. After this greeting, the marquis called at the home of his old comrade-in-arms Colonel Timothy Pickering, visited the museum of the East India Marine Society, and attended the reception and the ball in his honor, during which he gallantly kissed the ladies and not a few of their daughters.[22]

In the rainy afternoon, a crowd assembled in Essex Street to hear Lafayette speak. At the rear stood a sunburned young man, coolly scanning the mass of humanity from which he stood apart. Dick Crowninshield and the *Persia* had arrived in Salem just after Independence Day. In the buildings of the museum and the church, he saw that a movement was under way, and he was amused to hear about the church battle and the merchant Stephen White's efforts at leadership. In his few weeks ashore, Crowninshield, now twenty, had set up a South Danvers machine shop to fabricate parts for factories and carriage makers. He was good at this, but he was better at other things. During his long absence, crime had subsided; but Dick had reconvened the old gang, boys and girls and bottles, in the cave at Wenham Woods, and Salem and vicinity had begun to suffer from assaults on stores, barns, and homes.

Under their umbrellas, the people stood through an oration by the voluble Judge Story and a brief speech from the old nobleman. As the marquis and his entourage bade farewell and the crowd began to disperse, the first of them realized that something was wrong. Upon reaching into the pockets of their overcoats, they clutched and scrabbled and came up empty—their wallets had disappeared. By the dozens they lined up in the rain at Justice Savage's office, and the day ended in festive celebration, deep in the woods, by those who had effected a significant transfer of Salem's spending cash.

On summer winds, John Beckford and the men of the White bark *Eliza* had returned to Salem from Russia in time to see Lafayette.[23] Autumn came on, and Beckford grew restless. The merchants were holding back their vessels, reluctant to commit their specie. At last Stephen summoned Beckford to his counting-house and gave him a voyage to the Orient, by way of Rio. Beckford was now an East India shipmaster, headed for membership in the East India Marine

Society and toward his goal, and his mother's, of someday setting up as a Salem merchant.

In mid-October, seven foreign figures arrived on board the ship *Emerald,* whose captain, James B. Briggs, had acquired them for the society's museum: India mannequins perfectly modeled and painted and dressed in the actual garb of their vocations. President White was delighted and had them arranged in a group at the society's museum hall, on the second floor of a bank. Hundreds of visitors crowded the staircase to see these simulacra, alarmingly true to life.[24]

The Orient called to John Beckford, and he was eager to be off. He put together a good crew and sailed in the bark *Eliza* with two other nephews of Stephen White: William Story Jr., first mate, and Henry White Jr.'s teenage son William H. White, seaman. Beckford's younger brother Joseph decided not to make this voyage: Thanksgiving was coming up, and it was a very long way to Java. The boy's reluctance was soon validated by news of the fate of Captain John Upton and his fifteen-man crew on board the ship *Maine.* All but one had died of disease at Batavia, as had ten more on three other Salem vessels.[25]

Stephen White thought about the debacle at the First Church and Timothy Pickering's fierce desire to hold on to power. Positive, permanent change was needed, or most of the good people would leave. This was true even within the Pickering family. Henry, a hard-luck merchant who had published two volumes of first-rate verse, had been about to move to New York when White had hired him for the Asiatic Bank;[26] and Henry's older brother, the lawyer John Pickering, had quit his job as county attorney and put his house up for sale, hoping to move to Boston. Stephen could not forget that it was John Pickering who had taken up his brother John's rambling seafaring journal and turned it into a book—not for money, but for the cause of literature and Salem. Pickering was in many ways essential to the town. He was its great scholar and philologist, its Harvard overseer, its editor and essayist, the leader of its musical organization, a genius and a kindly spirit often overwhelmed by the demands of old enmities. It did not have to be like that: Salem could become a new place.

Looking inward, White, an Episcopalian raised as a Unitarian, found that he too wished to be renewed. Henry Colman had inspired a sort of fervor among his followers. To White, it was a revelation. Federalist merchants were ready to reject the claims of the past and to create an institution devoted to enlightenment. Reverend Henry Colman was the sort of change agent that was needed, a unifier of the best of both parties. Already, White's Marine Hall architect, Thomas W. Sumner, had designed a beautiful house of worship for Colman's adherents.[27] Meeting with Colman, White found the minister congenial and decided to join his church. Colman made a point of seeking out and cultivating old Captain White and his relatives and other connections, and they too signed on.

On December 7, 1824, the luxurious Barton Square Church was opened for divine service, with Henry Colman preaching on *The Proper Character of Religious Institutions.* The building had tall columns in the style of the temples of Athens, reminding everyone of the Greeks and their struggle for freedom, a cause to which many had donated. After services, the proprietors elected Henry Colman their pastor.

In the contest for president, eighteen states conducted a popular vote and six states held the election within their legislatures. Calhoun was chosen vice president. For president, Jackson came away with ninety-nine electoral votes to Adams's eighty-four, Crawford's forty-one, and Clay's thirty-seven. Jackson had won the first heat, but the contest would have to be decided in the House among the top three. Clay, Speaker of the House and Jackson's bitter western rival, believed that Adams alone had the experience and talent to carry out the "various, difficult, and complicated duties of the chief magistracy." In early February 1825, on the first ballot, thirteen states went for John Quincy Adams of Massachusetts, the clear winner over Jackson (seven) and Crawford (four).

General Jackson cried foul, but the Constitution said he had lost. For once, Jackson did not shoot anybody but quit the Senate in a fury and went home to Tennessee to plan the first campaign of his war on President Adams and the new secretary of state, Henry Clay.

CHEAP THRILLS. The Crowninshield brothers and
their friends frequented dives like John Mumford's
roadhouse and brothel, conveniently situated near the
Boston turnpike at the western entrance to the town.
Occasionally, an evening would end in mayhem.

8.

CELEBRATIONS

America's economic resurgence stayed well clear of Salem. A *Gazette* writer stated that "foreign commerce, at the present time, does not afford sufficient business for our population; great numbers [of people] pass off to other towns and cities to seek employment; our present population does not much exceed that of 1810, and our tonnage employed in commerce is now less than formerly. The business of the town is not sufficient to employ the capital, for we have frequently heard it remarked that a large proportion of the bank capital was loaned to businessmen in other places."[1] Although its world-wide commerce had supplied the capital for the mills of Newmarket, Franconia, and Amesbury, the seaport itself seemed fated to be a bystander at the Industrial Revolution.

And then something amazing happened: the discovery, in Salem's slack rivers and saltwater coves, of vast amounts of modern industrial power, good for thousands of factory jobs and a total reversal of fortune.

Standing at the shore of Salem's North River in June 1825, a few well-dressed men felt the thrum of the dynamo, latent and stupendous, driven not by falling water, but by the hydraulic-force equations devised by engineers. Authorized by seventy-one others, the men were investigating the possible creation of "cotton or other manufactures in this town, either by water or steam power, with liberty to employ surveyors, engineers, and agents."[2] Their consultant, the distinguished engineer Loammi Baldwin—his wife was a Pickering cousin—excitedly held forth about the best sites for the factories.

They could hardly believe what he was saying: Salem had an inexhaustible resource that could ensure its future prosperity. It was not a tidal dam at Collins Cove that they needed, but an enormous mile-long dam that ran across Collins Cove and the North River, connecting them by a canal. Buried in the mud of local waters was the promise of a manufacturing center to rival the new industrial city at Lowell—formerly East Chelmsford—with five-story factories rising higher than the topmasts of the largest ships. All it required was good advice and wise decision making. Baldwin had worked on high-profile Boston-financed projects, including the tidal Boston Mill Dam, recently built to create power for urban manufacturing. Salem, he said, had far greater potential for tidal power than Boston. It was like magic—the secret to Salem's success had been there all along. Baldwin's auditors squinted across the waters, imagining redbrick structures producing thousands of tons of goods for export. This discovery came just in time, while they still had some money not invested in the new industrial companies on the rivers of New Hampshire.

Water was a concept that Salem understood: the Salem peninsula was nearly surrounded by tidal water. John Pickering, Benjamin W. Crowninshield, Joseph Ropes, and J. White Treadwell made up the steering committee of the new Salem Mill Dam Corporation.[3] They had great faith in Baldwin, whose water power strategy required them to secure riparian rights, divert a river, dig canals, buy up land, and build roads and huge dams. Regarding the steam power that they had agreed to investigate, Baldwin dismissed it: water power abounded. But Loammi Baldwin was too busy working elsewhere to be their surveyor, so they hired his younger brother George. He rapidly drafted a survey, with impressive calculations of power. To secure water flow rights, the committee, chaired by John Pickering, vigorously negotiated with the riverbank property owners and got promises of cooperation. By mid-July, the surveying process for mill privileges was finished with "very encouraging prospects."

David Moody, who had overseen the Boston Mill Dam project, viewed the waterways with John Pickering's young brother-in-law, the lawyer Benjamin R. Nichols, who was good with figures; and they submitted a favorable report to the committee in autumn 1825. It was a moment to celebrate. Pickering decided that if Salem had the resilience and energy to reinvent itself, he would stay. He had done a very good job of clearing the way for the mill dam. That he had relatives advising him, that he had dismissed steam power—these things were out in the open. A bit riskier was his hiring of two people involved in the Boston Mill Dam, for they might naturally want to minimize its failings, which were many, amounting to devastating environmental impacts and a dead loss of hundreds of thousands of investment dollars. But even then the disastrous results could not be totally disguised. Anyone standing in front of the statehouse could look out at the Boston Mill Dam, with an alleged capacity for forty mill-powers, and see a grand total of three small factories perched upon it.

At Cherry Hill Farm in Beverly, in early summertime, Captain Henry White fell very ill. At seventy-four, he was at the end of an adventurous life in which he had fought the British as a privateer, languished as a prisoner of war, founded a large family, commanded merchant vessels on voyages all over the world, worked as a merchant, and finished as a contented farmer. He and his wife, Phebe, sixty-eight, had raised seven children, with Joseph, Stephen's former business partner, the only one missing from the group. In early August, there was a coming together of the family—Henry had many grandchildren—as the siblings watched over their father with their mother and their disabled brother, Francis, thirty-five, who had never left home. Abigail, the youngest, was thirty; Henry Jr., the eldest, was forty-six. Captain Henry White died on the afternoon of August 13, 1825; he was remembered publicly as "a patriot of the Revolution, distinguished for his private worth, sound sense, and inflexible integrity."[4]

After that Stephen had only one father.

On a fine sunny afternoon in October beneath the yellow-leaved elms of Chestnut Street, about one hundred very rich men smiled and chatted as they shuffled

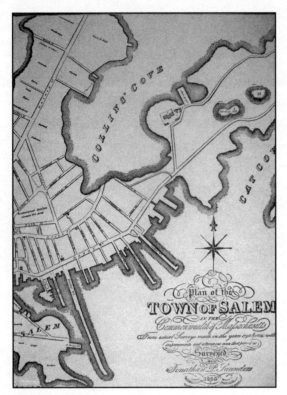

*THE LOWER END. Home to
Salem's seafaring families and
Republican merchants, the so-called
Lower End, or East Parish, fronted on
the outer harbor and encompassed the
Common and the proposed site of a
tidal milldam across Collins Cove.
Stephen White's wharf was the third
one northeasterly of the longest,
Derby Wharf.*

themselves into ranks outside of their elegant gathering place, Hamilton Hall.
They wore identical dark cutaways, slate-colored trousers, and black down-curving
cocked hats, with swords at their sides. When the band struck up a marching
tune, the members of the Salem East India Marine Society moved out smartly
into the street, following Stephen White, their president and master planner of
the grand event that lay ahead.

White had done well, for the parade included some of the region's most
distinguished men. Salem's own formidable array of national figures was headed
by his brother-in-law Joseph Story, forty-five, of the U.S. Supreme Court, along
with Nathaniel Silsbee, fifty-two, U.S. senator-elect and president of the Massachusetts Senate, and *his* brother-in-law Congressman Benjamin W. Crowninshield, fifty, ex–secretary of the navy, and Colonel Timothy Pickering, eighty,
president of the Essex Agricultural Society, former congressman, senator, and

cabinet member. From Boston came Mayor Josiah Quincy Jr., and from Cambridge came Reverend John T. Kirkland, president of Harvard. Such was the influence of Stephen White and his club of merchants that their guest of honor, at the head of the parade, was the president of the United States, John Quincy Adams.

They marched down the main thoroughfare, Essex Street, lined with buildings draped in bunting and big crowds of men and boys applauding, and the women and girls looking on from the windows above. To many, it was thrilling to see the great men of their town in procession with the president, the first northerner and nonslaveholder to be elected since his father, John Adams, almost thirty years before. John Quincy Adams stepped firmly, if a bit grimly, in leading the American procession. He was no smiling politician, but a steely diplomat on a national mission, certain of the unifying force of the new policies that he would soon place before Congress.

The members of the society marched alone—no woman or girl, no person of color, no laborer or mechanic, no builder of ships, not even a doctor or lawyer or minister went with them. These men, masters and merchants, had met great challenges, weathered hurricanes and storms of war, gone a-privateering, and survived the privations of British prisons. They had outsailed pirates and outbluffed rivals in a dozen ports; they had endured lulls in trade and smuggled their way through government embargoes and naval blockades. They had kept costly secrets, and sometimes they had betrayed one another in dangerous ports twelve thousand miles from home. They had followed their leaders in partisan and ritualized hatred of one another; but finally they had ended as comrades, united by wealth and salt water and their love of Salem. Row on row, the one hundred marchers made a brave show for the sailors and artisans and laborers and shopkeepers, wives and children and elderly parents, all dependent on these men and their money. Through their success, Salem would prosper.

These enterprising merchants, so handsome and confident, paraded past people who wondered about the future. Many were out of work or underemployed. Some of their friends and relatives had given up and gone west into the America in which opportunity shone brightly. Packed onto wagon trains and steamboats, they had taken their skills and dreams to counties and cities and lakefronts where the past did not impinge and castes did not exist. For them, Salem had quickly become a dream, a part of the past, back east. But Salem was real enough and had continued to push into its own famous frontier: the sea and the worlds beyond the blue horizon. With great dignity, the merchants marched along, holding Salem's fate in their pale, soft hands; and the people applauded.

Once, they had marched behind a man in a Chinese mask and a brilliant silk gown, in celebration of the Oriental cultures that had made their fortunes. The innocent exuberance of those days had been a casualty of the war. Now they marched as sedate gentlemen, passing the town's new Unitarian church, and the stores and Town Hall at Derby Square, and the tall mansion of Congressman Crowninshield, and they stopped directly opposite Stephen White's columned countinghouse, in front of the East India Marine Hall, on its day of dedication.

With its name incised high in the façade, and the names *Asiatic Bank* and *Oriental Ins. Co.* over the lower doors, the hall was a happy blend of glass and granite, commerce and culture. To White, it had fallen short: the most distinctive feature of Sumner's design, the third-floor pavilions, had been omitted to save money. Although it was still a handsome building, it was not the shining landmark that White had commissioned, a beacon reflecting sunlight out to the countryside and to the ships at sea.

At the head of the stairs, as they entered the huge second-story ark, the society members and guests encountered the Calcutta simulacra dressed in native garments. Along the walls were brightly painted idols, a bulky palanquin, decorated shields, wicked kris knives and crossed stands of spears, tall palm-frond fans, and, on the high walls above them, a sky of paintings: landscapes of Oriental seaports, portraits of turbaned banyans and dignified mandarins, portraits of the society's shrewd shipmasters and sleek merchants, and large paintings of the beautiful ships that had voyaged to the source of their wealth.

On this fine day, the new hall was decked out for feasting. The leading restaurateur, John Remond, served a dinner "in a style of magnificence heretofore

EAST INDIA MARINE HALL. Developed by Stephen White, the glass-and-granite building set a new standard in Salem. In its large upstairs hall, visitors encountered a group of alarmingly lifelike mannequins from India, surrounded by hundreds of paintings, artifacts, and specimens from the Orient.

unequalled in this town." Oratory followed, and superb wines accompanied ingenious toasts. The secretary, Stephen White's dashing cousin John White Treadwell, rose first and offered, "The President of the United States of America!" The assembly loudly saluted President Adams, who then rose and gave his own toast: "To the mariners of Essex, and their tributes, in peace and in war, to the glory of their country!"

More than twenty well-orchestrated toasts would follow.

"To commerce: the great civilizer of nations!"

"To the members of this Society: may their success as masters of good ships enable them to become owners of better ones!"

"To the trade to India: no commercial nation has been great without it: may the experience of ages induce us to cherish this rich source of national wealth!"

"To the navigators of the town of Salem: famed for nautical skill, correct discipline, and pure patriotism!"

Responding to White's call for unity, even the last Federalist, Timothy Pickering, offered "harmony among the various professions of society important to the prosperity of all." On this day in the East India Marine Hall, Salem was once more a great center of world commerce. Its bold merchants and brilliant navigators overspread the global seas and oceans, reaching to the last port of the rich Indies. Salem, they boasted, had no wage slaves toiling in textile factories; rather, its sailors gloried in "strong limbs, hard faces, and free-born manners—these are not the product of spinning-jennies!" Salem was no mill town but an imperial capital, representing the world of action and brains and enterprise, the freedom of the seas, the expansive vitality and limitless success of young America.

Josiah Quincy could be magnanimous as he offered a salute from his flourishing city to "the inhabitants of the town of Salem, who at all times, but especially in times of greatest peril, have stood to those in Boston in the relation of firm friends, generous rivals, and exemplary patriots." He made no mention of the greater celebration of that same day: in Manhattan, Governor DeWitt Clinton officially opened the Erie Canal, the incomparable man-made river connecting the inland sea of the Great Lakes and the Atlantic Ocean.

Outside, the crowd drifted away, already accustomed to this symbol of Salem's magnificence, put up by the great merchants for their businesses and their museum. It could be seen as a sign of the merchants' faith in Salem's future and their pride in its role in the world. It was also a monument to Stephen White. At last, his colleagues were sharing his view of Salem as a modern city, with great architecture and diversified businesses and institutions to match its capabilities. White had overcome everything that had formerly torn them apart, and for that they were grateful. So this parade to the new hall, with the president of the United States leading the way, was not just the march of hypocrites but symbolic of the new spirit of unity, which could forgive the inebriated members of the East India Marine Society for celebrating their trade with India and their commerce with the world.

Near the entrance to the Boston Turnpike, a few weeks after the opening of the hall and its museum of treasures, a different sort of celebration was held at Mumford's Hotel.[5] If Stephen White was the prince of merchants, John Mumford was the black king of shantytown, a tall, strong ruler whose own famous residence had a grogshop in the cellar and a brothel up the stairs.

With regal assurance, "King" Mumford served as a fence and broker, bridging two worlds, white and black, legal and lawless. White men came to him to buy cheap liquor, hire day laborers, spend time with a girl, or unload some hot goods, no questions asked. His trade was brisk, and his house was much frequented. Although he dealt in illegalities, Mumford was not reckless and generally stayed out of trouble thanks to protectors within the white community. He had begun in Salem as a carpenter, skillful and ambitious, and he had got his share of work and credit.

Travelers were always surprised to come upon a group of disreputable hovels as they entered Salem from the turnpike, but the locals had their reasons for loving them. Mumford's, shabby by day, was a portal to drink, dancing, gambling, and various other pleasures of the night. Caleb Foote of the *Gazette* had no use for the place and contrasted Salem's toleration with Boston's stringent anticrime policies. There, Mayor Quincy, leading the transition from town to city, was eradicating "the numerous sinks of vice and infamy" that had long infested the seaport. The city of Boston was being remade as shiny as the gold dome of the statehouse.[6]

Although Salem's selectmen had no legal basis for actions as drastic as Boston's, the constables finally did carry out a raid on Mumford's hovels and hauled in "three or four wretched women," presented to Squire Savage "as vagrants and peace-disturbers." Foote reported that the women were white and thoroughly unrepentant. "We doubt whether our state can furnish a parallel to this infamous nest of brothel-houses on the turnpike, white and black indiscriminately mingling in iniquity and debauchery of the most brutal and shocking nature. It is really astonishing that Salem has so long suffered such a stigma upon its character. It is astonishing that our selectmen, if by any stretch of their authority they can remove it, have for so long suffered such a nuisance to continue. The women who were taken yesterday were good-looking and might have been ornaments to their sex and society. One of them carried a beautiful infant in her arms, who smiled upon her face as she braved the indignant gaze of those who were assembled to witness her guilt. . . ."

When Justice Savage sentenced the women to sixty days in the charity house, they mocked him. "It is no uncommon thing," wrote Foote, "to see them laugh in the face of the magistrate when he passes sentence upon them, and tell him that they will very soon make their escape or that they had rather go to the work-house than not, where they can rest comfortably for a week or two." Editor Foote suggested that if no means were taken "to purge our town of such nuisances" and "if our police regulations are not to be mended," the public should find "some proper and efficient mode of punishing such offenders," though it meant building a house of correction "where they can be made to work without hope of escape."[7]

But the good times rolled on at Mumford's. A few weeks after, the constables made another raid during a wild bacchanal, wading into what the stiff-necked editor Caleb Foote called "the scum of our brothels, the offscourings of our grogshops, and the dregs and refuse of our Negro huts," all "mingled together in one indiscriminate mass." Then a man died there, overcome by drink, and Foote inveighed against "infamous brothelhouses" so disgraceful that "no person of decency can pass these huts without being mortified at their uncomeliness."[8] The town fathers, however, were unwilling to take action. Clearing slums and routing out criminals might be good for Boston, but Mumford's was, after all, something of an institution and not a place that was entered by accident or by anyone unprepared to make a steep and scary descent.

Two of its regulars were the brothers Crowninshield, Richard and George, aged twenty-one and twenty, dandies and young men-about-town. Their exploits had given them a dark fame. Dick was a wizard in his way, with his remarkable machine shop, but axles were not his real obsessions. His brother George had little of Dick's drive. George was a playboy and a bounder who enjoyed the theater and the society of whores and gamblers and ex-cons, and who traveled often to Boston and New York and New Orleans, usually to get clear of a bad situation or just to go slumming. George had no skill or training that might give him a career, but he did love to have fun.

On the late afternoon of November 9, toward dusk, the Crowninshields went hunting for some action. George and two friends, fresh from Boston, came by in a coach and picked up Richard for a night in the big city; but just outside the gates of the turnpike they pulled over. Mumford's Hotel seemed to beckon, as it had a few weeks before, when the Crowninshield boys had been among the party crowd during the raid. Now, the group decided to defer their Boston trip, and George's young gentlemen friends, William Rich and Daniel Wise, followed Dick and George down into the cellar to order a round of rum, perhaps the third of the day. The womenfolk claimed not to have any, but George insisted, and soon a very large man entered the room.

"Here's the General himself," said George, flicking his riding whip as he renewed his demand. John Mumford offered to send out for rum if paid. George ignored him and took the lamp and inspected the bottles on the counter until he found one that seemed promising.

"Does it chipper?" cracked Wise, in slang.

George allowed that it did indeed chipper and turned to his host, holding up the bottle in triumph. "You told me you had no rum, but I have found some," he said. "Mumford, 'twill puzzle the devil to take this from me!"

George proved his point with a long drink and passed it to Dick; and it went back and forth quickly among the visitors. When the bottle was empty, George set it spinning on the counter, and it crashed on the floor. He took up another bottle and spun that one, and it too fell and shattered. Mumford demanded payment for the rum, but the four drunk intruders mocked him and started dancing and whooping around the room, pausing to douse the fire and fling a bowl of potatoes and generally terrorize the Mumfords. When Mumford tried to stop them, George pounded him with his whip handle, and Rich kicked him, and Dick and Wise punched him in the head and hit him with an oil can. Satisfied, they relaxed and joked with Mumford about their earlier adventures in Boston. When Mumford went outdoors, Wise followed and soon made friends with a girl on the steps.

In her husband's absence, Margaret Mumford and her grown daughter, Betsy Wilson, invited the men to clear out, but instead Richard and George knocked them out of their chairs. When Margaret tried to escape from the room, George punched her. She fought back, and then he hit her in the forehead with an iron bar. General mayhem ensued, with Elizabeth and her mother battling the Crowninshields in the dark, punching, jumping, shoving, biting, and screaming. "Murder!" cried Betsy, whereupon Dick and William fled out the door, which locked behind them and trapped George inside. Richard too cried murder, and then Betsy's husband, Benjamin Wilson, and her large brother, William Mumford, pummeled George while rescuing Mrs. Mumford. Brained and bleeding, George advised them that he did not "value two thousand dollars to kill a Negro." This led to more chaos. Muffled screams and sounds of mayhem drew a crowd, and finally John Mumford burst into the room with a squad of neighbors, black and white, including the constable. Thus ended the evening's entertainment. Margaret Mumford sat weeping, and George Crowninshield, shoeless, watchless, and bleeding from the nose and head, laughed at his drubbing and thanked his rescuers. The constable led George away; and Dick, in his elegant coach, drove off into the night.

The "Riot at Mumford's" was given top billing in the newspapers for a couple of days—a major break with tradition in Salem, where editors were circumspect about local matters, especially those involving the nephews of a congressman and a senator. This case, however, was different. Everyone thought that Dick and George deserved a comeuppance, and everyone knew that Mumford's was a den of iniquity. Further, the story had the attractions of violence between men and women, blacks and whites, rich and poor, and a beat-up Crowninshield thrown in jail. It also featured the young lawyer Rufus Choate attempting to defend the indefensible. This was the case he had been waiting for since having passed the bar in 1823. In South Danvers, he had established himself as a Fourth of July orator, state legislator, and electrifying courtroom pleader; but he had not yet found the reputation-making case that would raise him high in Salem. The Crowninshields gave Choate that chance, and the rich manufacturer paid him well to rescue his sons.

The hearing attracted such a large crowd on Saturday that the local justice, Ezekiel Savage, moved the proceedings to the second-floor auditorium of the

Town Hall. At the end of the second day, before Choate had put on his case, the Salem *Gazette* editorialized about the trial and the conditions that it exposed. The reporter inveighed against John Mumford and his "infamous establishment." The peace of society "has long enough been disturbed by tumults and broils either at his house or in his neighborhood (the whole of which in fact is under his control) and justice has long enough slumbered at her post." The "great concourse of citizens" could not have asked for better drama. Justice Savage was not at all pleased with the public spectacle in his courtroom or with the revelations, attitudes, and behaviors of the witnesses.

Choate exceeded every expectation.[9] He blasted the prosecution for withholding John Mumford as a witness, and he ripped into the others' contradictory testimony. Skillfully, gradually, playing to the audience like a Shakespearean actor, he turned the trial around. It was not about drunk intruders who beat up women; it was about the Mumfords and their den of iniquity and the dark fascination that it held for young men, and the violence of past incidents, and the brutal beating that George had suffered. He summoned both blacks and whites to testify about the events of that chaotic night, and he used them as characters in a narrative that illuminated the terrifying and hellish world entered through the portals of the Mumford Hotel.

Ultimately, the newspapers portrayed Dick and George more as victims than as villains, but one editor did choose to release the court proceedings verbatim, concluding that "the folly and indiscretion of youth may entitle them to pity, but justice must be satisfied. A career of idleness and dissipation is inevitably closed by misery and disgrace. The arrest, the trial, the public exposure, the first lesson, must come: to these victims it has come; it is a solemn and, may it be, an efficacious, warning." The cynical brothers, however, would not be chastened. There was no repentance, no confession of fault or error. Faced with the Crowninshields' bad attitudes and obvious misbehavior on the one hand, and with Choate's unrefuted arguments on the other, Judge Savage ruled that the Crowninshields "had been the aggressors" and were to be "held answerable for the consequences" in an upcoming session of the court of common pleas. Mumford filed again, for $1,000 in damages; but when the actions were tried, the brilliance of the defense could not be overcome.

Choate's career was launched, the Crowninshields walked, the Mumfords lay low, and the crowds moved on. Judge Savage deplored the public spectacle and the mesmerizing effect of the magician Choate. Justice, he thought, should not be a matter of popularity or oratory. Savage was deeply disturbed by "the evil" in the case and by the fear of further trials and outrages that might, in their impact, amount to "a dreadful conflagration by fire"—the moral destruction of the town.

George Crowninshield, with his usual insouciance, laughed it off and celebrated—it had been a grand frolic, well worth the stitches and bruises, good for years of tall tales and free drinks. Dick Crowninshield, though, was furious at being held up for the amusement and scorn of the public. He was not who they thought he was. He did indeed feel the conflagration's heat; and he, and Salem, would never be the same.

Thanksgiving 1825 was a time of celebration for Stephen White and family. At their three-story fifteen-room mansion overlooking the common, they prepared for the holiday and its parties and dances. The prints and paintings and statuary were dusted, and the furniture waxed and buffed, and the plate and crystal polished to a high sheen. The family had much for which to be grateful, not least general good health, except for Stephen's sickly wife, Harriet. The Whites now had a beautiful church in which to worship, with a wonderful new friend in the minister, Mr. Colman, who would come to their house and sing with Harriet as she played the piano. Old Captain White was well pleased with Colman;[10] and he and Stephen had never been closer. Stephen knew that in the captain's will he had been named the largest beneficiary—a good thing, for he was deeply in debt to him.

At thirty-eight, Harriet and Stephen were the parents of three lively girls—Harriet, fifteen, Caroline, fourteen, Ellen, thirteen—and a son, Joseph, now eleven. They continued in friendly relations with Harriet's sister Eliza Story White, still widowed, raising three daughters for whom Stephen was both an uncle and a father figure. With six vivacious girls on hand—double cousins and virtual siblings—the White household was a hive of teenage activity. The two eldest cousins, Eliza Jr. and Harriet Jr., attended a notable girls' school in Boston.[11] Harriet and Stephen, ever ready to hold a convivial supper or an evening of music, were highly sociable and threw parties and sponsored balls, as did Eliza and many of their friends. With enormous wealth, personal attractiveness, lively children, and a love of display and finery, they were the exemplars of fortune's lifestyle.

The Thanksgiving season was a time of partygoing, and the Whites' predance soirees were not to be missed. The ladies favored long gowns of pale silk and white cotton muslin based on classical models, generally low-cut, gathered below the breast, often sleeveless. Unlike their dresses, so elegant in their simplicity, the ladies' hair might be elaborately done up, while the men wore theirs over the ears and the nape of the neck. For headgear, the men favored top hats of real beaver or narrow overhanging cocked hats. Cloaks were common: long dark cloaks lined with scarlet or shorter cloaks with red velvet collars. A short jacket known as a spencer was popular, as were frock coats in bright colors, and vests in shiny marseilles cloth with bright sprigs or in woolen kerseymere with lapels, buttoned over a white shirt with ruffles. Stephen White and most modish men had put aside their knickers for the new style of very tight trousers, tied in a bow at the ankles, with silk stockings and low-cut pumps, all the better for lively stepping to the music.[12]

The house, of course, was beautifully decorated. A party had no set supper— the general idea was for people to circulate freely, enjoying their conversations and their mobility, with no effort made to sit them down or to offer heavy foods. A night of dancing lay ahead and would be followed by the full-course seated dinner. Early in the evening, the guests would assemble at the White mansion on Washington Square and mix in the spacious parlors, ablaze with candlelight and lamplight and reflections in great pier mirrors, chandeliers, and crystal sconces. It could be very cold in the house, for there were few stoves and no furnaces, so partygoers would rush from room to room, huddling by the marble-fronted fireplaces to get the warmth of a big wood fire. Then waiters would appear and dodge in and out with empty plates for the guests, soon to be served with a first course of jelly and blancmange, a milk pudding. The waiters eventually returned with large trays of glasses of wine and lemonade. The partying continued over these drinks; and the return of the waiters, with oranges, nuts, and raisins, signaled the final phase of the soiree,[13] after which the company departed for a ballroom and the rest of the night's festivities.

At Thanksgiving, the one true holiday of New England—Christmas was generally not observed by these descendants of the Puritans—absent family members were remembered: relatives who had moved, sons and brothers at sea, the departed and the deceased. There was much to think of, for scores of Salem's ships were sailing across far-off oceans, in safety or in storms, headed toward unknown fates. At the moment, Stephen White had just one vessel in port and nine at sea: one bound for China; four sailing for or returning from Sumatra via Brazil; the *Elizabeth,* just cleared for Malta; the *Shawmut,* at Trieste; the old *Eliza & Mary,* in South America under Captain Benson; and the bark *Eliza,* believed to be approaching the coast with young Captain Beckford and his two cousins on board.

White's fleet never went to India anymore, but his vessels usually found good trading in other ports and good markets for selling hides, coffee, pepper, flavorings, spices, and the wine in which he had a specialty. The day might come when he would put most of his money into manufacturing, but he loved the business of ships and trade, and he was in no rush to turn his back on the sea.

T wo weeks after Thanksgiving, the bark *Eliza* arrived from Java commanded by Captain Barker, who had gone out as second mate. All three of White's nephews, he reported, were dead: Captain John Beckford, twenty-three; First Officer William Story Jr., twenty-one; and William H. White, sixteen, making his first voyage to the Orient. Disease and fevers had felled them, and all had died before the *Eliza*'s departure from Batavia.

Their families were devastated. William Story was a beloved eldest child, and young William White was the only son of the widower Captain Henry White Jr. Beckford's mother, the widow Mary Beckford, was inconsolable. John Beckford Jr. had been the hope of her family, the eldest and most promising son. Now he was as dead as his father, on a voyage for Stephen White, and Mary would have only memories of the excellence of her husband and son.

For Stephen White, a man of feeling, the loss of life in connection with his business was always grievous; and the loss of three young nephews on one voyage was horrifying. There was no cure for it—it was a hazard of commerce—but that did not make it any less tragic, and it did not relieve him of feelings of guilt toward these young men, beloved kinsmen, and their families. Captain William Story would bear up, and his family; but Stephen feared it would kill his widowed brother, Henry, already sick and bankrupt.[14] Mary Beckford, he knew, would never, ever, forgive him.

9.

JUBILEE

Dick Crowninshield cleared out for the winter, far from the cold and the notoriety of Mumford's. He would never have chosen to be at the center of a public incident, but his brother had been in mortal danger. George, his favorite and his disciple, simply did not have the brains or the discretion to do what needed to be done. It was a problem, for Dick had ambitions to create his own red-light district in Salem, offering drinking, gambling, dancing, and whoring.

But that would have to wait, for he went as a passenger to Charleston, South Carolina, where the rice planters lived like lords. The city was handsome, with broad streets and tall churches and many mansions and beautiful fragrant gardens concealed by high walls and palmettos. Along the promenade, by the harborfront, the local beaux and belles made a famous strolling parade not unlike that of Washington Square in Salem; and, like Salem's, Charleston's gentry loved music and dancing.

As the story came back to Salem, Dick, nephew of a congressman and a senator, was warmly welcomed into Charleston society. It was a relief for him to play the young gentleman, to be someone else—and it was interesting to see how well he could do it and how easily he passed for a scion of the gentry among these trusting people. In his role as Fascinating Richard, visiting among the aristo families, enjoying their conversation and their generosity and their gracious manners, he would drink their wine and dance with their lovely daughters, passing for a normal sort of man. He made new friends among the town's

JOHN PICKERING VI. Lawyer, essayist, linguist, editor, musician, developer, philologist, and first president of the American Oriental Society, John Pickering (1777–1846) agreed to head up the Salem Mill Dam Corporation as the best means of effecting Salem's economic rescue.

young bloods, and he cut a dashing figure, very poetic and romantic, with flowing artificially curled hair, and a long face with a prominent chin, and a small, lush mouth; and some of Charleston's mothers began priming their daughters for a match.

But Dick needed no such assistance, for he had fixed on the eldest daughter of a very wealthy house and had paid her the usual attentions of a suitor, which were returned. She was barely seventeen and a great reader of novels and virginal idealizer of romance; and she was famously beautiful. He had fallen hard. She returned his feelings and made him happy. For once in his life, Dick felt a true, pure emotion and a connection to another person that seemed like love.[1]

In Salem, Joe Knapp cut his own impressive figure. In fashionable homes and at private musical venues he carried himself like a matador, with a haughty grace that made him a favorite among the sweethearts of the town's ballrooms. A twenty-one-year-old sea captain, Joe Knapp was a tough, shrewd fellow, cold-blooded and ambitious. At fifteen, he had borne the hardships and crudities of the sailor's life; at eighteen, callous and determined, pushed by his self-made merchant father, he was the bully of a crew; at twenty, he was sailing as master of family-owned vessels. This had put him among the elite of respectable young society. As Captain Knapp, shipmaster, he had earned respect from shipowners, deference from his crewmen, opportunities for riches and a good marriage, and possible ascent to partnership in a merchant house. In certain circles, Joe was a star.

Knapp's father had worked hard to build his Union Wharf shipping business, but the son had no interest in a life of toil. He was as good an actor as a dancer and passed for a gentleman. It was a thin disguise, for Joe was most happy as a raunchy sailor, running wild in foreign ports. On Essex Street, though, he posed like a fashion plate in Corinthian doorways and lounged in the lobby of the Lafayette Coffee House among the other pomaded bucks; and he moved with ease through the dances, tea parties, and churchgoing of female-dominated genteel society.

If Joe was something of a poseur, the next oldest Knapp brother, Nat, really had the qualities that Joe impersonated. Nathaniel Phippen Knapp was a popular senior at Harvard College, in that day more an academy than a university. Nat had enrolled from the public and private schools of Salem in 1822, exemplary as the sort of bright middle-class boy that old Harvard was welcoming into its august halls alongside the sons of rich merchants and professional men from families well-known in the annals of New England. The Knapps were not among them.

The years 1823 and 1824 had not been good ones for Captain Joseph J. Knapp's business. With the slowdown and the costs of providing for a large family of teenagers, he had turned to his old patron and former employer, Captain Joseph White, who in January 1825 had readily loaned him $3,000, secured by the Knapp homestead—the house in which White himself had grown up. With the loan, he was able to cover Nathaniel's college expenses, pay off debts, and purchase a brig, *Governor Winslow,* 148 tons burthen, for his little Caribbean fleet.

In November 1825, young Joe Knapp joined the East India Marine Society, although it was not clear that he actually qualified. The invitation must have come personally from the president, Stephen White, the beau ideal of the smart

set in Salem and the father of three daughters who would soon be of marriage-
able age. Ever alert to opportunity, Joe Knapp transferred his allegiance from
the East Church to the new Barton Square Church. After about a month at home,
he prepared to depart in command of his father's *Governor Winslow*, bound for
Martinico, the sugar island off Venezuela, with a chief mate, a crew of six, a cabin
boy, and a cook. It was hardly a glamorous enterprise. The outward cargo of
cured fish, lumber, and cheap furniture would not fetch much at St. Pierre. At
home, after the federal government's cut, little was left for the owner, from whose
proceeds the captain took much of his pay. Without the likelihood of large profit,
a shipmaster was simply hauling freight for other men, like a seagoing trucker.

As a lawyer or a physician, or even a minister, Nathaniel P. Knapp, Harvard
man, would have fine opportunities, especially if he left Salem. The Knapps'
older sister, Abigail, was married to William H. Low, a hustling young merchant
grown frustrated in Salem. They planned to move to New York City to join a
large middle class that prized books, music, conversation, liberal religiosity, and
a self-conscious propriety and outright teetotaling temperance that was something new. The big, rich, new cities welcomed men like brother Nat, who could
leverage his learning and contacts; but the rest of the Knapps might well be
marooned. As it was, all too many Salem ships remained at the dockside, waiting for months between voyages, with the western wind blowing through their
rigging. In the past, Salem had recovered from wars and embargoes, but to Joe
Knapp and his friends Salem felt becalmed while other places were surging forward. Some advocated transforming the seaport into a manufacturing center, but
Joe did not see how he could transform himself. Since boyhood, he had worked
to reach the goal that his father had set for him. Now, as Captain Knapp, he
might never make his fortune on the high seas—a fortune that had been part of
the promise of Salem for two hundred years. Luckily, he told himself, he did not
need to think too hard on these things, for he had seen the look in pretty Mary
Beckford's eyes.

In his congressional address of December 1825, presenting a visionary program
for the nation's future, President Adams declared that the purpose of government

was to improve the condition of the people governed—a position totally inimical to that of the states' rightists and slaveholders—and so he set forth his initiatives: a transportation system including new roads, bridges, and canals; a Department of the Interior; a naval academy and a national university; an astronomical observatory; a uniform standard of weights and measures; a voyage of discovery along the Pacific coast. He intended to make America, "the nation blessed with the largest portion of liberty," into "the most powerful nation upon earth." But Adams had not seen the huge wave that was rolling toward him, in the form of a furious General Andrew Jackson, a terrible loser, who felt, with all of his murderous heart, that the election had been stolen.

Jackson and his minions incited public outrage at the so-called corrupt bargain by which Clay had delivered the presidency to Adams. Three years in advance, Jackson began a new presidential campaign. In a blitz of articles, speeches, and rallies, and with the founding of partisan magazines and newspapers, Jacksonians everywhere vilified Adams as a dangerous, immoral, possibly insane man capable of leading the nation into disaster. The Hero, unwilling to foment a civil uprising, patriotically waited in exile among his slaves and supporters at the Hermitage, preparing for the day that the great injustice would be corrected.

Among other unforgivable statements, Adams had mentioned the need for better relations between the government and the Indian tribes. To his opponents, the Indians were squatters on American soil, red savages blocking the tide of white civilization. Adams was working with the Cherokees and trying to help the Creeks, they said—but what was he doing for the working white man trying to get his own piece of America?

Even then, Adams might have succeeded if he had simply retaliated. He was, however, a well-bred diplomat caught up in a western-style brawl. Adams resolutely took the high road, ignoring obvious slander and counting on the people to support their elected president. To his supporters seeking patronage, he insisted on merit, not loyalty. Urged to build a propaganda machine, he refused to demean himself and his office. The result was that the Jacksonians dominated Congress and passed their own legislation in defiance of the aristocrat from Massachusetts. Adams's adherents, like Joseph Story and Stephen

White, were appalled at the democracy that would raise up a blood-spattered demagogue as its idol.

John Pickering's Salem Mill Dam Committee had worked hard to create the conditions for industrial development. By the early spring of 1826, all was in readiness. Stephen White had done his part in the legislature, having managed the passage of legislation favorable to the mill dam corporation; and he had just been elected to Salem's seat in the state senate while continuing to serve on the Governor's Council. The committee members had listened to concerns about everything from the ownership of upriver property to investor liability to the costs of construction and the level of hydropower generated by the dams. Certain that they now had all of the answers, they proposed that the subscribers build a very large dam—a mile long, fifty feet wide, and five feet above the level of highest tide—to create a holding basin and a receiving basin. A canal, they explained, would run from one basin to another, generating between fifty and seventy mill-powers. The legislature had granted a charter for the Salem Mill Dam Corporation to hold property worth up to $700,000 and to build dams and to sell or lease water power and mill privileges. For the first time, limitations on the liability of individual stockholders were granted, for Massachusetts had little experience with the laws of business corporations.[2] The stock would be issued in five thousand shares, not exceeding $100 each.

Pickering's committee conceded that their model, the Boston Mill Dam, had "little success" and "small profits." However, Moody, its superintendent, thought it might still become "one of the greatest manufacturing establishments in the country."[3] The "Salem establishment," said Pickering, would be far more productive and cost-effective. As for being overrun by uncouth millworkers, the committee felt that newcomers would seek to fit in with the "large population of good habits and principles." To those who feared that "the habits of [Salemites] have so long been commercial that it will be difficult to turn their thoughts and to apply their talents to new occupations," the committee declared that Salem people were as enterprising as any in the world.[4]

Finally, factories would benefit Salem in many ways: "direct management of local industry," the ability to "keep our capital and our enterprising young men at home," a rise in real estate values, and the assurance that "the commercial and other business of this town, as well as its population, instead of declining or remaining stationary, would be advancing." Most important, Salem "would preserve its comparative importance with other sea-ports—and a solid foundation would be laid for the permanent prosperity of this ancient town and its vicinity."[5]

Duly impressed, the subscribers accepted the report, added two members to the committee, and authorized it to take measures to form a company "for the purpose of making the proposed mill dams and other works, and of establishing manufactures in Salem."[6] The project, it seemed, was now under way, with John Pickering firmly in command—and none too soon. People had been reading about the next big thing, the railroad. Like so many aspects of onrushing modernity, this too seemed to threaten Salem, whose fleet of wind-powered ships was the only sure employer of its people.[7]

In the spring of 1826, Joe Knapp was back in Salem, having completed his Caribbean voyage in the *Governor Winslow*. No doubt his father was willing to stake him to another, but Joe was looking for a better connection. Recycling the limited funds of the Knapp family was not what he had in mind. Instead, he approached his father's former wartime partner, Stephen White, as one who might do a big favor for a young shipmaster and fellow East India Marine Society member. White was willing to consider it—he was thinking of a European voyage for the *Caroline,* and her regular master, Captain Proctor, was unavailable. White was preoccupied with worries about the health of his wife, Harriet. He planned a vacation in the Catskills and at fashionable Saratoga Springs with their eldest daughter, Harriet, and niece Elizabeth, now graduated from finishing school and introduced to society as "accomplished young ladies."[8] White was also concerned about his relationship with Mary Beckford. As housekeeper for their adoptive father, Beckford saw the closeness of the two men and the many ways in which Stephen was favored. She was jealous of the advantages conferred on his children, and his dead brother's, as if they were royalty, going off to school in Boston, taking trips to spas, hobnobbing with every rich family and famous visitor, attending all the balls and parties for miles around, hosting glittering soirees in their great mansions on Washington Square. Stephen understood her envy but attributed it to the unhappiness of a "weak" person,[9] easily carried away. There was only so much that he could attend to in a very busy life, and he had to remain focused on politics and commerce and the news coming back from the other side of the globe.

His bark *General Stark,* commanded by A. D. Caulfield, had touched at Brazil and sailed on to the Indian Ocean and a terrible storm. She had been reported at Mauritius, east of Africa, shorn of her foremast and mainmast, half-wrecked, limping in under her mizzen spanker. Fortunately, word had just arrived that the *Stark,* repaired, had been within a week of completing a full lading of pepper at Kuala Batu. Caulfield's colleague, Captain Moses Endicott, had made a reputation as a geographer of Sumatra, turning his soundings and surveys into detailed handmade charts that he sold to other shipmasters. Endicott, commanding Pickman & Dodge's ship *Packet,* had gone to six different ports to make up a cargo, and his wanderings had given him a troubling picture of the Pepper Coast. Early in January, the officers and most of the crew of an English brig had been killed through the treachery of a sultan while seeking pepper at Asahan. In a second instance, the American ship *Maine* was targeted for attack at Mingin. Armed men from two canoes, claiming to have pepper for sale, had got on board the *Maine* before the captain had sensed danger and ordered his crew to drive them from the deck.

At Trumon, Endicott had learned of the probable cause of the violence toward visiting ships. The Dutch had attacked and taken an island and a small outport between Sinkil and Tapakuli. "Very much disturbed at this outrage," the Malays were planning to counterattack as soon as possible. Already, the rajah of Trumon—whose brother had slaughtered the men on board the British brig—had written politely to the king of England for help in dislodging the Dutch invaders.[10] Sumatra was becoming a more dangerous destination, requiring only the smartest of shipmasters. The military actions of other nations had turned many of the rajahs into potential enemies rather than reliable trading partners—and Salem's shipments of opium had contributed to instability among the populace of younger men, unpredictable addicts whose cravings could lead them into piracy.

Captain Caulfield had done well in a crisis far beyond the reach of White or his agents in the Orient. A successful voyage to Europe was a very different thing, and White decided to give young Joseph Jenkins Knapp Jr. a shot at command as a favor to an old family friend, Captain Knapp Sr. The son was a legitimate master mariner; he was well regarded around town, a member of the Barton Square Church, socially ambitious. Perhaps he also had a talent for profitable voyaging. In June 1826, Captain Joe Knapp weighed anchor and stood out to sea as master of Stephen White's *Caroline,* bound for Charleston, then to Hamburg, back to Charleston, over to St. Petersburg, and back to New York.

Soon after the sailing of the *Caroline,* Salem was rocked by the collapse of the merchant house of Peirce & Nichols. The spectacular failure of this firm could not have been predicted. So powerful was the tide of Salem's prosperity that no major Salem shipping firm had ever gone under. Its founder, Jerathmeel Peirce, had been in business since the 1780s and had brought along highly regarded younger partners, including his son-in-law Captain George Nichols, a founder of the Barton Square Church, and his son Benjamin Peirce, a Harvard man who had just been appointed a director of the Salem Mill Dam Corporation.

Jerathmeel Peirce, a very old and honorable merchant, was devastated. He instructed his creditors to take everything, down to the crockery on his kitchen shelves. Aghast, they urged him to stay where he was, but he insisted on being reduced to the level of Jerry Peirce, the poor young leather dresser who had wandered into Salem one day in 1768. With no end to his sadness, Peirce terrified the other merchants.

Captain Nichols went down with the firm but accepted his fate stoically, having weathered many a real gale and murderous typhoon. If he must die as a merchant, he was eager to be reborn as something more useful. His minister, Reverend Henry Colman, dreaded the visit he had to make, to bring consolation to a fallen merchant, the victim of a plague so swift and terrible that it made people think of a vengeful God. Trembling, Colman arrived at Chestnut Street and ascended the stone steps to the front door of the ruined man. Captain Nichols greeted him with a smile and took him by the hand into the airy parlor, with its hangings and paintings and mahogany, and sat him down on the satin sofa.

Nichols explained that the situation was hopeless: he had gone "in a few years from affluence to complete destitution." His firm had prospered after the war, but then had come "a long series of disasters"—the depression, shipwrecks, losing voyages, "bad management." Now they were bankrupt, although credit had been offered to recoup. Nichols had decided against it. The times were unfavorable for trade, and he had no assurance that future voyages would produce better results. "I have divided my property equally among my creditors," he said. "And now I must begin life again, with nothing to look to but my own resources." Backed by his thrifty, plucky wife, Nichols had "kept up a good heart and felt I should still be able to support my family comfortably." When Colman asked how he would do so, Nichols replied calmly, "I never felt less anxiety in my life, Mr. Colman. The Being who gave me my children will assuredly take care of me and of them if we only strive to do our duty."

"Captain Nichols, I envy you," said Colman.[11]

Although he would lose his grand house on Chestnut Street as well as his business, George Nichols was determined to remain in Salem—and to find a way to pay for his eldest son's education at Harvard. The younger boys could join their father in a business. He moved his family to Warren Street, near Chestnut, and he took in his fast-fading father-in-law, Jerathmeel Peirce, and Peirce's daughter Betsy.[12] Nichols knew that he was not the only one in trouble, so he became an auctioneer of furnishings, unwanted vessels, and foreclosed houses.

Salem's commerce, spread out worldwide under straining canvas, was completing its second year of general unprofitability. In the summer of 1825, a brief recession hurt all shippers; a year later, in retaliation for the Monroe Doctrine, Great Britain denied American vessels access to its ports and those of its colonies—open with near reciprocity since 1822.[13] Samuel Williams, Salem's eminent banker and commission merchant for forty years in London, suddenly failed. No one was certain of the causes or the solutions, but all could agree on the consequences: "a depreciation of property, a cessation of the usual returns of investments, and a general stagnation of business." Salem's merchants frankly discussed their difficulties. The tariff forced them to drop certain kinds of imported goods altogether, but it did not prevent them from loading other goods or from trading from port to port in the world. However, their energy and activity only took them deeper into a global malaise. The exception was the United States, internally expanding, affording good returns to the capitalists invested in manufacturing. Higher levels of growth and productivity were the results as more immigrants arrived in the seaports and more people of all backgrounds settled the interior and flocked to the cities. These waves of national prosperity did not reach Salem's shores.

"A Merchant," writing in the *Salem Gazette,* asked, "How many merchants, manufacturers, and bankers have been ruined, and from causes which no eye could foresee, and no caution guard against? The state of commerce is beyond the power of anything human to control; it lies deep and concealed, and if statesmen and politicians have depth of intellect enough to reach it, they have not the ability to apply a remedy or a corrective." Salem investors, having shifted much of their money out of trade, now saw the value of their holdings in banks and insurance companies starting to slide.

Outwardly, Salem still looked good. "In all probability," wrote *Gazette* editor Caleb Foote, "there has never been a time in which our shipping was in so good order, or so well built and found, or our [ship] masters possessed of so much skill in navigation and trade. No insurance company has as yet suffered diminution of capital, and all, if dissolved, would return at least par. . . . The problem is too many companies, including those of the metropolis which have agencies in this town. The present course will lead to ruin."

In August, at a conference of the shareholders of Salem's insurance companies, the meeting's chairman, Judge Story, made a few observations on the depreciation of insurance stock, noting that the value of insurance premiums had fallen by 50 percent since 1820. After a long discussion, he suggested that it was time to take action. Each company should hold a meeting to see if investors wished to set a minimum premium rate, to offer a uniform rate of credit, or even to dissolve their companies. At that moment, dissolution at par would free up a good deal of capital for other purposes, such as the Salem Mill Dam.

Story's advice was taken and the meetings were held, at which the shareholders decided to preserve their insurance companies and ride out the storm.

In the summer of 1826, Joe Knapp's brother Nathaniel Phippen Knapp was graduated from Harvard with every prospect of a fine career. Under the new name of Phippen—more distinguished than Nat—he was ready for the typical postcollegiate track: the boys were at liberty to pursue any one of the professions through clerkships. Knapp had some interest in theology but decided to find a place with an attorney, reading the law and filing pleadings until he could join the bar. Essex County's lawyers were among the best in the state; and their leader, Joseph Story, had already achieved the highest peak of legal ambition. Nat/Phippen was grateful for his privileged start toward a life among educated men, with the prospect of a steady income from his professional activities. No doubt his father was as proud of him as he was of Joseph Jr., the shipmaster, and grateful that at least one of his sons would become a gentleman. Captain Knapp had to keep making money for the benefit of his two younger daughters, Sarah and Ellen, and two more sons, Samuel and William; and he would do all he could for his son Joe, and for his next son, Frank, fifteen, already a working mariner, already doubting his calling.

Nat Hathorne, living in the Knapps' neighborhood, had different aspirations. Having graduated from Bowdoin College in 1825, "Hath," a quiet, sardonic fellow in college, had returned to the "tall, ugly, old, grayish"[14] Manning house, to which his mother, the widow Betsy Manning Hathorne, and unmarried sisters had also retreated from their place in Maine. They were insulated from the world by a small but steady share of the gradual sell-off of Manning lands Down East. His family's lethargy soon overtook him, and he sank from Salem's sight except on nights when fire alarms rang and engines rumbled through the streets, and he could lose himself in the excitement and the blazing spectacle.

Never connected to the life of the waterfront, a bit of a stranger to other Lower End families due to long boyhood sojourns in Maine, Hathorne had few local friends and little interest in socializing. During the day, he would read; in the evenings and well into the night, he worked on his stories and a half-finished novella,[15] determined to create a body of work that would admit him to the society of American letters. In the meantime, he spent too much time alone, imagining himself as the fictive Oberon Fanshawe, author. The Mannings, having paid for his education, expected him to be like Nathaniel Knapp and read the law or pursue some other profession, or at least clerk at their stagecoach office. No one thought he would make a clergyman, but no one thought he should be an author other than his mother and sisters and, sometimes, himself.

He was indeed a writer, but he was happier as a summer horse trader with his uncle, touring the jovial taverns of rural New England. In Salem, he collapsed back into himself. He became a night-being, like a ghost sprung from the old Hathorne graves at Burying Point. Others were as nocturnal, tripping out to the inns and cellar grogshops on the waterfront; but none wandered as far afield, and as frequently, and none was as liable to terrify himself. He voyaged under cover of darkness, wandering without purpose and wondering if he were mad. Of the others, shapes seen at a distance, he knew that none had spent an hour staring into a mirror or an afternoon lying corpselike on a bed, door locked, blinds drawn, hidden from his beautiful sister, lost in the smoke of his mind. When the trance broke, he wrote furiously to get some of it down; and when it scared him, he threw it into the fire. Between the dream of fame and the shadow-life, he made no progress and got no help. No one knew him as the author of stories of lost faith and sabbat orgies and people turned to stone. If he was known at all, it was by a few drinking companions and by old ladies who remembered him as a curly-haired child.

In the summer of 1825, he showed his stories to his older sister Elizabeth. Incest and murder were the subjects of *Seven Tales of My Native Land*; and a publisher, he said, was looking at the manuscript. For a few weeks in the summer he went off horse-trading. Then he returned to Salem and resumed his half-life, occasionally selling anonymous sketches and poems to the papers, patiently waiting for word about his manuscript. Late in August 1825, the *Salem Gazette* ran his morbid poem "The Ocean," about mariners like his father, lost on a voyage from Salem.[16]

In Charleston, Dick Crowninshield's courtship progressed with great success. It was not long before the girl's father saw what was afoot. His daughter was obviously infatuated, and his wife approved; and Crowninshield, a plausible fellow, seemed to be serious about becoming a husband. She was very young to be so deeply involved, but if the stars were aligned and the money was right, the thing might be encouraged. With a life of wealth and respectability now opened before him, Richard proposed marriage to her and was accepted. Her father, promising to consider the matter, wrote to some knowledgeable acquaintances in the North. Three weeks later, he received his answers.

Dick was done for: the furious father banned him from the house and forbade his daughter ever to speak another word to her true love. Charleston was outraged at its nefarious deceiver and shut him out of its dances and mansions. Desperately, he arranged for messages to be smuggled in and out, but his proposal of elopement was refused. When she went off to a ball one evening in the company of condoling friends, Dick followed the carriage in the dark and pressed a note into her hand.

He may never have seen her again. Dick later claimed to have had a midnight visitation: "I saw, or thought I saw, as through a floating and mist-like veil, the features of Mistress J., but how changed! Sunken and hueless and set in death. . . . The spell passed from my senses; I sprang from the bed with a loud and agonizing cry. All without and within was silent as the mansion of the dead. There was not a trace of what I had witnessed in my dream."[17] Crowninshield booked passage for Massachusetts. A few women held on to the memory of the romantic northerner, and the dances went on as before.

Upon his return, Dick was a specter, so pale and haggard that even his mother did not recognize the frightening man at their door.

10.

DREAMS OF NEW BLISS

George Crowninshield and a friend, George Needham, sailed from Salem in October 1826, for a winter sojourn in New Orleans.[1] By far the largest city in the South, the Big Easy attracted footloose visitors from around the globe. The two Georges plunged in, and one night they met a nineteen-year-old from Belfast, Maine. John Palmer was good, raffish company—a true piece of Yankee flotsam, out in the world on his own, a deckhand who had voyaged to London, Gibraltar, and Havana and had come ashore to run a store for a while.

Palmer had been sailing before the mast for nearly two years, collecting adventures and near disasters. On his first voyage, to England, he got a dose of high-seas reality when his shipmaster had sailed right past an American brig in distress. Next, he had sailed to New Orleans, a place quite shocking to young sailors making a first visit. "Here, for the first time," he would write, "the picture of vice was held up to my view in every form imaginable; here, for the first time, I saw the sabbath utterly disregarded; worse than that, for it was, morally speaking, blasphemed. Gambling houses of every kind, open; horse races, boat races, bull baitings, puppet shows, balls, theatres, open; and every kind of amusement on that day, afloat, that the city of New Orleans could produce."[2] Afterward, he had banged around on voyages between Europe and the Caribbean, accumulating more evidence of the strangeness of the world.

RAJAH PO ADAM. On the Pepper Coast of Sumatra, Po Adam (here holding his sword) was the man to see. He had a fondness for Americans and supplied hundreds of tons of peppercorns to Salem shipmasters and supercargoes, who enjoyed the hospitality of his bamboo palace at Kuala Batu.

Salem's investors turned to the Salem Mill Dam project with great interest and some desperation. They had failed in their efforts to get control of the falling values of insurance rates and bank stock, so now the mill dam, which had begun as an effort to create a few factories to employ the local poor, had become Salem's best chance for economic health. The owners of the 2,687 shares of stock had all agreed to pay assessments when requested. No bills had yet been sent out, but John Pickering, president of the board, purchased thirty acres of land on Collins Cove as the first step toward construction of the dam and canal. The stockholders voted that "the work ought to proceed" after a $3 assessment was collected, due by September 13.

The thirteenth was not a lucky day. Much to the amazement and disgust of the board of directors, many of the shareholders did not pay their assessments. Pickering was furious. After all of his work—more than a year of unremitting voluntary effort, undertaken only for the betterment of the town—there was no support! If each share was valued at $50 or so, how would they ever raise the money if they could not even get the first $3? The directors promptly gave up and stated that it was "not expedient to proceed in the erection of the proposed Mill Dams."

Salem's leading citizens, well organized and well intended, had failed, shockingly, to introduce the means for large-scale manufacturing in their community. On October 5, John Pickering read the stockholders his report. He generously blamed unforeseen reversals in commerce and "change in the situation of the town and of individuals" as the main causes of "discouragements to the proposed undertaking," and he concluded by submitting resolutions to terminate the entire undertaking. The stunned stockholders voted to reconvene in two weeks.

The moment of crisis had arrived. Proponents like "Z" wrote the editor of the *Gazette* that he was astonished at opposition to "the great and redeeming enterprise," this "long-cherished hope, and, we may add, this last refuge of the town. . . . If we are willing to see our population migrating by the hundreds from the town to abodes more propitious to their industry and talents; if we are willing to witness the wasting progress of decay and dilapidation and ruin preying like a consumption upon this ancient seat of enterprise and wealth; if we are willing to see our real estates sinking by certain and rapid declension into worthless possessions, *and all those noble edifices which have been so recently erected and so justly admired as ornaments of the town, soon standing out only as the more prominent monuments of desolation;* if, in fine, we would behold the grass growing up in our streets and upon our wharves, like the melancholy verdure which decorates the grave, then let us calmly fold our hands and sit down to await this consummation of our folly with all that resigned and patient despair which has nothing further to do but to write its own epitaph."[3]

Many were not willing to let the project die, but others saw the $3 turndown as fatal. The whole cost of the project did not exceed the expenses of four voyages to the Orient—and certainly that kind of money could be raised in Salem. Indeed it could, if a few merchants had undertaken it. But a shipping partnership was not the model; instead, everyone in Salem had been invited to invest in a corporation in which a single dissenter could block forward progress.

The mill dam stockholders met on October 19 at the Town Hall. Lawyer David Cummins set forth all the reasons for going forward, and the vast majority, 320 to 45,[4] overrode the negative report of the board of directors. To assist the directors, Stephen White, Rufus Choate, and Joseph G. Waters formed a new subscriptions committee.[5] The directors, however, had seen enough: John Pickering, Joseph Peabody, and three others resigned. Peabody had invested lightly in the mill dam, having already sunk his nonshipping money into manufacturing at Newmarket and Dover. Pickering had done all in his power to save Salem, but he was out of steam. He moved to Boston and renewed his old intimacy with Bowditch.

On November 18, the Salem Mill Dam Corporation stockholders chose a new nine-man board of directors headed by the shipwright-cum-merchant Benjamin Hawkes. This group represented the many mechanics and middling investors who stood to gain from the large construction projects. In early December, confident of their authority and determined not to fail, they voted to sue delinquent stockholders. They also voted to fulfill former contracts for timber and plank and to begin the building of the dams in springtime. Then they negotiated the cession of low-water rights at Collins Cove; and finally they levied $7 per share to pay for the initial phase of construction. In the meantime, the directors appeared at a special town meeting to request a grant of land on Salem Neck, a much smaller piece than those they had received from the town in 1825.

The vote went against them. Incredulous, the proponents called for a division of the house. They lost by 51 votes out of about 470 cast. On January 15, the treasurer reported that the great majority of the 451 shareholders had failed to pay the $7 fee. The directors conferred for a few minutes, then broke off the meeting.

By the time George Crowninshield met him, Palmer knew New Orleans's night town well enough to serve as a guide to the rich boy and his pal Needham. When they decided to move on, he went with them to Charleston at the end of March 1827 for a month's vacation. In the company of the two Georges, Palmer did not have to work for a living; they paid his way to New York for a few days of hell-raising and then went on to Providence. In May, at South Danvers, Crowninshield introduced him to his impressive brother Dick, the machinist. Dick saw possibilities in Palmer and took him into Salem for drinks at the Lafayette Coffee House. Two other men sauntered into the darkened barroom. One, Fisher, was fresh-faced; the other, Hatch, was older and hard-looking. Just released from Salem Jail, they had come up Prison Lane to the Essex Street mansion of Captain Joseph White. For weeks, they had talked about the old captain's treasure chest, a common fantasy object of the jailbirds, who imagined it at the foot of the old man's bed, full of rolls of gold doubloons, glowing pearls, and glittering diamonds and rubies. Standing before the reality of the solid brick three-story White residence, however, Fisher and Hatch had looked at each other in amusement and had gone up-street to drink a farewell to their fantasy.

They were waiting to place their order when they realized that the half-drunk men in the next booth were plotting a crime. They grinned and listened carefully: in fact, it was the same robbery that they had intended. The moment was too good to waste, so they went over to meet them—and there they found the infamous Dick Crowninshield. Fisher and Hatch told him what they had just been doing in Essex Street, and they all had a good laugh. Crowninshield introduced them to his boothmate, a man they did not recognize, called Palmer.[6]

Back at South Danvers, Palmer met young Frank Knapp, aged sixteen, older than his years, edgy, surly, and hung over. The Crowninshields and Knapp were about to depart for New York. The brothers joshed their young companion, who had just stolen $300 from his father for the Manhattan spree. Palmer had other plans. He and Needham took off for Belfast, Maine, the starting point for several weeks of gambling and grifting that ended in New York City in late June. Palmer, returning to Maine alone, tried to straighten out his life but soon became entangled in a plot to raise funds for Needham, who had been arrested for robbing the mail stage. Palmer was caught breaking into a store and sentenced to two years in prison.

In Manhattan, the Crowninshields quickly ran through Frank Knapp's stolen funds and sent him home. Frank's family had worried terribly about the boy, who had vanished without a word. Now he had to confess to his father—not everything, but enough that Captain Knapp realized that Frank was in danger. His son, he knew, had a wild streak; but he had not thought he might become a criminal. He consulted with his son Phippen and with his own mother, old Mary Jenkins Knapp, living with them at eighty-six; but his mind was elsewhere. The captain's wife, Abigail Phippen Knapp, was gravely ill, and on July 21 she died, aged just forty-six years, leaving him with the care of three teenagers and three younger children, one only seven. Captain Knapp did not know what to do about Frank, other than to keep sending him to sea on voyages of the *Governor Winslow,* under the eye of his older brother Joe.

The Crowninshield brothers found another Salem companion for their next escapade. Early in August, they went off with young Joseph Fisher on an adventure that began with a week in Boston and moved on to Manhattan, where, as at Boston, they prowled hotel lobbies looking for loose luggage and broke into the guest rooms to swipe jewelry.[7] On a good day, they would go from floor to floor, pinning their loot to the inside of their coats. Fisher slipped up and was nabbed at the National Hotel with a stolen watch. The police got him to turn on the Crowninshields. They "had persuaded him to leave Salem and accompany them on a marauding expedition; that one [brother] took him to the Franklin House and sent him up to search the bed rooms, where he broke open a trunk and stole a watch. . . ." All three, jingling, were arrested and imprisoned. The Crowninshields' lawyer elicited from Fisher a confession of various robberies in Salem and New York and fastened on him "so many prevarications" that the jury acquitted the brothers. Sent home, Fisher was sentenced to four years in prison for the Salem robberies. Dick and George went on with their lives, leaving a trail of wreckage.[8]

Despite all of Stephen White's efforts, Salem drifted and crime was now a serious problem. As more working-class people and sailors lost their jobs, there was greater desperation and more illegal activity. The town's police force of old men came out late at night to shuffle through the streets, while brigands attacked wayfarers and burglarized stores and warehouses. Stephen White and the Society for the Detection of Thieves and Robbers were overmatched. Working by night and by stealth, following well-laid plans, and executing the most daring and improbable raids, the gangs robbed stages and wagon teams, cleaned out orchards and barns, rolled travelers, and broke into stores and houses to carry off whatever was valuable. The "systematic and hardened villainy" of "nefarious agents" was the result of thoughtful planning and cool audacity, directed from the shadows

No less alarming, the mill dam project verged on collapse. Early in 1827, the failure of Peirce & Nichols, owners of fifty shares, led the second-guessers to think that the stock would not be sufficiently subscribed to pay for construction costs. One of them, Samuel Endicott, had another problem: he had subscribed thirty shares for three relatives, absent at sea, without their permission. What were the chances they would want to buy now? Better to stop the whole thing before he became liable for another $3,000. Others were as anxious. The directors brought suit against Endicott, former director Joseph Ropes, and others who had not paid the paltry $3 assessment on their shares.

The industrial age in Salem had opened with the construction in 1827 of a steam-powered lead factory owned by Francis Peabody. At twenty-five, Colonel Peabody was the rumpled second son of Captain Joseph Peabody, Salem's richest shipowner, and the younger brother of the elegant merchant prince J. Augustus Peabody. A few years earlier, returned from his European tour, Augustus had Salem holding its breath: would he move to Boston or New York, or would he stay in Salem? He was handsome, refined, ambitious, and eager to make his mark; and his decision to pursue a career in his hometown had been an enormous affirmation of its future, despite Bowditch's departure. In the side yard of his own homestead, their father had built a Boston-style bowfront mansion for Augustus; out back, he had built a laboratory for Francis. In 1823, old Captain Peabody had started a lead factory that had not met the expectations of Frank, who then had founded his own works in South Salem, to make vinegar and white lead. Frank's product was better than his father's, and it kept improving, because Frank surrounded himself with other brilliant young men—not well educated, not affluent—who loved science and machinery more than anything. The waterfront there became an interesting place, with Peabody's new factories and a determined group of young inventors hard at work. The promise of the mill dam and its dozens of factories kept them enthralled. With its arrival, they would be operating equipment, managing production processes, inventing new devices,[9] and applying the concepts for which Harvard professor Jacob Bigelow had coined the term *technology*.

To smart boys everywhere, it was exciting to see factories going up and to read about the new inventions registered at the patent office. The president himself was an inspiration, as the proposer of scientific and infrastructure improvements, but his stirring proposals met with contempt in the House of Representatives and in much of the press. Jackson's adherents considered their man the president-in-exile; Adams was an impostor. Although his supporters fired back, the diffident Adams paid a terrible price for his refusal to compromise or to engage in political patronage. From within the government, the Jacksonians undermined him; from without, they formed a new national party, the Democrats, to defeat him.

In Massachusetts, Story and other Republican conservatives conferred about how to rescue their movement. Judge Story and his friends had tried to align their politics with the socioeconomic changes that were creating a culture of middle-class people who were mobile, well-read, and abstainers from alcohol. As their leader, Adams was doomed. The most plausible solution seemed to be to replace him with Daniel Webster, a man of high standing and popularity. But they could not let national politics become a matter of personality—that would be giving in to the democratic demagoguery they had feared all along. Somehow, they had to build a coalition that could translate as an electoral majority against General Jackson. They reached out to Henry Clay. By fusing the West and the North, and holding on to some of the middle states, they could build a party that would win in America.

In the spring of 1827, tragedy visited the beautiful house of Stephen and Harriet White. Despite the deaths of friends and relatives and the difficulties of a fading commerce, their home life was a refuge of happiness. All four of their children were now healthy teenagers. Harriet was described by her brother as "an interesting and lovely woman, one of the most perfect and engaging I have ever known."[10] She and Stephen, both forty, anticipated a long life together. Now, in May, Harriet was stricken with what appeared to be tuberculosis, the dreaded "consumption" for which there was no cure. She sank fast, to the horror of her family and many friends. Joseph Story, dealing with the grave illness of one of his children, was devastated at the condition of his beloved sister. On June 10 he wrote to his friend Daniel Webster, just elected to the United States Senate, "She may not live for a day—indeed for the last three days she has been expected to quit us hourly."[11] She died nine days later.

Stephen no doubt drew closer to his sister-in-law Eliza and turned to his foster father, Captain Joseph White, as he always had. This time, too, he could count on his friend and pastor, Henry Colman. Judge Story, still a poet, wrote:

> *Nor mind nor rank escapes the common doom—*
> *Youth feels the withering touch of slow disease;*
> *Oft Beauty's triumph sparkles near the tomb*
> *And Genius droops in ruins. Yet on these,*
> *In contrast strong, the setting sun of Age*
> *Oft shines with mellow luster, cheerful, free;*

And Sorrow, poring o'er her blotted page,
Dreams of new bliss; Care wakes to ecstasy;
Night is not darkness all: stars gem her silent sea.[12]

Bliss, of a sort, had found a new foothold. Up the hill from an abandoned shipyard on the South River, a country road ran toward the Derby farm; and there, in the borderland between warehouses and cornfields, on the knoll that was the picnickers' Mount Pleasant, Dick Crowninshield had established a night town for his revels, directly opposite the winking seaport.

Off the highway on a new road, Peabody Street, stood the house of David Foley, an Irishman, perhaps a veteran of the Crowninshield factory. By day, another Irishman, John Pendergrass, kept a grocery on the first floor, while a newsroom upstairs attracted young men looking for company and a drink or two. After sundown, Foley's turned into a roadhouse, with an assortment of illicit entertainments, liquors and wines, games of chance, connections to paid companionship, and bargain prices on goods of unknown origin. Other houses in the neighborhood began to light up as well. Sally, Betsy, Nancy, and Mary Jane might be seen coming and going with their tipsy escorts.

Dick Crowninshield, in from the woods, was behind it all. As host of an evening of South Salem carousing, he offered something new in town; and the constables stayed away. Salem's ever-growing crowd of out-of-work or underemployed men was looking for cheap thrills. Mariners, stuck between voyages, thwarted in their careers, came by to satisfy tastes acquired in the red-light districts of New Orleans or Marseilles. Gambling operations, with several organized games of chance, guaranteed good times for patrons every night, in addition to whatever else might transpire. Dick hired fellows like Benjamin Needham as croupiers and enforcers, to see to the profits but to be sure that things played out enjoyably. The crude alternative, Mumford's, could not compare; and in September 1827, for the first time, John Mumford was arrested for operating houses of prostitution.[13]

Dick's little babylon attracted a big following. Harvard students rode out from Cambridge for an evening of fun; and Boston rich boys, too drunk to know quite what was happening, would find that they had been fleeced of $200 or $300 in the course of a night. Their host generally kept out of sight, unlike his brother George. Dick was a businessman first, interested in making money, and he was a celebrity, unsmiling and unsettling, with a reputation for violence that kept everyone in line. Joe Knapp admired Dick and feared him. When ashore, he was a regular customer, as was the wild boy Frank Knapp, who, unlike Joe, was not planning to marry, and did not attend a church, and certainly was not trying to impress anyone in the ranks of regularly conducted society. Dick's night world made Salem bearable for Frank and his inebriated friends, drifting loose in a town that seemed not to want them.

One native of the region, visiting New England after ten years away, found it transformed by manufacturing and nearly unrecognizable except for Boston. Boston had grown and changed, but somehow it was the same, only better, full of energy and intelligence and handsome new granite buildings in the classical style. There was, he observed, "a greater concentration of bustle, business, and life, than in any other city. . . . In wealth, in enterprise, in the grandeur of its mansions and churches, it seems to me still to retain its proud preeminence." This was the Boston that Salem's young people visited, the Boston of Nathaniel Bowditch and John Pickering and thousands more drawn to a hot spot of the new culture. "General intelligence and taste have more than kept pace with its improvements in other respects," decided the visitor. "Boston, out of question, is the American Athens."[14]

In November 1827, Captain Azor Marshall and Stephen White's bark *General Stark* arrived in Salem Harbor. It was one of the last Salem-to-Sumatra pepper voyages. Most were now starting at Boston or New York, sailing to Europe, then on to Sumatra and home via Antwerp or Hamburg, with the final cargo unloaded at New York. Thanks to the commerce made possible by the Erie Canal, Manhattan had become the metropolis and mart of America, where prices were highest and demand strongest, for coffee and pepper as for everything else.

Sumatra remained an irresistible target for Salem merchants, and several Salem brigs could still be found along the west coast, from Mingin to Kuala Batu, bargaining for the harvest. Captain Moses Endicott of Salem, at sea in command of the *Suffolk,* had solved one of the biggest problems in the Sumatra trade. Years of meticulous soundings and surveying had resulted in a set of hand-made charts of the upper Pepper Coast, more accurate by far than any others in existence. In Salem, these charts were copied and supplied to grateful shipmasters; and Endicott's former first mate, Captain James D. Gillis, published his own charts extending the Sumatran coastline farther north with equal precision.[15]

Even as they contributed to safer navigation, Endicott, Gillis, and other Salem shipmasters realized that the long-standing harmony of their trade with the rajahs was being jeopardized by other Westerners looking for quick profits. The Dutch were carrying out military raids to the south, and expanded trade had inevitably brought shoddy dealing from captains who cheated by altering the pepper scales and even, in some cases, by sailing off without paying.[16] Most of the vessels along the coast carried very valuable specie and big ladings of opium, which made them targets for the more warlike of the young sultans. Sometimes they did attack a European vessel or a country vessel from the other islands; but the king of Atjeh disapproved, and the older sultans and rajahs tried to keep things cool in order to maintain fruitful and reliable trade.

The new rajah Po Adam of Pulo Kio, a headland near Kuala Batu, made a specialty of friendship with the traders of Salem. A Muslim like all the others, Adam had come to the Pepper Coast from his native Atjeh as an ambitious trader and translator, speaking broken English and working with the Americans to secure cargoes and help them with local protocols. Eventually, both sides came to rely on the newcomer, and he amassed enough money and power to set up his own fortified village, with his own harem and adherents, and boats, warehouses, and weapons. As the chief of Pulo Kio, he had been made a rajah by the king and had earned the envy of his rivals up and down the coast. Nevertheless, Po Adam, ever courteous and ever eager to be of service, became successful as the talkative host of Salem shipmasters who, even while visiting ashore in Adam's pleasure dome, made sure that the men on board the vessels kept up a sharp watch at all hours for the swift, silent proas and their treacherous crews.

The master of Stephen White's ship *Caroline,* Captain Joe Knapp, arrived by packet from New York in mid-October 1827. Much had occurred since his departure sixteen months before, bound for Charleston and Europe. Not least was the death of Joe's mother, Abigail, and Stephen's wife, Harriet. Perhaps there was some commiseration, but it could not have counted for much. Joe had kept White guessing while he was at sea, crisscrossing the Atlantic from Charleston to Europe, then back to Charleston for rice, then over the ocean and up the Baltic to Kronstadt and a visit to St. Petersburg. White was dismayed at Knapp's performance: he had not stayed in touch or taken advantage of changing conditions. For his insubordination and poor results—the net of all of those cargo turnovers was a losing voyage—Joe Knapp would not be commanding any more vessels owned by Stephen White.[17]

Joe defended himself but hardly cared about White's bad opinion. He had been doing a lot of letter writing, as it turned out, to his favorite dancing partner, Stephen's cousin Mary White Beckford. Mary, seventeen, had agreed to marry Joe, now twenty-two. When he arrived in Salem, their announcement caused a furor within the family. Old Captain Joseph White had a great fondness for young Mary. He did not approve of her marrying so young or of Joe Knapp as a partner—his prospects were poor, his character was questionable, he was a gold digger. Stephen, of course, supported the captain, but Mrs. Mary Beckford fought back. She had the greatest respect for Joe Knapp, he was a wonderful young man; and Mary and Joe were deeply in love. She appealed to Henry Colman. Joe was his parishioner, and Joe's Mary was a dear young friend. The man of God called on Captain White to see if he could not persuade him. The old gentleman remained immovable. He was convinced that Knapp was taking advantage, and he warned them and their mother that they should not expect a reward for this. He did, however, agree with good Mr. Colman that if there was to be a marriage, there ought to be a wedding. On November 6, 1827, in a ceremony at the Barton Square Church, Mary White Beckford became the bride of Captain Joseph J. Knapp Jr.

*ANONYMOUS. Nathaniel Hawthorne (1804–1864)
was graduated from college in 1825 and went home
to Salem and obscurity. After his unsigned novel
Fanshawe (1828) sank without a ripple, he turned to
writing dark tales and fantasies, some of which were
finally published by Samuel Goodrich of Boston, who
found Hawthorne "cold, moody, distrustful," as
befitted one who dealt in "grisly specters of jealousy,
remorse, despair."*

II.

TWILIGHT

I n May 1828, Salem received word that a new tariff had been enacted and that Senators Nathaniel Silsbee and Daniel Webster had voted for it. With last-minute adjustments, the bill had been made generally favorable to New England's manufacturing economy. Webster spoke impressively, reviewing the course of New England's earlier opposition to tariffs in hopes of protecting its commerce. But the Tariff of 1824 had "settled the policy of the country," and New England had been forced to turn from foreign trade and toward manufacturing. Webster noted that the new tariff would do further damage to shipping, but no one was willing to fight for it, not even Benjamin W. Crowninshield, Salem's congressman. The vote was close, 105 to 94, and the South was furious at the likely impact on overseas markets for its cotton and at a precedent of federal action so drastic that slavery itself might be the next target. This "tariff of abominations" inspired talk of secession in South Carolina and a regionwide embrace of the concept of "nullification," by which a state could simply refuse to recognize the primacy of federal law.[1]

Salem's own manufacturing effort was troubled. Having lost their latest lawsuit against former directors, the Salem Mill Dam Corporation directors also lost confidence in the water power projections of Moody and the Baldwins. The argument within the investor ranks became public. Outsiders were treated to the spectacle of a famous, wealthy place that was noisily, desperately struggling to join the ranks of communities quietly prospering all over New England and America. Few stopped to consider the incredible difficulties involved in trying to reinvent a seaport as a modern manufacturer.

The Salemites turned to Daniel Treadwell, a Boston engineer, for reassurance about their project; and at the same time the shareholders decided to bring in new leadership. In May, they elected Stephen White and a committee of six to recommend measures to carry out the corporation's programs. White was joined by a merchant, a teacher, an editor, a doctor, a contractor, and a shopkeeper.[2] They could see that Frank Peabody's new lead factory was chugging away by the harborside of South Salem, powered entirely by steam. All were eager to hear about Treadwell's findings, none more than the town's poor, still looking for jobs, still watching their friends and relations leave town. One of them, Miss Clemmons, wrote a sing-along about the mill dam and a poem, "Lines Composed on the Dullness of Salem, &c."[3]

> There's many a gentleman in this town
> Whoso now they do look around,
> And in their hearts with grief they say,
> Oh, how Salem does decay.
>
> It is a sad thing for to tell
> Gentlemen will trifle with the canal;
> Gentlemen will turn and let their hearts fail,
> And o'er the town cast a gloomy veil.
>
> If we could all be of one mind,
> How quick we would make Salem to shine,
> And her commerce would not cease,
> And manufactures would increase.
>
> It is a sad thing that it should be,
> Party or spirit so disagree,
> When love and friendship ought to reign,
> And Salem ought to be maintain'd.

Stephen White and his committee read Daniel Treadwell's report and nearly choked on it. What Treadwell told them was horrifying. There would be no industrial city in Salem, no Lowell-like profusion of factories and boarding-houses, no mounds of new products waiting to be teamed and shipped from the wharves. They were not visionary developers, but silly dreamers. They had deluded themselves with their vision of a roaring dynamo. The Baldwin projection of seventy mill-powers and 50,000 spindles was a joke—they would be lucky to get twelve mill-powers and 7,700 spindles for all of their money. The mill dam was not even needed: steam power would cost no more and would not require the disruption of rivers and coves and the creation of canals. In June, the Treadwell report was made public.

Those who could not wait any longer packed up and left. Some went to Boston to enter retail business or to engage in foreign trade; others went to Baltimore, to join expatriate friends as shippers; some went on to New Orleans, the great mart of the Caribbean and the Mississippi. Most went to the booming metropolis of New York City, where Salem-bred Jonathan Goodhue still presided as the prince of merchants. One of Salem's Union Wharf entrepreneurs, young Joseph Howard, who had been running a Salem packet line to New York and Baltimore, settled in Brooklyn. He quickly made the transition and reconnected with other young Salem friends in the next year or two, most notably the ambitious Salem apothecary Seth Low. Many Salem-owned vessels were now sailing from the port of New York, and the transplanted Salemites prospered as business agents and commission merchants with excellent contacts overseas and up and down the coast. Low thrived in the New York drug and opium business; and his brother, William H. Low, was hired by the merchant house of Russell & Company, China traders with offices in New York and Boston. William and his wife, Abigail Knapp, sister of Joe and Frank, moved all the way to the Orient and settled at Macao, the British-Portuguese port opposite Hong Kong, conducting a legitimate trade with Canton and also smuggling thousands of tons of opium past the Chinese gunboats to help feed the dragons of addiction.

The spring's disasters continued with the sudden death of the leader among the empire's younger merchants, J. Augustus Peabody, thirty-one, felled by tuberculosis. He and his father, Joseph, now quite old, had jointly conducted a mercantile enterprise with revenues far higher than those of any other in Salem. The Peabodys were among the last owners to build their vessels in local shipyards, and to trade to China, and to send their vessels out with Salem cargoes, and to have them return to Salem wharves with foreign goods to be unloaded and sold.

With the death of Peabody, it seemed that something in the Salem structure had given way, and the people felt a new vulnerability. "His unexpected demise startles us, as though the monster Death had, in visible form, rushed before our eyes and snatched from us one in the richest vigor and bloom of manhood. We feel, and that most solemnly and truly, that neither wealth, nor usefulness, nor the deep interests of society, can stay the terrific blow."[4] Of the remaining Peabody sons, George was still a boy in school, and Frank's interests did not include sailing ships and commerce.

Daniel Treadwell was not the only disabuser of the mill dam investors. In response to their lawsuits, the courts told them that their corporation was defective and their system for investment illegal. Joseph Story had designed the corporate structure, and Stephen White had persuaded the legislature to give them special standing on liability. But corporations were brand-new things in America, far trickier and more fragile than had been thought. Salem would have to start over with a new corporate entity if it wished to become a major manufacturer, and it was not clear that Salem's reserves of confidence were equal to that prospect.

In September 1828, Salem's rich men were as affluent as ever, and twenty-four households sent their sons into the freshmen classes of New England's colleges, fully seventeen at Harvard.[5] In an old-fashioned burst of pride, they produced a bicentennial festival, "The Landing of the Pilgrims at Naumkeag," hosted by the Essex Historical Society just as Adams was facing reelection. Salem had first been settled by the English in 1626, but not by the Puritans until 1628, when the first ship arrived under the direction of John Endicott. Already, in 1827, Joseph B. Felt had published his 570-page history, *Annals of Salem*. Salem's historical importance as the beachhead for the Great Migration of Puritans was validated by the festival's guests, including the governor, the senators, many judges, and heads of various historical societies. At dinner they were to be joined by the president of the United States.

Before noon, the marching band struck up the tune and the parade moved into Essex Street, led by Chief Marshal Stephen White. At the North Church, after the singing of original Salem hymns, Joseph Story stepped to the lectern. In describing the Puritan pioneers' friendly relations with the Indians, he invited the audience to reflect on the disgrace of the modern practice of dispossessing the Indian tribes of the South and West. Salem's indignation was not shared by the majority in America, where ethnic cleansing was an acceptable price for the black earth of ten thousand new cotton plantations, worked by slaves.

At dinner, the celebrants learned President Adams would not be joining them; but the festivities proceeded and many toasts were made, temperance movement or not. Old Tim Pickering offered "the great principles of our immigrant fathers: liberty, civil and religious—*este perpetua*." "The merchants of Salem," offered a Boston capitalist: "the most intelligent and the most enterprising on the face of the globe." Isaac Parker, chief justice of the Supreme Judicial Court, pronounced Salemites "wise, frugal, enterprising and industrious. May a free commerce and returning prosperity make their venerable town *what it was* in better times!"

The festival of self-congratulations was over, and all the famous people went away, some of them on a huge Boston steamboat larger than any sailing vessel. And then Salem was itself again, a little too quiet.

The Salem police log was filled with bad behavior in the summer of 1828, during which the night watch had been laid off. In one hot week, street corner loungers vilified an "infirm old lady" as she shuffled along at night, and they "grossly insulted" a high-caste mother and daughter. The bloods and sports of Dick Crowninshield's playground held chariot races in South Salem: "While they were chasing each other over the ground, the shaft of one of their chaises [ran] into the breast of a horse traveling in the opposite direction and he was killed on the spot—three young women were in the carriage, one an invalid." "Idle vagabonds" ruled the streets after dark. Gangs of boys blocked the sidewalks so that "peaceable people are driven into the gutter." Salem seemed unsafe; the town needed to adopt the efficiencies of a city.[6]

Some blamed the crisis in public morals on the new Salem Theatre. Developed by a Boston impresario, it presented the plays of Shakespeare, Goldsmith, Sheridan, and contemporaries. A ticket entitled the bearer to enjoy a drama or melodrama, a set of songs and recitations, and a comedy for dessert. For years, the citizens had debated the merits of performances and whether they served to uplift and entertain or to distract and degrade. The matter was settled by the construction of the capacious brick theater, after which the newspaper editors, pleased with new advertising revenues and a regular source of dramatic fare, dropped any pretense of moral concern and became enthusiastic fans, never failing to publish reviews, opinions, and puffery of the stars.

Stephen White's committee had devised a new formula for advancing the Salem Mill Dam Corporation's business. Delighted, the shareholders voted to revise the bylaws and to complete the subscription of the stock.[7] The mill dam project still had the support of the Charitable Mechanics Association, deeply committed to the apprentice system by which crafts were perpetuated. The association's leaders realized that their apprentices and young journeymen were headed into a future that belonged to the well educated as well as the well trained. Inspired by English mechanics' organizations and by the Essex Lodge of Freemasons, which had sponsored a series of public lectures in 1827, the association offered lectures early in 1828 "to increase the personal knowledge and cement the friendship of its members with each other, and prove a source of great advantage to the apprentices." Francis Peabody was their first speaker. As the owner of a successful steam-powered factory in Salem, he gave a course of lectures entitled "Steam, the Steam Engine, and Their Utilities." Peabody illustrated his points with apparatus and model engines demonstrated by his self-taught colleague, Joseph Dixon. Aided by the apothecary Jonathan Webb, Peabody then gave another series of presentations titled "Electricity."

Salem was not alone in its interest in these matters, but it was one of the first places to create a free lecture program showcasing the scientific processes by which society was being transformed.[8] Ironically, these processes were destroying the traditional quality-intensive apprentice system, for in the new economy, the bosses wanted laborers and semiskilled workers, not specialists; and they would not pay extra for those with training as craftsmen. Most young men would not be apprenticed into a craft but drafted into the mass workforce for factory work, canal building, road building, brick making, drayage, and construction.

Stephen White himself was deeply involved in the most startling of all the visions conjured by steam and science: the railroad. Having built their metropolis by grabbing all of the resources of eastern Massachusetts, Boston's leaders tried to envision the factors by which their city would keep rising as the future came rushing up. The first American railroad began with the laying of tracks at Baltimore in July 1828. Anyone with a map could see that a Boston railroad line to Albany would create an overland tributary of the Erie Canal; and another one to Providence would keep Boston's port the major exporter of the region's industrial output. Toward the end of 1828, legislator White served as a director of the state's internal improvements commission, studying the advisability of building Boston railroads.[9] Ultimately, the legislature would decide that this important work should be undertaken by the private sector.

While Salem was struggling with its future and the intractability of corporate mechanisms, a young man named Fanshawe was killed off and consigned to the flames, along with other creations of the frustrated writer Nathaniel, now Hawthorne.[10] Like Phippen Knapp, he had changed his name to accord with his new identity.

Living in a new house in North Salem with his sisters and mother, Nathaniel had scribbled furiously. He tended to come out only after dark, like the denizens of Wenham Woods or South Salem, whose doings had found their way into his stories—the existence of a moonlit, outlaw demimonde in Salem was the most interesting thing going, other than nighttime conflagrations. In three years of writing, he had produced many pieces—a novel, two collections of short stories, some sketches, and some poems—most of them unpublished, but a good output for a young writer who was not being paid. *Seven Tales of My Native Land* was finally returned by the would-be publisher.

When he finished his novel in the early fall of 1828, he was only twenty-four and stood on the brink, he thought, of fame. He paid a Boston publisher to bring out *Fanshawe* anonymously in October. It was full of the angst of the sickly, love-struck student hero: "Fanshawe had hitherto deemed himself unconnected with the world, unconcerned in its feelings, and uninfluenced by it in any of his pursuits. In this respect, he probably deceived himself. If his inmost heart could have been laid open, it there would have been discovered that dream of undying fame, which, dream as it is, is more powerful than a thousand realities. But, at any rate, he had seemed, to others and to himself, a solitary being, upon whom the hopes and fears of ordinary men were ineffectual."[11] Fanshawe's love object, of course, prefers his friend; there are backwoods mysteries, a pirate with a secret, a bumbling professor, a merchant unable to get home across the sea, deep chasms, a maiden in distress, sobbing pines, and gusts of portentous wind.

The novel was advertised (as *Fanshaw*) briefly in Salem, and it did not sell, although it did get a good review in Boston. Dismayed at his rejection by the reading public, Hawthorne reclaimed the unsold copies and burned them on chilly nights. Perhaps he was not a novelist, but a writer of poems and tales.[12] If so, he would have to do something about his damp, morbid stories of zombies, doomed lovers, and witch sabbats, too full of betrayal and incest and damnation for the new-named author to sign them.

Scurrilous, filthy, sundering, and interminable, the presidential campaign finally slid to an end, and General Jackson, whose minions had been trashing

Adams for four years, won by a landslide, taking all the votes of the West and South and some of those in Maryland and New York. Delaware and New Jersey had joined New England in standing firm for President Adams, who lost in the electoral college 83 to 178.

Timothy Pickering, now a melancholy widower, had lived long enough to cast a ballot against his old enemy Adams. Publicly, he had continued as president of the Essex Agricultural Society, corresponding widely on the best methods of the scientific farming that had transformed New England into the most productive region, per acre, in the country. Further, in a long lifetime of fighting for Indian rights and for the abolition of slavery, Pickering had taken up a final cause: that of Greek independence. Elected in 1828 as chairman of the Essex County Committee to Relieve the Suffering of the Greeks, he urged that money and supplies be sent to the civilian population until the day of liberation from the Turks. Pickering could not count on donations from the opium barons of Boston and Salem, who were drug dependent on the goodwill of the Sublime Porte of Constantinople.[13]

In January 1829, Pickering fell ill and was bedridden for the first time since his army days fifty years before. Fortunately, he was not well enough to read John Quincy Adams's incendiary new publication, *Federalist Treason*. Pickering died within a week, in his eighty-fourth year, the very last of the High Federalists. None of his political goals had been met; and the United States remained one nation, indivisible, with democracy in charge, Indians on the run, and slavery overspreading much of the land.

His beloved farm in Wenham, with a big farmhouse and oversize scientifically designed barn, was put up for sale right away, and the high bidder, at a bargain price, was Mrs. Mary Beckford, who bought it with her own money. Her daughter Elizabeth and son-in-law John Davis agreed to manage the farm as a business and a family retreat.

The Salem Mill Dam Corporation would not die. Abandoned by the aristos who had once sought to reinvent Salem, the project had been rescued despite the Treadwell report. Stephen White's reorganization of the corporation was a hit, and people enthusiastically purchased all five thousand shares of newly issued lower-priced stock. No decision was made about the shares in controversy, thirty reserved to Endicotts and two hundred held by insolvent parties—technicalities that could be handled in future. The really important thing had been accomplished: the corporation was back in business, with the financial support of all of the middle class and the fond hopes of the working people. Salem would yet have a manufacturing future, even if Joseph Ropes and Samuel Endicott were still trying to hold up the proceedings, claiming that Treadwell had uncovered an overoptimistic evaluation that amounted to fraud. Once again, the corporation decided to sue Ropes to dispose of this legal impediment to its renewed progress.

In March 1829, Andrew Jackson was inaugurated; and Joseph Story, as a Supreme Court justice, was on the scene. Thousands of people poured into Washington. Full of spirit, the jubilant Jacksonians reveled in their victory and in the defeat of John Quincy Adams and all that he represented: the rich, educated, top-dog easterners who had always run things, from the beginning of America, from George Washington down to James Monroe and Adams himself.

Adams was long gone. When Jackson had not paid a courtesy call in the weeks before inauguration, Adams had packed up and left town as he had come in, quiet and grim. His father, he thought, would have approved. President Adams went home, not to Boston but to the old homestead in Quincy; and soon he would return to Congress as a representative and haunt the House for the rest of his life, trying to stop its members from doing their worst.

Story observed the takeover of the capital by the men of the West: "The reign of King Mob," he wrote, "has begun." But Story did not despair. Adams's loss had been foreseen: he had never been a politician, a stirrer of the masses and a rouser of popular support. Webster was in the Senate now, famous as "Black Dan," a superb orator with a bully pulpit and a firm friendship with Clay. Things might not go so well for the Hero, and, if they did not, Webster and Clay would have their chance.

Jackson did not make Adams's mistake of retaining good men regardless of party. He was the victor, and his adherents grabbed the federal spoils. In Massachusetts, the few prominent Jacksonians—one was Stephen White's cousin Andrew Dunlap, the new federal district attorney in Boston—were in a position to prosper. On the state senate slates that spring, White was placed at the head of the Jacksonians; but he disavowed any interest. He was a National Republican, and he did not want to serve in either legislative house this year—he would continue as a member of the Governor's Council, period. His wishes, however, were ignored, and he was elected to the lower house;[14] and he and Stephen C. Phillips worked on a plan to build up their new party toward the elections in spring. They were willing to tussle with other Adamsites to be sure that the party developed along the proper "liberal principles."[15]

For the first time in their political lives, White and Story were not in charge of political favors, and they could do little to help their friends in the post offices and the custom houses of Essex County. Joseph E. Sprague was thrown out as Salem postmaster—his father-in-law, Bailey Bartlett, the county sheriff, could help him—and in the big brick building at the head of Derby Wharf, the collector of customs and his entourage of tide waiters and measurers and surveyors vacated the offices that they had held for decades.

At Union Wharf, Captain Joseph Knapp, merchant, was doing all he could to keep his little fleet at sea. He had bought the brig *Rover* with the intention of employing his son Joe in trade with South America. Joe, however, was enjoying married life ashore and told his father to find someone else. Old Captain Knapp relied on others to consign freight to make his voyages profitable; but in 1828 and 1829, more men left town or invested in stocks rather than send adventures to the West Indies. Captain Knapp did not have the capital to expand overseas or to acquire larger vessels; his formulaic Caribbean trade and freighting had always paid off. Now it did not.

Captain Joe Knapp did agree to command his father's brig *Governor Winslow* on a voyage to Martinique, sailing in September 1828 with brother Frank on board as mate and a crew of six. After trading for a cargo, they began the voyage home in company with the schooner *Rapid*, commanded by a Knapp cousin from Newburyport, for safety against pirates. Upon arrival in Salem, they found that a Union Wharf shipper, Stephen W. Shepard, had just learned of the loss of his small 120-ton brig *New Priscilla,* seventy-five feet long, commanded by David Hart. The specie for the voyage had been driven down from the banks "in several four-horse stages and delivered at the wharf" to the six-man crew on sailing day. After a couple of short trips between Cuba and Charleston, Captain Hart had departed Charleston in late January. Three weeks later, the captain of a New York vessel, approaching the Dog Keys near Matanzas, Cuba, spotted a brig and a schooner together, lying to the wind. As he approached, they both filled away and tacked for a few minutes; then the schooner sailed off. Coming up with the brig, the New Yorkers found that she was the *New Priscilla,* deserted, with her boat gone. They concluded that the crew had been murdered by the schooner men, which made the *New Priscilla* the only Salem vessel known to have been lost to pirates.[16]

Although Joe Knapp's voyage in the *Governor Winslow* had merely been unprofitable, the killing of Hart and crew caused more doubts about making losing voyages to the West Indies. However, no one else—Stephen White especially—was offering Joe a vessel, so in March 1829 he cleared Salem in the *Governor Winslow,* with Frank and several of the same crew members, bound for St. Thomas once again.

When Joe and Frank returned, their father explained his predicament. Prices continued to fall, and freight was not to be found; he could not afford to ship cargoes of his own; the market for West Indies goods seemed to be fading. The tariff had raised the duties on molasses, his major importation, and the temperance movement was reducing the demand for the rum distilled from that molasses. The more he tried to make money, the more he lost. He did not know how much longer he could stay in business—and he was not alone. Except for Robert Upton, who traded up the rivers in South America, Union Wharf's shippers were in trouble.

Joe Knapp had lost his chance. Even if he could get a real command, the merchant vessels, he saw, would take him nowhere. His whole life had been premised on a career in trade to the Orient, making long voyages with high profit margins. Instead, he was plowing a north–south saltwater furrow in his father's old brig.

Now that he was a man, married and ambitious, his career was over. For this he had risked his life since he was fifteen, doing all that was expected of him. Stephen White had plenty of vessels but would not give Joe another chance. An open command had just gone to Lewis Endicott, the new husband of White's niece Mary Fettyplace. Joe had no other merchant relatives; his brother-in-law Low was already gone from New York to work for Russell & Company in the Orient.

In Salem, he could not get ahead. Yet he did have certain advantages: Mother Beckford had been supportive and generous, and all of them were spending more time at her Pickering farm. Joe could not see himself as a farmer, nor could he be a shipmaster without a voyage or a vessel. Salem's dullness was oppressive, but his bride had brought him plenty of money, and he did not mind spending it in Dick Crowninshield's gaming rooms, with some left over for brother Frank.

Well-established merchants and solid old-line businessmen, fighting hard to stay afloat, suddenly lost their grip and went under. John Andrew, who had married a Forrester, died suddenly in July 1829. A merchant in the Russia trade, he had built the largest house in Salem, overlooking the same quadrant of the Common as that of his brother-in-law John Forrester and *his* brother-in-law Stephen White. Andrew's enormous brick mansion was so extravagant that even its shallow rear porch had three-story columns; and its interior furnishings were as costly and luxurious as money could buy. When the accountants were done, it was found that John Andrew had died hopelessly insolvent, leaving creditors with huge losses and his family with almost nothing.

In Boston, Bowditch navigated the Massachusetts Hospital Life Insurance Corporation by improved actuarial principles, and he introduced new mechanisms for investment and pension funds. He had the money now, and the time, to produce an edition of *Mécanique Céleste by the Marquis de La Place, Translated, with a Commentary,* and in 1829 he brought out the first of four volumes. As his sons had entered Harvard one after another, he, John Pickering, and Joseph Story had become so deeply involved in the college's curriculum and finances that in 1828 Bowditch had forced John T. Kirkland out of the presidency. Salem people now ran the college, and Story managed the election of Josiah Quincy, the mayor of Boston, as its new president. Quincy made a point of discussing with Story and the lawyer-statesman Nathan Dane the sad state of Harvard Law School, which had enrolled just one student in 1828. Quincy believed that the school must be put on the principles of scientific law to meet the legal and legislative needs of the country. Dane agreed to endow a professorship for the judge. Story could remain on the Supreme Court and could publish on whatever he cared to lecture about—perhaps commentaries on the Constitution. Only he, they said, could build up the law school into a national resource; but he would have to move to Cambridge.

Story and his wife, Sarah, considered what would be lost in moving from Salem with their two surviving children, Mary, fourteen, and William, ten. They were pillars of society, much beloved among friends and especially relatives, the Whites, Storys, Forresters, and Fettyplaces. Joseph Story had arrived in Salem with nothing but brains and energy and had found it the perfect place for his ferocious drive to become a lawyer, politician, and judge—one of the most important people in the country.

But that Salem was gone, along with the world of trade of which it had once been the capital. Repeated tariffs, and world peace, and the forces of science and technology—the brute power of the dynamo, of turbines and falling water and steam engines, speed, and production—had overcome wind-driven commerce and left Salem on the ebb tide, still trying to create a manufacturing future. Cambridge and Boston, already arrived at a suave modernity, offered the Storys dozens of congenial friends and abounding prospects for the happiness of their children. At the law school the judge would be running things, lecturing and writing without having to teach, and taking good pay for creating an institution embodying his values and principles and extending them to the next generation. If America was not going to be his legacy, Harvard Law School would do.

On September 3, 1829, his friends gave Judge Story a memorable farewell dinner in Salem. Bostonians abounded. Dr. Bowditch, as he was known, was among the honored guests, as were Harvard's Josiah Quincy, Mayor H. G. Otis of Boston, Senators Webster and Silsbee, distinguished judges, eminent professors, and the Honorable John Pickering, Boston's new city solicitor. There were "toasts and sentiments worthy of the occasion" and a wonderful meal. Salem's leaders acknowledged their "exalted esteem for Judge Story's private virtues and their high admiration for his abilities and profound learning as a justice and his invaluable services as a judge."

Story was deeply moved. At Hamilton Hall, the scene of so many glamorous balls and dinners, he "made a most eloquent and feeling address to his fellow citizens, from whom he was about to separate, and dwelt on the circumstances of his residence among them for thirty years and his emotions on parting from early and fast friends."[17]

In the wake of Story's departure, new rumors arose on the waterfront and swirled around Chestnut Street and Essex Street and Washington Square. John Forrester was said to be facing ruin like that of the deceased John Andrew. Smaller merchants continued to sell out and move away to the larger ports. Even the banks were not safe from a rising tide of crime. In mid-September, a well-prepared gang used crowbars and other heavy tools to break through the outer doors to the vault of Merchants Bank. A final effort to crash through the walls ended in failure, and the robbers fled. Their only actual prize was that day's deposit, left in a desk drawer, belonging to Stephen White's Society for the Detection of Thieves and Robbers.

At Union Wharf, several businesses were said to be failing, and many owners were hard-pressed to assemble a cargo or find a consigner of freight. Hawthorne's uncle John Dike, a packet line operator, and Captain Joseph J. Knapp were among those in serious trouble. Insolvency and bankruptcy were common, and crime was thriving.

The fleet of vessels owned in Salem was still numerous but diminishing, partly from sales and partly by losses—a total of 25 vessels were lost by shipwreck in only two years. Early in 1828, about 163 vessels had sailed for Salem owners engaged in foreign trade: 35 ships, 8 barks, 95 brigs, and 25 schooners. By the end of 1829, the total was reduced by 20—but in fact more had been lost and new vessels had replaced them. There were 33 full-rigged ships, less than half of them trading to the Indian Ocean.[18] The fleet was shrinking, and at the same time Salem was overextended. Its merchants had pushed the mariners into oceans and markets where they had rarely or never gone before, at great risk, keeping them out in the world for three years and more, sometimes stopping at places where the natives were savage to the point of cannibalism. But the merchants were adamant: no island or port was too remote, obscure, or dangerous if there was a chance of profit. Far out in the Pacific, seventeen thousand miles away, Salem had developed a trade with the Fiji Islanders. In exchange for guns, knives, whale's teeth, and trinkets, the Yankees got China cargoes of sandalwood, tortoiseshell, and especially bêche-de-mere, or sea cucumbers, a foodstuff prized at Canton. On blazing hot tropical beaches, Salem crews stripped down to build large open barns for curing sea slugs by the ton. The anchorages were always bad, and the Pacific typhoons could be as fatal as the mercurial islanders. Several vessels were engaged in this trade, with the brigs *Fawn* and *Niagara* cleared away the year before and the large ship *Glide* recently sailed.[19]

Stephen White intended to keep his ships at sea, although he was not prepared to send them into the wastes of the Pacific. In the face of others' failures and losses, and of his own mistakes, he planned his voyages with great care, based on the freshest information and the best scenarios for market value. He visited regularly at the Union Reading Room to check the out-of-town papers, and he made the rounds of the insurance offices and taverns, to listen and discuss with a shrinking group of the empire's viziers. He insisted that his captains use every possible resource to get first-quality goods and find healthy markets once they got out into the world, which for him consisted of South America, Europe, and the Orient. He employed about one hundred men at sea, and he owned eight large trading vessels, having sold the ship *William* to New York owners in 1828 and the brigs *General Brewer* and *Eliza & Mary* before that. None of his vessels carried more than 260 tons burthen, and few of them sailed with a Salem cargo. Almost all of his 1,500 tons of freight now went out of and into the harbors of Boston and New York.

J oe Knapp agreed to sail in command of his father's *Governor Winslow* once more, a forlorn hope. He would go for Guadalupe with Frank as mate, and their regular crew of Hill, Reese, old Israel Phippen and his son, and a couple of others. Joe did not bother to stay for the celebration of the Fourth of July; the day before, they cleared for the West Indies. He drank his way south and found things pretty dull at Pointe-à-Pitre. He drove her home quickly on another losing voyage, and on the evening of September 22 he arrived at Salem, done with seafaring.[20]

Mary and Joe spent a couple of weeks visiting her mother in the afternoons when old Captain White was out of the house. Mary Beckford was still working as his housekeeper, unhappily, shutting herself up in her back parlor overlooking the garden. At night, she would sleep in the room over the kitchen or go home to Bridge Street and the Beckford house, partly rented out, where her teenage son, Joseph White Beckford, resided when not at sea. It was clear that the wedding had driven the captain farther into the circle of Stephen and Stephen's family and of Eliza White and her girls, two of them now married to wealthy Bostonians. It seemed best for Mary and Joe to go live on the farm with the Davises—there was plenty of room and no reason to stay in the seaport. In October they moved to Wenham, whereupon Captain White summoned his lawyer and changed his will to increase the money that would go to Eliza White and Stephen White at the expense of Mary Beckford.

On October 21, Captain John Francis Knapp, nineteen, sailed in command of the *Governor Winslow,* bound for the West Indies with the usual crew. Right on schedule, Frank had become a shipmaster.

*THE GODLIKE ONE. Daniel Webster (1782–1852) was a
formidable presence in Congress and the courtroom. Peerless as
an orator, Black Dan had presidential aspirations and the support
and friendship of Stephen White and Joseph Story. White would
give him plenty of money over the years, and pay him an assassin's
fee for a deliberate act of vengeance.*

PART THREE

INTO THE DARKNESS

Can evil in the city be,

except the Lord be pleased?

—ASHLEY BOWEN OF MARBLEHEAD, 1773

(FROM "ON SMALLPOX")

THE HOUSE THAT TRADE BUILT. In 1814, during the war, Captain Joseph White, 67, had acquired John Gardner's eight-year-old mansion from the mortgage holder (a nephew of both men) for a bargain price. Designed by Samuel McIntire, situated on Essex Street near the Common, it was considered the finest house in Salem.

12.

NIGHTFALL

S tephen White was losing the battle to save Salem and its people. With his son Joseph now at Harvard and his daughters eager to move to Boston, White's main reason for staying was his aged mentor and chief creditor. The old gentleman lived quietly, socializing often with relatives and a dwindling circle of friends, serving in one last business role as president of the Salem Laboratory, a chemical producer. In Boston, Stephen served on the Governor's Council and in the House of Representatives. As a founding member of the new Prison Discipline Society of Boston, Stephen was chosen to head up a legislative panel to recommend changes at the state prison, "a veritable training school in depravity." He also took part in the national movements to release debtors and the insane from jail and to decriminalize debt altogether.[1]

White thought that he might remain a Salemite while living a part-time Boston life, developing the new National Republican Party with Webster and pursuing business, policy making, and the social opportunities open to rich, handsome widowers. In the capital, though, he needed a residence suitable for his daughters' forays into society. That problem was solved with the opening of the Tremont House, the first luxury hotel in America, on October 22, 1829, near Boston Common.[2]

The gray granite structure was four stories high and half a block long. Its Doric portico opened into a new conception in America: a grand public lobby with chandeliers, mirrors, and elegant furnishings and novel amenities like laundry service, a reading room, private drawing rooms and dining rooms, plumbed bathrooms, and a formal dinner served at a European-style restaurant every day at half past two. The Tremont House was a spectacular success, and among its long-term guests were the three beautiful sisters, Harriet, Caroline, and Ellen, the so-called White Witches, belles of Boston's invitation-only ballrooms, and their hopeful father, very handsome in his cloak and his evening clothes and dancing pumps.

Along the shores of the North River, big piles of lumber and stone awaited contractors and their crews. Plans had been drafted and approved, and the directors of the Salem Mill Dam Corporation only awaited word from the lawyers to commence their enormous project. John Pickering and Rufus Choate argued the case against Joseph Ropes, a former director refusing to pay his assessment; and on November 6, the judge found for the corporation.

Ropes appealed. The new trial was set for April at Ipswich. The building materials lay by the river through the end of another year.

Captain Joseph White, eighty-two, was very ill for much of the winter of 1829–1830. To his lawyer, Joseph Waters, he dictated a will disposing of his fabulous wealth. As the empire had begun to contract in the early 1820s, he had moved his money out of commerce and into office buildings, Boston row houses, mortgages, promissory notes, and large stock positions in various banks, factories, and insurance companies.

He kept his wharf but leased most of its buildings to a boatbuilder and a lumber dealer. His nephews and nieces and their children "were objects of his care and bounty," according to Stephen White, "and if they did not share alike, they were all patronized as his kindred, in such a manner as he thought proper. He had his partialities, and he did not hesitate to show them. His nephew, Stephen White, in early life found favor in his eyes, and never for a moment lost his affection. The old gentleman, generally, kept a will by him, and the fact was known, nor did he wish to keep it a secret to his friends, nor was it doubted but that Stephen White was a legatee in it, a much larger one than any other relation."[3] Captain White was "determined" to keep all of his property in his lifetime[4] and so to influence the financial fates of several families by virtue of his hidden will.

The cousins Mary Beckford and Stephen White, once close friends, had grown distant. Beckford had every opportunity to earn the captain's gratitude as well as his largesse; whatever unpleasantness had occurred, it was, Stephen thought, entirely the doing of resentful Beckfords and Knapps, who might have been more careful to respect the wishes of their very wealthy old patron. Dismayed but unwilling to retreat, Mary Beckford stayed on in the captain's house, at her sitting room overlooking the garden.[5] Most of the work was done by Miss Lydia Kimball, a maid there for sixteen years, and by Benjamin White—no relation to the captain—a teenager who had been houseman for two years. White had provided handsomely for both of them after his demise.

In the dark days of December, death hovered in the White mansion. The old gentleman slept much and breathed with difficulty. Mary Beckford's daughter Mary Knapp was a frequent visitor, and Mary's husband, Joe, was in the habit of coming by in the late afternoon to sit in the parlor and drink the captain's brandy. Joe had a key—or two keys: he had made a copy of the key to the captain's locked treasure chest, and one day he opened it and read the will. His mother-in-law's share was much smaller than the Whites' and especially Stephen's. Joe told her about it. A vast fortune hung in the balance, just out of his reach but not beyond imagining. In his cups, young Captain Knapp was master of the house and all of its beautiful things.

Joseph White was so sick that he thought he was dying and told his relatives that he wished "to go off like a flash." Death held no terrors for one who had lived so long and buried so many. He had a sudden, sharp attack and sank low toward the end of the month; and Mary Beckford summoned Stephen White from Boston. Joe Knapp told her that he was sorry she had done so, for White would use it as an opportunity to tear up the notes on the loans he owed.

Captain White wrote that it was his "wish and desire that when I decease that no minister may be called on to attend my funeral, that my corpse may be carried the nearest way to the grave, that no mourning may be worn, and that only a few of particular friends attend my corpse to the grave, that the funeral is not to be a public one but only to be attended by my nearest relations, that my corpse be laid as near my wife as can be made convenient."[6] It was not by his choosing that, in the first week of the new year, the captain felt his strength return.

In his terrible illness, the old merchant had not been quite as unaware as some had thought; and on January 8 he summoned his lawyer and again revised his will.

In South Salem, as the sun set on a February afternoon, grocer Pendergrass and his clerk put away their wares, lit the lamps and candles, brought up chairs and tables, and set out bottles for gamblers. Upstairs, similar preparations were taking place, and in a little while the first customers appeared. Two hours later, the building was buzzing with a crowd of pretty painted girls and eager, tipsy young men, sailors, students, merchants' clerks, and Dick Crowninshield's shills.

Colonel Benjamin Selman, the rakish leader of Marblehead's militia regiment, showed up with his entourage for a night of fun. Joseph Hatch and John Quiner, petty criminals, listened in as Selman and the Crowninshield brothers discussed the old subject of Captain White's treasure chest. Hatch murmured something to Quiner about Dick's needing new material. Daniel Chase, a sport from Lynn, drifted over and joined Selman in the conference. Pendergrass listened, too, and glared at Hatch and Quiner to let them know that he was on to them. Smirking, they slid away toward the corner.[7]

By mid-February, Captain White was out of danger altogether. The newspapers and magazines had stories of remarkable doings in science and technology, in manufacturing and transportation, in the struggles of nations to throw off their kings. Reverend Henry Colman, a frequent caller, was a font of information about these matters. Colman had a farm just outside of Salem, and the two men discussed scientific agriculture. Mr. Colman was nearly a member of the family, sitting up with the captain, sometimes reading aloud from his own books of sermons. In worship service at the new church in Barton Square, Colman prayed for the recovery of his patron, who held the mortgage on the Colman farm. He had ingratiated himself with the whole family; he had been astute, helpful, and very careful not to make a false move.

Slowly, unexpectedly, on a chilly afternoon after the late March thaw, a few snowflakes fell, as light and melting as ash. Within an hour the first flurry had thickened to a squall, followed by the howling of a desolating two-day blizzard. At just the moment that people had begun to look forward to spring, they were buried. Snowdrifts blocked the roads and rose in waves against the buildings. Salem looked like Pompeii. Then the sun came out, and it all melted away.

On April 6, 1830, by morning messenger, Stephen White, forty-two, learned that he had been elected to the state senate. His colleague Levi Lincoln had won the governorship, and Joseph Sprague had won the office of county sheriff, succeeding his late father-in-law. It was a clean sweep for the National Republicans in South Essex and in the important state offices. Senator White accepted congratulations at the Republicans' Union News Room. Stephen called on his father and found that Mrs. Beckford had left for Wenham to care for her daughter Davis, taken ill.

Stephen had a fresh copy of the *Register* and read it to the captain.

The big news was the Webster-Hayne debate in the Senate. Stephen's friend Daniel Webster had responded to Robert Hayne of South Carolina, the champion of nullification, the principle that the states were not bound by federal laws, which came with an implied threat of secession and civil war. The perpetuation of slavery was behind it all. The South feared that the federal government—in Congress or in Story's Supreme Court—would put an end to the South's "peculiar institution," even though "northern manufacturers derive greater profits from the labor of our slaves than we do ourselves." Webster, speaking before a packed Senate chamber, responded that the Constitution and Supreme Court were unmistakable on the subject of nullification: no state had the right to interpret federal laws as it chose. He concluded with a ringing description of America as a union of many parts, diversely peopled, embarked toward a grand destiny under "the gorgeous ensign" of "Liberty and Union, now and forever, one and inseparable!" Webster had won the oratorical showdown, and he and Clay, now making common cause, might still find a solution to balance the various regional interests while the South developed an alternative to slavery.

In the Union Wharf shipping news, Robert Upton, the new owner of Judge Story's house, was landing large amounts of Maryland corn and stocking lots of cocoa and flour at his store, while Thomas Pingree was selling two hundred barrels of whiskey and taking on freight consignments for his schooner *Christopher Columbus,* bound to Norfolk and Richmond.

Robbers were hard at work, and William Sutton of South Danvers, up near Crowninshield's factory, offered a $100 reward "for the detection of thieves" and the recovery of a bale of very valuable superfine white flannel, evidently thrown into a wagon "heard by a number of neighbors to start off with great rapidity about 8 o'clock."

The financial columns reported that the Commercial Bank and the Asiatic Bank, with capital stocks reduced to $200,000, would soon decide whether or not to distribute dividends. There was a notice placed by auctioneer George Nichols, Captain White's choice as the new manager of the chemical works, who advertised the sale of Stephen's large Beverly fishing schooner *Regulus* and shares of insurance and bank stock.

And there was another notice, offering an impressive assortment of goods that had made it past the tariff: Bologna hemp and roll brimstone; patent cordage of all sizes, Russian and American; pipes of white brandy; Russian tallow candles; Weesp and Schiedam Holland gin; bales of velvet corks; barrels of balsam copaiba; boxes of Sicily lemons and oranges—available at White's Lower Wharf for purchase in bulk from Stephen White, Merchant.[8]

At Cherry Hill Farm that afternoon, Joseph White enjoyed the sights and sounds of these early days of his eighty-third springtime: the shrilling of the peepers and the cawing of crows; the livestock wandering in the stunning sunshine; the farmhands and horses, busy at the plows, opening the dark fields to their furrows.

He had thought that he might not see the farm again—that he would not survive into the season of renewal, with its promise of abundance and another year of life. Arm in arm with the tenant farmer, he took a short walk in his boots, pointing his cane as they spoke of plantings and fields and crops. The manure, a compost of seaweed and cattle dung, was fresh in the ground, and its chilly stink hung over all of Cherry Hill. After a while, he returned to the dooryard and told his servant Benjamin to wait for him. He entered the ancient house, low-studded but solid and spacious, the scene of so many good times and jolly parties in days gone by. He went upstairs to his chamber and stood at the window to take in the wonderful view of distant steeples and harbors and the horizon of the wide world. Here his brother Henry had spent his last years, a contented farmer, as happy as a boy.

Dead these five years, Henry White had owed a large debt to his son Joseph's widow, Eliza Story White, but she had not been able to collect from Stephen, the administrator of Henry's estate. Eliza was extremely protective of her daughters and their prospects, which hinged largely on the size of their dowries. Already, her daughter Elizabeth had made a good marriage to the Bostonian Samuel C. Gray, a nephew of Billy Gray. Her other daughters, Charlotte and Mary, deserved the same chance. To old Joseph White, any unpleasantness between Stephen and Eliza was unacceptable, and so, to "preserve the harmony that had subsisted between the two families," the captain took over Stephen's debts to her and her children, paying 5 percent interest and securing them with his own real estate. It was an excellent compromise, and one that he could well afford to make, for he already owned the farm and, in his new will, had named Stephen White and Eliza Story White and their children as his principal heirs. At no additional cost to himself, he had purchased what he hoped was another year or so of peace and love among the Whites.

Benjamin had the chaise ready, and the captain settled back for the trip home. It had not been a long visit, but it had been satisfying to see his fields and the men who worked them. Already he thought of the trip back in a few weeks, when the nights would be warm and the air sweet and the land freshly green. Then he could begin to enjoy his seasonal residence as the squire of Cherry Hill.

Home at Essex Street, Miss Kimball served a simple meal to Benjamin and herself and the captain. He did not expect much, with Mrs. Beckford gone off again to Wenham—she had been summoned by Joe Knapp. Captain White remarked on the state of the farm, and the fishing fleet at Beverly, and the orchards at Orne's Point. After dinner, they sketched a few plans for the next day. Outside, the night had turned damp, with hazy moonlight and sudden gusts of heavy mist, fresh from storms at sea.

A tall, lean man strolled down one of the side streets, unhurried and unobserved. The houses loomed dark and silent above him, some black, some dimly glowing at windows and doorways. The old town lay still under the moving sky. Nathaniel Hawthorne knew the scene so well by day, and he loathed the dullness of the people and his own aching dullness. He stopped to savor the murky ambiguities of the night. Aloft, the trees sighed in the breeze, naming the departed.

In Salem, few men died but many disappeared—dozens each year, young men mostly, fathers and sons, brothers and bridegrooms, gone over the horizon on their voyages, never to return, some because they found the world a wide and interesting place, and some because they had been dumped into the sea or buried in a foreign grave. Salem men vanished all the time, and sometimes they just went west. Few, however, vanished into their own minds, thinking of "those strange old times, when fantastic dreams and madmen's reveries were realized among the actual circumstances of life."[9]

Out at South Danvers, in the big house adjoining the factory, John Palmer, just released from prison, was staying with friends. After spending two weeks under the name of John Carr in a Salem hotel, he had moved into the chamber of the Crowninshield house that he had occupied in 1827. Dick and George[10] paid him a little money, brought him food and drink, and let him out to help with forgeries and burglaries. He passed counterfeit bills for them, and he was in on the heist of several bales of very valuable flannels.

Early in April, they received visitors from Salem. Frank Knapp and William

Allen came riding up on white horses. From his hiding place in the mansion, John looked down as Dick and William ambled off toward the factory. George and Frank rode away. After a couple of hours the men returned, and then the two visitors departed. Dick and George came upstairs and talked to Palmer about committing further crimes, more dangerous than ever. Palmer suddenly realized that he, the notorious ex-con, might be more useful to them as a fall guy than as a partner.

Next day, he told the brothers that he had to catch up with an old pal in Boston. They tried to get him to stay, but Palmer thanked them and said he would see them later and started walking.

At a mansion on Derby Street, the young lawyer Phippen Knapp and his father were meeting that night with Joseph G. Waters, Esq., to complete proceedings on the bankruptcy of Captain Knapp. His largest creditor was Captain Joseph White. This dismal work involved much lawyerly back-and-forth and much miserable silence on the part of the senior Knapp. Twenty-five years as a merchant was coming to an ignominious end, on a windy night, in a flurry of paper. After a while, it was clear that he was not really needed—here, as on the wharves, as in the town and its taverns, he was now a phantom, done with the life he had made for himself and his family, finished as a productive inhabitant of the seaport. There was no disgrace in it, or so he was told: no money in shipping, no cure for the times. Captain Knapp excused himself from the lawyer's office and trudged home, up the lane from the quiet wharves to the family house. He knew he could not sleep, so he sat downstairs in the dark, very glad that his wife had not lived to see this night of infamy.

A few doors away, Captain White nodded in the parlor wing chair, finishing a small glass of port. The candlelight shone on dim, shapely furnishings, picking up the glints of mirrors and sconces. On one wall, obscured in darkness, were small wedding portraits, sixty years old. There was his bride, Elizabeth, practical and pretty, a brunette with clear blue eyes, wearing a low-cut pink gown trimmed with lace. Her groom was a lean, long-faced, hard-looking young shipmaster, with dark hair, a prominent nose, high cheekbones, and gray eyes. Over the fireplace was the new portrait, one she had never seen, of the rich old man that he had become. He nodded to his likeness and held out his candle to go up to bed.

Early in the morning, in the lifting darkness before dawn, as the town stirred to life and the birds tried out their songs, Benjamin White whistled in the back kitchen, poking at the fireplace ashes and tossing in some kindling and a couple of logs, to start a new fire for Miss Kimball.

Spring came slowly in Salem, and they were not past the reach of a last snowstorm. The night had turned cold, with a piercing breeze from the sea. By the mantel clock, it was nearly twenty past six, and soon the others would be rising, the old man in his chamber and the maid, Miss Kimball, in the room above the captain's. Perhaps she was up already. Ben stood closer to the fire, but he did not warm up—somehow the cold had got in, like an intruder. The back door was shut tight, so he got up to check Mrs. Beckford's room. In the hall he felt a fresh draft, and then he noticed the open window and the curtains swaying.

With a shock, he saw the top of a plank propped against the outside sill, a plank that someone had used to break in. Benjamin closed the sash and hurried up the back staircase, two steps at a time, to the third-floor landing and rapped on Miss Kimball's door and asked if she was all right. After hearing her calm voice, he descended one flight and hesitated outside the captain's room. The door was ajar at the front of the hall, and he stepped into the dark warmth of the room and said, excusing himself, that there had been some trouble. The captain lay still in his four-post bed. He was near deaf in his left ear, so Benjamin repeated himself, louder; but the old gentleman did not stir.

He went to his bedside and saw that the captain was dead. No, not dead, not that only: Captain White had been killed.

Benjamin ran upstairs to tell Miss Kimball, and then he ran into the street to rouse the neighbors, and then he sprinted across the Common to the house of

Stephen White. Stephen dressed quickly and returned with Benjamin and found a few people already gathered in Essex Street. Benjamin and Stephen entered the house, and a frantic Miss Kimball met them on the upstairs landing.

People in the street stared at the house, murmuring and pointing. The rosy brick façade seemed to glow in the morning sun, three stories of the finest architecture in Salem. Its windows reflected the sky, and its door did not open. In the front yard the crocuses blazed in jets of color. Then, from around the corner came Dr. Samuel Johnson, hurrying from his house in Brown Street. He went up the steps of the entry portico and stood at the door for a moment, framed by its columns. The people wanted to follow him, to penetrate the mystery of the rich man's house; but when the door moved he slipped inside alone.

Stephen White met the doctor in the hall and conducted him to the chamber. The shutters were open and the curtains drawn back; the room was full of light. Captain White lay on his right side, under the rumpled covers, diagonally across the bed. The young physician could see the marks of violence. He felt the still throat, touched the cool bloodstain on the front of his thick flannel nightshirt, and stared at the old man's left temple, where flesh and hair formed a little crushed-in bowl. Whatever the damage to his chest, the skull had been fractured, deeply, from a blow of terrible force.

Who would do such a thing?

13.

THE SALEM MURDER

Stephen White stayed calm. He called for his driver, Stratton, and dispatched him to Wenham to fetch Mrs. Beckford. He conferred with Dr. Johnson and agreed that an inquest should be held, immediately if possible. He and the servants, Benjamin White and Lydia Kimball, checked the house for burglary, but nothing was missing. He went out back and stood in the yard, looking at the plank and the window that someone had left unlocked. He noticed, in the mud, the distinct impressions of the soles of a pair of shoes or boots—the killer's tracks, to be measured carefully. He summoned the coroner, Thomas Needham, who quickly assembled a jury of bystanders to witness the medical examination.

Solemnly, uneasily, the jury men filed up the stairs and shuffled into the spacious chamber of death, with its iron-bound trunk and beautiful furnishings. Dr. Johnson waited until all were assembled, then directed their attention to the depression in the skull and the unbroken skin. The body, reported the doctor, was nearly but not quite cold. White was rather fleshy, and there had been little bleeding, perhaps because the blow to the head had stopped his circulation.

Without moving the corpse, Dr. Johnson pulled back the bedclothes and had the bloody nightshirt stripped away by his assistant, Dr. Hubbard. To their horror, the jury men saw a number of knife wounds. The doctor took out his probe and found five stabs to the heart, three to the chest, and another five to the side, indicating that the captain's arm had been lifted as the killer finished his work. There was no evidence of a struggle. The cause of death could have been

REAR WINDOW. Overlooking the garden out back, this window opened from Mrs. Beckford's sitting room. On the evening of April 6, someone who knew that the sash was unlocked had climbed up a plank and entered the Captain's house.

the blow to the head or the knifings—take your choice, said Dr. Johnson. It was his opinion that Captain Joseph White had been alive just three or four hours before.

The selectmen and their tiny police force had no experience in solving major crimes. Incredibly, the treasure chest was shut tight; and on the captain's dresser lay a golden rouleau of Spanish doubloons worth $1,000. Robbery must have been the motive—yet by all appearances, it was not. This bizarre fact fascinated the people of Salem and added deeply to the mystery, for it meant that "the sole and single purpose seems to have been the taking of life."

Soon, the inhabitants were in the grip of terror, imagining how they would be slaughtered in their beds. Offices closed, and men with pistols and swords sat in their stair halls. At hardware stores the locks, crowbars, chains, knives, cleavers, and ammunition flew off the shelves. Families holed up in their apartments and houses, fearing the spectral nighttime enemy and the invisible hand of death.

Official Salem reacted with indignation. The murder of one of its oldest, richest citizens—and one of the largest holders of its municipal debt—called for mobilization of all relevant resources. These, however, proved to be very few—it was not Boston. The police force had no detectives. The various low-level courts had no subpoena power, and the town had no agency through which to collect information or filter citizens' observations. Thwarted, the selectmen could do no better than to post a $500 reward and print up handbills. The town's creaky constables were "directed to make the most diligent search for the assassin," without benefit of any clues or descriptions. The judges grilled Benjamin White and Lydia Kimball, and they arrested Joseph White Beckford, a grandnephew, who had been observed on his way to Marblehead late that night. But he had an alibi, and they released him.

As Salem swirled in fear and outrage, Reverend Henry Colman arrived at Captain White's mansion to be with the heirs. There was plenty to drink and plenty of reasons to drink it, for the tension was thick. Mary Beckford suspected that Stephen White had been behind the arrest of her son. She sat with her family members: son Joseph White Beckford, daughters Eliza and Mary and their husbands, John Davis and Joseph Knapp Jr., and Joe's brothers Frank and Phippen. Stephen White and his four children—son Joseph, the Harvard student, and three daughters, Harriet, Caroline, and Ellen—sat with Eliza Story White and her three daughters, Charlotte, fifteen, Mary, eighteen, and the very pregnant Mrs. Elizabeth Gray, twenty. Stephen's brother John White was there, and Frederick Bessell, Frank Story, and the Story-Fettyplaces. They received small groups of relatives and close friends, a few old widows, and even fewer old men, survivors of the captain's generation like Joseph Peabody. Crowninshields and Silsbees stopped in to pay their respects and reminisce, as did the banker John White Treadwell, the captain's cousin, who sat with them and had a drink or two and eventually mentioned that he was executor of the last will and testament, in the possession of lawyer Waters. To Stephen White, privately, Treadwell confided that he had nothing to fear, nor did the daughters of his deceased brother Joseph.

At five thirty on the afternoon of April 8, the physicians returned, at the request of Stephen White, to conduct an autopsy. Dr. Abel L. Peirson, a Salem surgeon, led the examination, assisted by Dr. Johnson and a few of his pupils. When he was finished, Dr. Peirson said that Captain White was sturdy and much healthier than most men his age. The head bash was fatal. The blow, he said, must have been very severe, or the instrument very heavy, or both, judging from the impact and the gaping cracks in the skull. The stabbings, he thought, involved two knives, one about five inches long, with a hilt that accounted for the broken ribs, and one that was longer and flatter. From this, he posited that two men had done the fatal work.

Stephen White, acting "for the heirs of the deceased," placed a newspaper notice that first appeared on April 9. It was headed, ATROCIOUS MURDER!!! $1000 REWARD!!!! One thousand dollars could buy a homestead outright. The reverberations of the "Salem Murder," as it was dubbed, quickly spread across the state and region, and Senator White's friend, the newly reelected governor Levi Lincoln, encouraged "extraordinary efforts" at detection with a matching reward of $1,000 from state coffers.

The people of Salem, of course, talked and gossiped: someone must have seen the killers; someone must have encountered the persons who had so brutally ended Captain White's long life—unless it was Benjamin White and Lydia Kimball, unfaithful servants, or Captain White's heirs themselves. If it was not burglary, still it must have been a robbery—someone must have profited.

On Friday afternoon, Stephen White and his cousin Mary Beckford led the funeral procession up Essex Street from the White house. The coffin, draped in black on a horse-drawn bier, was followed by the somber Mr. Colman, Bible in hand. An "immense concourse of people" trailed the family past the watching mansions, to the East India Marine Hall. They turned down Prison Lane and then on to Brown Street. At the corner made by the headhouse of the ropewalk—in which, it was said, two men had been lurking before the murder—they turned left onto the narrow lane of Howard Street, past the Branch Church along the cemetery fence to its gate. They entered the graveyard, facing the gray castle of Salem Jail; and the funeral carriage carried the captain's bones to a massive granite block set in place eleven years before for the burial of his daughter, Elizabeth.

To the hundreds who stood amid the gravestones, Mr. Colman gave a speech that was more about outrage than consolation. He closed with a prayer, and Captain White's coffin was lowered into the long night of the tomb. Colman spoke again: a meeting would be held that evening at Derby Square to see about finding the killers.

At the Town Hall, some men made speeches, but the panicky townspeople wanted action and authorized a small group of the gentry to form a Committee of Vigilance "consisting of seven men from each ward, with power to search every house and interrogate every person on any point that could lead to the detection of the murderers." The selectmen were to double the police force and to "establish a very numerous voluntary watch" in the neighborhoods, starting that very night. After the meeting broke up, the committee came together and chose a secretary, Stephen C. Phillips, to record their secret proceedings. The steering subcommittee was made up of Dr. Gideon Barstow, John White Treadwell, and Philip Chase, three of the many protégés of Stephen White. As much as they wanted to find and punish the killers, they wished even more to clear the name of their dear friend. If the rumors did not abate, White's reputation might be permanently damaged, and Salem's with it. He had already told them that he would be moving his household to a suite at the Tremont Hotel in Boston. He was placing the investigation in the hands of his friends on the Committee of Vigilance; by midnight they were in full control of the effort to solve the Salem Murder.

The town seethed with mistrust as neighbor eyed neighbor, suspecting the worst. The large rewards, a total now of $2,500, had set everyone against everyone else, rivals and suspects, all hoping to be the first to stumble upon the truth, re-vealed by the slip of a tongue or a conversation overheard. In a town full of ter-rified hunters, everyone was fair game. Added to the horror of assassination was the fear of being carried off in the night—not by killers, but by the agents of the committee, summoning citizens from their parlors and out of their beds and escorting them through the streets to the Essex Place chamber of inquisi-tion. There the suspect would find himself forced to answer to a tribunal of twenty-seven angry men determined to force a break in the case.

At the waterfront, not one vessel had arrived from Sumatra since December, and few were preparing to sail for the Orient. Packets continued to come and go at Union Wharf, and brigs and schooners arrived from South America and the West Indies and made ready for coastal trips. In every forecastle, the scuttlebutt was the same, genuine bewilderment that someone would go to all the trouble of killing Captain White without plundering his treasure chest. It seemed an awful waste of a crime.

Speculations flew about the town like the spectral spirits of old. For night walker Nathaniel Hawthorne, the murder raised the ghost of his ancestor Judge John Hathorne, the grim magistrate of 1692, presiding fatally over Salem's witch-craft hearings with his own committee of the vigilant. Yesterday, there were ru-mors about Stephen White; today's rumors concerned Nathaniel's own cousin John Forrester Jr., a hard-drinking Harvard student who ran with a fast crowd. Arrests would soon be made, if only to give some relief. Hawthorne did not feel the need to leave Salem; he had always enjoyed a good fire.

But John Palmer stayed away, terrified of the witch hunt: "All were excited; a general uproar had taken place; two-thirds of the town's people were raving mad, the rest crouching like a lion for his prey, eagerly, furiously hunting up every-thing for the express purpose of sending down the vengeance of the law on the perpetrator, or perpetrators, of the murder; and him who could relate anything of importance must have the evidence of his own innocence in his own hand, or he would literally be torn in pieces, almost hung, for being able to tell the truth." Under the alias of John Carr, "I knew not what course to take," he wrote. "I tell you that my mind was *perplexed*, and that I could only act with caution: I changed my name, not that I feared being arrested as a murderer; I never *feared* it; I had but one fear, that was that I should never be able to unfold what your public prints styled a mystery—a mystery."[1]

Palmer knew too much, and he suspected more, and the fabulous sum of the reward money made him bold. On April 9, he paid a visit to the Crownin-shields and found that he "had lost their confidence. They wanted to know where I came from, and where I was going. I led them astray in everything, both in my feelings and in regard to my views and intentions." After a brief and disturb-ing conversation, he returned to his hideaway in nearby Lynnfield, "disgusted with a wayward life; disgusted with every evil act of my life. It was horrible to be obliged to suspect an acquaintance of the crime of murder; it was no less horri-ble to conceal it; and I determined to divulge my suspicions to a friend."

On April 12, at Providence, he called on an uncle who managed a hotel and told him about the murder and his suspicions about the powerful families be-hind the crime. The businessman told his disgraced nephew not to expect any-one to believe an ex-convict, but to keep his mouth shut, choose a new name, and "migrate to the western country." It was excellent advice, given when it would have done the most good if followed.

As usual, John Palmer had other ideas.

The Committee of Vigilance was the ultimate oligarchy: above the law, it had assembled swiftly in elite outrage. It met at the White countinghouse and oper-ated with a fund of one thousand White dollars. Its sole legal adviser was the brilliant Rufus Choate. Each evening, the gentlemen entered at the pillared por-tico opposite East India Marine Hall to do their grim business, reviewing evi-dence, receiving requests, interviewing the eager and the afraid, dispatching messengers into the dark shuttered streets to summon more victims.

The committee was chaired by Dr. Gideon Barstow, merchant and former congressman, assisted by White's dear friend Stephen C. Phillips and other White friends and relatives—William Fettyplace, John White Treadwell, Frank-lin Story—among the twenty-seven. They felt justified in their methods as they tried not just to solve a murder, but to save Salem—from the bad opinion of the nation's press, from criminals, from their failure with the mill dam, and from the loss of an honorable reputation. At the end of a week of investigation, the Committee of Vigilance had done nothing to allay the reign of terror but had succeeded in churning up great amounts of fear and loathing.

From his home in Cambridge, Joseph Story wrote to Daniel Webster[2] about "the horrible murder." The killing had set off a panic in the entire region, "not confined to Salem, or Boston, but seems to pervade the whole community. We are all astounded and looking to know from what corner the next blow will come. There is a universal dread and sense of insecurity, as if we lived in the midst of a banditti." Story believed that plunder was the objective, contrived by "a deep scheme, by persons who were adept in their vocation and irretrievably wicked, damned spirits. Its success is astonishing; its malicious deliberation unparalleled."

Stephen's involvement in the Prison Discipline Society gave him special influence. Two Salem emissaries visited the state prison at Charlestown to see who had been released earlier in the year. They spoke with inmate Joseph Fisher, still buried alive by the Crowninshields, for whom he had taken the fall for the hotel spree. Three years into a four-year sentence, he saw a chance to go free. He told his visitors about the moment in 1827 that he and Hatch had overheard Dick Crowninshield and a man named Palmer discussing Captain White's treasure chest. The names of Crowninshield, Palmer, and Hatch went into the notebook and came back to the Committee of Vigilance.

Fisher had an echo in New Bedford. The jailer there wrote to Stephen White that Hatch,[3] Fisher's hardened friend, was willing to testify to what he had heard while hanging out in Dick's night town. The Committee of Vigilance summoned Hatch and his friend John Quiner,[4] and the names Benjamin Selman and Daniel Chase were reported. Despite the convergence of the Fisher-Hatch stories, the committee had to consider the sources. They were listening to criminals and lowlifes, one of whom had a strong motive of vengeance toward Dick and George. The brothers were suspects in any major Salem-area crime, but they were also Crowninshields and had to be handled with respect.

Every night for two weeks, the Committee of Vigilance hauled in citizens and grilled them: the stable hand, the college students, the shopkeepers, the constables, the bartenders. One suspect, a man named Joseph Antony, had admitted his involvement in the Crowninshield gang. Rather than arrest him, though, the committee had referred him to Stephen White, by whom he was hired to spy on the Crowninshields.[5] A bank manager, John Southwick, told about his vigil at a window overlooking Brown Street behind Captain White's estate on the night of the murder. He and Captain Daniel Bray, sensing something untoward in the behavior of a couple of loiterers at the mouth of the ropewalk there, had stood in the dark of a bedroom in Bray's house, watching the comings and goings of the pair below. Captain Bray affirmed his story. Neither mentioned any names. The Committee of Vigilance knew it was making progress, but toward what? They kept their own counsel and let the rest of Salem wonder and tremble.

Before the end of the month, a terrifying incident forced the committee's hand. On the night of April 27, Frank and Joe Knapp were heading home from Salem to the Wenham farm in a carriage. As they recounted it, they were assaulted by ruffians on a country road, two against three in a wild melee. The robbers had clubs, but the Knapps lashed out with swords and canes and drove their attackers into the woods. Next evening, the committee hosted Joe and Frank, two more respectable citizens—and members of the extended White family—who had been targeted for death. This attack came on top of the report of Salem break-ins at both the Knapp house on Essex Street and the Beckford house on Bridge Street. The Knapp brothers had taken to wearing pistols and carrying dirks.

On May 2, the committee made its move and arrested four men for murder: Daniel Chase, Benjamin Selman, George Crowninshield, and Richard Crowninshield Jr. The next day, a grand jury heard from Hatch, his companions, and members of the Committee of Vigilance. By one vote the grand jury returned indictments on May 5, a month after the murder of Captain White, alleging that Dick Crowninshield had struck the killing blow while the other three had conspired and assisted. It was a guess, perhaps desperate, but the public needed answers. Dick's acquaintances snorted: he would never have killed the old merchant and not come away with the loot.

Dick amused himself in his cell, writing letters and composing poems, planning new adventures, awaiting restoration to his throne among the sports and whores of night world. He knew that the case was a long shot, based on flimsy hearsay and completely lacking in motive. To his sister Sarah's birthday wishes, he responded on May 15 with a set of mawkish rhymes ("Unhappy day! You'll find me in a gloomy cell, and thoughts of keen sensation in my bosom swell," etc.) and a letter full of Byronic posing: "How visionary are the anticipations of this life! . . . But a few days since, I enjoyed contentment and liberty. I had the most flattering prospect of passing a cheerful summer with you, unconscious of the malicious and hellish schemes contrived to blast our characters, our all in life. Now doomed to spend our youthful days in the solitary cell of a gloomy prison, I sometimes imagine it a vision. Would to God it was so! But I know too well the reality of the reverse. Had the Committee of Vigilance requested us to give an account of ourselves, we would cheerfully have done it to their entire satisfaction. The perjured State's Prison convict that they intend to bring as evidence against us will be none to their credit. What prompts him to this perjured confession? Is it in anticipation of getting pardoned? Or is it wealth?"[6]

Captain Joseph J. Knapp Sr. was still trying to cope with the loss of all of his property. He continued to reside in his house, which now belonged to the estate of a murdered man. He had no idea of how to start over, and he was shaken at the death of Joseph White and the vicious attack on his own sons Joe and Frank. His son Phippen was the one calm presence in a home in which the housekeeper and younger children were afraid to fall asleep.

The strangeness of Captain Knapp's life was mildly compounded on May 15, when he received mail from Maine. Dated May 12 at Belfast, the letter was signed by Charles Grant Jr. of Prospect, who described himself as "an utter stranger." He started by requesting a loan of $350, "the refusal of which will ruin you." Grant wrote "that I am acquainted with your brother Franklin and also the business that he was transacting for you on the 2nd of April last; and that I think you was very extravagant in giving one thousand dollars to the person that would execute the business for you. But you know best about that, you see that such things will leak out." Captain Knapp thought the letter nonsense; his son Phippen, the lawyer, thought otherwise. Father and son saddled up and rode off to Wenham to place it before Joe and Frank. Joe laughed at it: the letter was "a devilish lot of trash," and he might have tossed it into the fire, but in a bit of bravado he advised that it be given to the Committee of Vigilance.

Next day, May 16, the committee received another letter signed Grant, posted in Salem that morning but dated May 13. He wrote that he and Stephen White had killed the captain: "I struck him on the head with a heavy piece of lead and then stabbed him with a dirk; he made the finishing strokes with another. He promised to send me the money next evening, and has not sent it yet, which is the reason I mention this." On the same day, Stephen White received a letter just posted at Salem and dated at nearby Lynn, May 12, signed "N. Claxton 4th," ordering him to "send the $5,000, or part of it, before tomorrow night, or suffer the painful consequences." White, unaware of the Grant letters, gave the Claxton message to Gideon Barstow of the Committee of Vigilance.[7]

Four men languished in jail, with nothing more than convicts' stories to hold them there. Meanwhile, the accumulating evidence was forcing the committee toward a new possibility, which, while highly distasteful, did provide a clear motive: the man who had stood to gain the most by the death of Joseph White had been both his principal heir and his executioner.

Stephen White, the leader of Salem society, the chief agent of enlightenment and civic progress, stood before the committee members in his cloak and his expensive bottle-green coat, with his silk top hat in his hand, the picture of poise and elegance, summoned from the grieving mansion on Washington Square to the hall of vigilance in his own countinghouse. His friend Dr. Barstow seemed anxious; most of the others, White's trusted colleagues, sat in silence, some looking down at their hands, some staring at him. White took his seat, wary but hopeful, ready for whatever news they had, knowing it could not be worse than the blows he had already taken.

When Rufus Choate began laying out the evidence against him, White could not believe what he was hearing. He rose to his feet, suddenly realizing that he stood alone in a star chamber, without rights, unprotected by the law, unrepresented by an advocate, in peril of his life. He was stunned, but not for long. He looked into the faces of these men, whom he had known his whole life, and saw how it was. For years he had spurred them toward a vision of Salem's greatness; for years they had borrowed his money and sat on his boards and marched in his parades—friends, brothers. In an instant all of it was shattered, and he was adrift.

14.

CONFESSION

Looking for Grant, Joseph G. Waters, Captain White's lawyer and the committee's agent, arrived in the town of Prospect, Maine, two hundred miles from Salem. On May 24, as Grant came into the post office for his mail, two constables jumped him and carried him off to Belfast Jail.

The young prisoner, about twenty-three, "had hard work" to tell his story to Waters, who seemed "like a man traveling in a whirlwind, afraid to go on, feeling it impossible to stop." He recalled that "every word that I uttered was caught on the point of his pen, and with the same movement dashed in the ink, and then on paper, for fear that it might escape his grasp. What then? All kinds of promises made, to get more!"[1] The prisoner knew that a true inferno awaited him at Salem. Waters asked Grant who he really was, and the prisoner answered, Palmer, John Carr Roberts Palmer Jr., of Belfast, recently a prisoner of the state, and more recently, under the name of John Carr, a sojourner in Salem and in Danvers, dragged deep into mysteries as a guest of the Crowninshields.

Waters wrote to the committee that his captive "has insinuating manners, and possesses an acute mind."[2] Palmer wanted immunity from prosecution, and Waters told him he would get it; but then Palmer was refused a visit from his father and the written assurances he had sought. Palmer denied posting the letter in Salem on May 16 in which "Grant" confessed that he and Stephen White had done the killing. Palmer insisted that he had sent only one letter, from Charles Grant Jr. of Prospect, Maine, dated and posted May 12, intended not to extort, but to save himself and flush out the killers. "My belief, that the conspirators

A YANKEE ROVER. John Palmer, a young sailor from Belfast, Maine, was fated to spend much of his time in Salem under lock and key. He had a taste for adventure and a talent for bad company, as in New Orleans, where he had first beheld the shocking "picture of vice" and made the acquaintance of the feckless George Crowninshield.

were of such influential families that it was dangerous to meddle with them, was my greatest difficulty, yet I was determined to make an effort." He had meant for the letter to go to Joe Knapp and had not realized that it had gone to the father. The payment of hush money, he said, was to have incriminated the real conspirators, whom he claimed were the Knapp brothers and, perhaps, Mrs. Mary Beckford. Asked how he knew these things. Palmer replied that, pre-murder, while at the Crowninshields', he had found out about the Knapps and their interest in killing Captain White; post-murder, he had feared being framed.

At the conclusion of a long day, Waters sent word to the Committee of Vigilance, relating what he had learned and urging the arrest of the Knapps. As for Palmer, Waters wrote, "I cannot but feel an interest in him, and sincerely hope that he will be able to convince all of his innocence."[3]

Unaware of these proceedings, Dick Crowninshield wrote to his sister as if he were some sensitive divinity student who could not get home for vacation: "I much admire the poetry you sent in yours, and think it quite appropriate to circumstances. Excuse me for not acknowledging the reception of the rose in my last." He enclosed a poem about her rose, a reminder of "the lovely hours I ne'er again shall find." He added that he and George had been visited by a cousin and his friend; and Dick asked Sarah to bring books: Cicero's *Orations* for George, and, for himself, Hutton's *Mathematics,* Walsh's *Commercial Arithmetic,* and Moore's *Irish Melodies.* The jailer, he said, was very obliging, their food was wholesome, and the lawyers were attentive. "In gratitude, I acknowledge the innumerable obligations we are under to our friends for their perseverance in the cause of innocence. I see nothing warrantable in this barbarous punishment. I think the savage of the western wilds, who never saw a Christian, would not inflict the like cruel punishment on his greatest enemy, without a more substantial evidence. But alas!—they have struck the excruciating blow. If they have any conscience it will rebuke them for the heart-rending pangs they have caused."[4]

The officials of the Salem Mill Dam Corporation finally had their day in court. Although it had lost many of its champions along the way, the mill dam was finally about to be realized; and if it did not rescue Salem outright, certainly it would provide good jobs and valuable exports for hundreds of the least affluent of its citizens.

The Supreme Judicial Court met in mid-April to consider the appeal of the Endicotts and Joseph Ropes. There was much to review: the incorporation documents, the torturous history, the terms of the stock offerings, and the procedures for reorganization. At the time of the corporation's restructuring, the Endicotts' 30 open shares and the 200 units owned by bankrupts had been the only orphans among the 5,000 newly purchased shares. Now the judges made their ruling: the 230 shares were fundamental to the value of the corporation; without them, the stock offering had been illegal.

After many years and many blunders, the owners came to a fateful decision. In May, 1830, the Salem Mill Dam Corporation was formally and permanently dissolved.

Captain Moses Endicott, thirty-seven, welcomed the demise of the mill dam project, which meant that he was no longer in the pathway of a lawsuit. He was trying to ascend to the ranks of merchants and bankers. He and his wife, Sarah, resided in an elegant, brand-new brick triplex on Chestnut Street, and he had shed his Old Testament name for a brand-new modish one, but Charles M. Endicott found that people still called him Moses, which always brought a testy correction. He hoped that no one associated him with his *Persia* shipmate from years before, Dick Crowninshield.

Endicott was happy to be sailing once more for the Orient. Upon his return, he might have enough wealth to pursue the mercantile career that he had earned through his own exertions and his status as a descendant of Governor Endicott, founding Puritan. After packing up his books and his handmade charts, he had his sea chest delivered to the large ship *Friendship,* one of the last to sail directly from Salem into the world—although he had orders to sell the return cargo of pepper at New York. She would need a swift passage to reach the west coast of Sumatra by the end of the harvest. The *Friendship* had been acquired by Silsbee, Pickman & Stone in the liquidation of Peirce & Nichols; although not new, she was sound, handsome, and proven as an East Indiaman. He had a good crew, including two holdovers from her last voyage: John Barry, twenty-four, of Salem, again sailing as second mate, and a fellow from Genoa or Leghorn, now of Salem, known as Gregory Pedechie. The other fourteen were young and mainly Salem born, including two African Americans, the steward William Francis and the cook Lorenzo Mizell. As first mate, Endicott had hired Charles A. Knight, twenty-eight, a short, brisk, cocky sort, to keep the crewmen hopping.

On May 25, the owners came down to the dock for the send-off. Family members and friends, boys, dogs, drunken sailors, and old salts made a little crowd. With a few chests of opium in the hold and a barrel of specie in the cabin, Captain Endicott ordered her topsails set. They filled in the light breeze, and the *Friendship* slowly pulled out of the dock and glided into the harbor. In a few minutes, with her big sails shaken out, she gave a salute, bound for the other side of the world.

The roar of the cannon echoed off the buildings of the waterfront and sent the seagulls squawking over the many vessels riding at anchor.

On the evening of May 26, while lounging at the farmhouse in Wenham, Joe and Frank Knapp heard riders approaching. They looked at each other, at their guns on the wall, at the woods behind the house. When the knock came, they opened the door and submitted to the agents of the Committee of Vigilance. That night they took up lodgings in Salem Jail, joining Richard and George Crowninshield and Benjamin Selman and Daniel Chase. When the jailer told Dick about the Knapps, he slumped back on his cot in a sweat.[5]

The excitable Reverend Henry Colman had been kept busy attending to his congregation, conducting funeral services, and helping the stunned and grieving family. He had consoled Stephen White as he dealt with the possibility of being arrested and unable to protect his children. Now he had a parishioner behind bars: the young sea captain Joe Knapp, whom he had joined in marriage with his dear young friend Mary White Beckford. And then it got worse: on the night of Joe's arrest, Mary tried to kill herself. She was discovered in time to be saved.[6]

On Saturday, May 28, Squire Savage began the examination of the Knapp brothers by laying out a shocking case against them. Just a few days before, Salem had been horrified that these two young men had had to fight for their lives; now they appeared to be blackhearted villains, plotting a murder for months, writing the letters that had framed Stephen White. The Knapps denied everything. Reverend Henry Colman saw his chance to be a hero. He discussed the allegations with the vigilance men and "obtained their consent to visit the prisoners."[7] Then he went to the Knapp house and conversed with the downcast Mrs. Beckford and her daughter Mary and other family members; and that morning, right after Savage's examination, he went to the jail.

Acting as both Joe Knapp's minister and as an informer to the Committee of Vigilance, Colman came away from the meeting convinced of Joe's guilt, "for he did not deny it" when asked if he had conspired to kill Captain White.[8] Joe understood that anything he said to the clergyman was protected by the priest-penitent rule in law; but he was wrong, for Colman was a double agent. After reporting to the Committee of Vigilance and lying to Phippen Knapp about agreeing to meet him before returning to the jail, Colman proceeded to Joe's cell. Joe felt that he must unburden himself to the man of God, who found it thrilling to hear Knapp's calmly told tale of murder.

When he finished, Joe was a wreck. Could the case against him be proved? Colman replied that some of the vigilants believed that the evidence was "complete and conclusive." Colman asked who Palmer was, and Joe did not know. Colman said that the offer of a pardon was in play: it might go to Palmer instead. Without legal counsel, Joe did not realize that he was being bluffed, for Palmer had not even committed a crime. Joe was distracted—"a good deal of the time he said nothing"—but he also kept asking whether the charge could be proved.[9] Colman told him that "if he was innocent, by no means to state anything to involve himself"; however, if he chose to confess, Colman would keep silent and arrange with the government to give Joe formal immunity. The minister then departed.

Depending on the role he chose to play, Colman held the lives of several persons in his hands. As a minister, he might live with terrible knowledge and never say a word; as Joe's protector, he might save his life; as the friend of the incredibly wealthy Stephen White, he might clear an honored name; as an agent of the Committee of Vigilance, he might solve the whole case, for which there was a great reward. In the midst of murder and terror, he, Henry Colman, could end the madness in Salem.

At three o'clock Colman returned, in company with Phippen Knapp. Joe had heard from one of the Crowninshields that Palmer was a notorious liar being brought from the state of Maine. Was that true? Colman said that he believed Palmer was on his way. Joe asked again about the evidence against him, and Colman replied that "the two letters put into the Post Office are traced to you." These were the Grant and Claxton letters, mailed by an innocent friend. Knapp whispered that he wished to confess as a state's witness and proceeded to tell them more details of the murder plot and the place of concealment of the murder weapon, a wooden club. The lives of Joe and Frank were in peril. One of them should seek the state's protection, Colman advised, and Joe was a married man and perhaps was less implicated. Joe liked what he heard. Phippen said it must not be done without Frank's consent.

Colman and Phippen left the cell. Phippen started toward Frank's door, thinking that he would visit privately, but the minister trailed behind him, expectant. Phippen asked Colman not to get the club except in his presence, and Colman agreed. Then they sat down with Frank and told him that Joe had confessed. Before his brother could speak, Phippen said, "Frank, Mr. Colman has proposed that you take a trial, and that Joe make a confession and have the benefit of immunity. The Committee of Vigilance will guarantee it, but we want your consent. With immunity, Joe will live; and you will likely prevail in a trial." Frank hesitated only a few seconds, then said, "I have nothing to confess; it is a hard case, but if it is as you say, Joseph might confess if he pleases, and I shall stand trial." For his response, Phippen considered Frank "a hero" and told his colleague, lawyer Robert Rantoul, "I wish to God that Frank was in Joe's place and Joe in his—they would as soon get anything out of the stone walls as out of Frank."

That afternoon, Colman reported to the Committee of Vigilance that Joseph Knapp Jr. was prepared to confess. The committee authorized Colman to go that night to the attorney general in Boston and get a letter "promising the protection of government." Colman did so and returned to Salem by noontime. At one o'clock, committee members Barstow and Fettyplace went with Colman to the Branch meeting house, across the graveyard from the jail; and there, in a rathole under the northern stairs, Colman fished out a machined wooden bludgeon with a beaded grip and lead inserts in the barrel.

At Joe Knapp's cell, Reverend Henry Colman showed him the immunity letter, and they talked about the club and about the attorney general. After a while, Colman took out his notebook and his ink bottle and pen and said: "Now, Joseph, let us begin. Please make an explicit, exact, and full disclosure of every circumstance of the murder." Joe sighed and closed his eyes, then started talking.

In a pained monotone, Joe said that in January he had entered Captain White's chamber and opened the famous iron chest and found that it contained some silver plate and a will devising $16,000 to his mother-in-law, Mrs. Beckford, with much larger amounts going to Stephen White and others. Joe calculated that in the absence of a will, much more of the captain's fortune would descend to the Beckfords and Knapps. This thought had led to others. In February, he advised his brother Frank "that I would not begrudge one thousand dollars that the old gentleman, meaning Captain Joseph White of Salem, was dead." When Frank asked why, Joe explained about the inequity of the will—remove it, destroy it, kill the old man, and the Beckford-Knapps would have theirs and stay rich for decades. Besides, "Stephen White had injured me in the opinion of the old gentleman and, I had no doubt, had also prejudiced him against all the [Beckford] family; and that I thought it right to get the property if I could. I mentioned to him also in a joking way that the old gentleman had often said he wished he could go off like a flash."[10]

Joe continued with his confession, relating that Frank had showed interest, and the two had plotted murder as if they were charting out a voyage. Joe would take no direct part in it. "One way was to meet him on the road, but the old gentleman was never out at night. Another was to attack him in the house, but Frank said he had not the pluck to do it." Frank then thought to sound out the Crowninshield brothers. Although Joe doubted, Frank rode out to their house and proposed murder. George offered to kill the captain anywhere outdoors, but not in the house; Dick said he would do it indoors if George would back him. George refused, but Frank met with Dick thrice more: once by the Salem Theatre, once by the Universalist meeting house, once by the Southfield Bridge in South Salem, where Dick had held his nightly revels.

Joe told Colman that one afternoon in March, Dick had been ready to knife the captain in his carriage on a visit to Chestnut Street; but White had returned before dark. Early in April, as Joe concluded that the murder was not going to happen, Dick and Frank met again, and Frank told Joe to make arrangements to get Dick inside the house. On Friday, April 2, Joe removed the will from the chest, took the key from the door to the captain's bedroom, and unlocked one of the windows in Mrs. Beckford's back parlor. That night, Joe met Dick Crowninshield on the Common and confirmed that he would pay $1,000 "if he would fix him, meaning Captain White." Dick smiled and showed Joe "the tools he would do it with, which was a club and a dirk. The club was about two feet long, turned of hard wood, loaded at the end and very heavy. I presumed it was loaded, and ornamented at the handle, that is, turned with beads at the end to keep it from slipping—I took hold of it, I think I lifted it. The dirk was about five inches long on the blade, having a white handle, as I think—it was flat, sharp at both edges."[11]

At that point in the confession, Colman and Joe were interrupted by the arrival of Phippen Knapp, outside the cell, requesting entrance. Colman told him to stay out, that he and Joe were not finished.

Joe resumed: Dick said that he could not get George to back him, that he would meet Frank on Sunday evening. They met after Joe had attended Colman's church services in Salem and gone home to Wenham. On Tuesday afternoon, Frank had come to the farm and confirmed that Mrs. Beckford would not be in Salem that night. Frank finished his tea and rode off, saying, "I guess he will go tonight." At the farm on the next morning, Wednesday, April 7, "Mr. Stephen White's man came up in his chaise and informed us that the old gentleman White was dead; and Mother Beckford said she would go right down with him. My brother Frank came to the farm that day about noon—he asked if we had heard the news; we told him yes and how we heard it. After dinner he told me aside how it occurred. He said Richard Crowninshield met him, I think, in Brown Street, in Salem, about ten o'clock in the evening, and that he, Richard, left him and came round through the front yard, passed through the garden gate, pushed up the back window and got in by it; and passed through the entry, by the front stairs into Captain White's chamber; that he struck Captain White with the club while asleep, and, after striking him, he used the dirk and hit him several times with the dirk, and covered him up, and came off, and met my brother again in Brown Street, or by the Common, I think about eleven o'clock." Frank had then hurried home to bed a block away; Dick had walked the four miles home, strolling out through Paradise and along Dark Lane up into South Danvers.

Henry Colman and the Committee of Vigilance hastened to leak summaries of Joe's confessions to the newspapers.[12] Nothing could have been more damaging to the prisoners. The Knapps and the Crowninshields, Selman and Chase, would be tried for their lives in a town where everyone had discussed all the roles and movements of every plotter and player in the cold-blooded assassination of Captain White.

The summaries did not include Joe's final remarks in his second confession: "My brother Frank told me two or three times that I had better let the business alone; that I was looking altogether on the bright side and did not consider the danger. I told him I had weighed the matter pretty well, as I thought; and that I would run the risk of it."[13]

15.

IMPS OF HELL &
DEVILS ROAM

Stephen White had done his best for Salem for fourteen years, supported by Joseph White, the man whose generosity and love for Stephen had caused his death. Now it was time for vengeance.

Several on the Committee of Vigilance had been willing to let him take the fall for their town and their inability to bring an end to the disgrace of a notorious crime. His whole career, his devotion to Salem and its institutions, his loyalty and energy—all were trumped in a flash by a pair of fools and three letters. In Salem, had it ever been about anything other than pride, and envy, and money? Boston was his new home. He and his bloodstained treasure would not return.

Of course, White would do everything in his power to send the conspirators to the scaffold, a few graves over from the tomb of Joseph White. Whenever he felt himself lapsing back into the gentleman who had advocated for prison reform and rehabilitation of criminals, he thought of his brother Colonel Joseph White Jr. and resolved to do what was right. Joseph would have paid the cost of real justice. The Crowninshields were already doomed. Stephen conferred with Judge Story and made his decision: $1,000 had bought the death of his father, and $1,000 would buy the services of Daniel Webster toward executing the Knapps.

Black Dan was willing.

White could hardly wait for the trials to start.

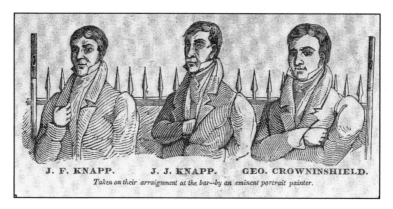

J. F. KNAPP.   J. J. KNAPP.   GEO. CROWNINSHIELD.

Taken on their arraignment at the bar--by an eminent portrait painter.

ACCUSED. *Frank Knapp, Joe Knapp, and George Crowninshield were ushered into the courtroom together to hear the charges. With Dick Crowninshield gone, their lawyer thought that none could be indicted as a principal or subjected to capital punishment. It seemed that only smiling George believed it.*

On June 3, John Palmer arrived in Salem in chains. In spite of Waters's good opinion, Palmer, the ex-convict, was charged with killing Captain White by means of a hatchet. This false accusation put him in a cell, although he had protested: "What had I done to create all of this confusion? Why, I had told the truth—what do you think!—told the truth, and turned the world upside down." But it was his fate to be a prisoner. The constables had placed him in irons, neck and heels, and carried him out of Belfast Jail in a strongbox to a mail stage headed south.

In Salem, he wrote, he was met by the "citizens of the city or town of peace. I was amused, and I was terrified, for they came rolling on with the impetuosity of tornadoes." He knew that if the powerful, upstanding Stephen White could be framed, he himself was fatally vulnerable. "Do you think this was a visionary fear?" he asked. "I refer you to Stephen White. Who sent suspicion down upon his head like a torrent? Who vexed his soul to agony? I would ask, Who did this, but the conspirators!" If the conspiring Knapps could trick the committee into suspecting White, "a man whose character was spotless, one who was beloved, was honoured, one whose nature was all kindness, and *generosity,* would I stand safe? Let the impartial answer this question; I say I had no idea of trusting myself to their goodness!"

Palmer's tale never varied. On the afternoon of Friday, April 2, at the South Danvers Crowninshield house, he had seen Frank Knapp and William Allen ride up on white horses.[1] A couple of hours later, the Crowninshields visited him and proposed a murder for hire. He would be given one-third of their thousand-dollar fee for the killing of old Captain White, on the order of Joseph Knapp. Palmer claimed that he had told them that murder was beyond him. "Come, Jack," Dick had said, "we'll meet the old gentleman tonight, and overset his carriage—a terrible accident."

Palmer had asked about Knapp's motive. Knapp wanted the will destroyed, Dick had told him. "Both destroyed: the old gentleman and his last will and testament." Again, Palmer said, he had protested: "I am not your man." Next day, Saturday, Palmer had cleared out early in the afternoon and stayed away. He dreaded going back to prison and thought about informing on them; but he had laughed it off, knowing that no one would believe an ex-con. And it was all probably a joke anyway, a black joke of the sort that Dick enjoyed.

The murder had occurred four days later, and after that Palmer had returned twice to the mansion in South Danvers. He had visited briefly on the night of April 9, then stayed for two days at the end of the month. They had fed him, as before, and had hidden him in the room. He had joked with them, dirk at the ready, and finally Dick had loaned him four five-franc pieces, part of Joe Knapp's payout. Then he had run.

Visited in jail by Colman, White, and Waters, Palmer kept explaining that he could not have gone to the authorities and related his suspicions without the risk of being arrested for slander or locked up as a lunatic. Having learned of the killing, he had told what he knew, several times, to his uncle at Providence and to Waters at Belfast and now to the Committee of Vigilance, verbally and in writing: an explanation. He had not accepted counsel because he had not done anything wrong—well, about those stolen flannels found at South Danvers, he kept mum, but the flannels were hardly the point.

Yet to Dick they *were* the point. The missing Sutton flannels had been discovered, per the newspapers, at the workshop of Richard Crowninshield Jr. It galled him to be portrayed as a petty thief. He had always said that he would never submit to ignominious treatment. Dick Crowninshield read his tomes on mathematics and hummed tunes from his book of Irish melodies. He chatted with his lawyers and the jailer, Mr. Brown, and he seemed his usual confident, inscrutable self. But he was thinking a lot about hell, and he stopped writing poems of innocence.

> *Ungrateful wretches; why do ye crave*
> *The life our heavenly maker gave?*
> *Why confine us in the gloomy cells*
> *Where nothing save grief and sorrow dwells?*
> *Detested fiends, be banished hence,*
> *Among your kindred go boast your sense,*
> *Where imps of hell and devils roam*
> *Go and seek out your native home.*

Dick amused himself by tormenting Palmer, whose cell, he had discovered, was under his own. He imagined what Palmer was doing, what he was saying, the pleasure he was taking in bringing down the Crowninshields, his friends, who could have killed him and no one would have cared. In the nighttime, Dick would lie like a python on the floor of his cell, hissing into the crack: "Palmer, what have you said? Palmer, is it you? Palmer, Palmer, why don't you speak, Palmer?"

On June 5, Dick learned that a special session of the Supreme Judicial Court would begin at Salem on July 10. The fatal machinery had been set in motion, and it focused his mind. However poetic and grandiose his nature, whatever his talents for denial and escape, he was now locked up in a cell like a pig in a pen. His magnificent daring, his fearless soul—these would not save him. About a week later, Franklin Dexter, the Boston lawyer, was visiting his clients Joe and Frank Knapp. At the end of the day, Dick called him over and asked his opinion on the law of principals and accessories. Dexter thought that Dick would be indicted as principal in the murder, and the other five would be accessories. If Dick was not convicted, Dexter thought that the government would try Frank Knapp as a principal in the second degree—but probably could not make a case. The lawyer departed, and Dick began to think.

Concluding that no one else was culpable of a capital offense, Dick Crowninshield now saw the way out. He would not have to explain about flannels; he would not have to sit in the dock as a thief and a cowardly killer of sleeping old men. Though the "ungrateful wretches" of the prosecution would make him seem stupid and greedy, he was, he thought, heroic, with the courage to move through the big dark rooms and the long hallways, up the creaking stairs, steadily toward the goal. In a world of fantasies, Dick was real. He had not even bloodied his clothes, and he had given the old man what he had wanted, an ending in which he went off like a flash.

Unlike Dick, Joe had made many mistakes: using Frank as a go-between, stealing an out-of-date will, talking too much, writing the letters, faking the assault. He had not kept cool. For his part, Dick should not have played games with Palmer; and it was hard to know why he and Frank had been so careless in Brown Street, lounging in plain sight as if they were invisible.

Dick looked out the small opening in his cell door and stepped back. Like a magician, he held up his handkerchief, a nice big silk one from Bengal, colored and patterned; and he slipped off his neckerchief. It would do. He knotted them together and pulled hard, and then he tied one end to an iron bar in the window. He had to work quickly, before someone came along.

He had killed Captain White, and now he was done. He could never be found guilty or be exhibited as a bad example. If his life had been pointless, it did at least have its moments; and other men would not have to die because of him. He had not failed at much, except the biggest things, and he would not fail now. He sprang forward like a panther, and the knots held; and he pulled back his feet and willed his full weight against the noose.

When they found him a little later, too far gone to be revived, Dick's bent knees were about two inches off the floor.

Crowninshield's death on June 15 brought relief to the Knapps. People talked. Bets were placed. Without a principal, accomplices could not be convicted. Common wisdom said they might be tried on conspiracy and sentenced to long terms, but they were young men and would eventually get their lives back. In Salem, there was some sympathy. The Knapps came from a good family, deeply involved in the seaport and its institutions, and both were shipmasters.

George Crowninshield was upset at his brother's suicide, but appreciative, too. Good old Dick. In the dead man's cell they had found two letters, one to his father requesting that his corpse not be dissected and a longer one for George, a useful parting gift: "May God and your innocence guide you safe through this trial. Had I taken your advice, I would still enjoy Life, Liberty, and a clear conscience." George had to grin. "But I have not, and perceive my case to be hopeless. Therefore I have come to the determination to deprive them of the pleasure of beholding me publicly executed, as after I am condemned they will not give me the opportunity, and may God forgive me, George, this is an awful warning to you, and *I hope it will be the means of reforming many to virtue*. Albeit they may meet with success at the commencement of vice, it is short lived, and sooner or later if they persist in it they will meet with a similar fate to mine. Oh! George, forgive me for what I have caused you and others to suffer on my account, and my last benediction rests upon you. A long, a last, adieu."

No doubt Dick's letter would be helpful, but George was planning to walk away from all of this anyway, for he had been careful to spend the night with a prostitute on April 6. In court, George imagined, he could smile and bow. They might not give him a parade, but no one would hang him for sleeping with a whore.

In fact, that year there were no parades in Salem on the Fourth of July, which fell on a Sunday and thus put the whole populace in church, to pray and reflect. The town's high morals and vaunted principles did not count for very much if two sea captains could hire a senator's nephew to kill an honorable old merchant—and if a minister of the gospel allowed himself to be used to incriminate his parishioner. Nor did Salem defend itself against new charges, alleged by the reporters gathered in town, of a "disgusting affair" in which a rich man was rumored to have raped a local woman, with no investigation and no arrest.[2]

Monday, July 5, was a day of heavy silence in the streets of the demoralized town, in which the only public event was a speech at the Tabernacle Church, given by a Bostonian for the benefit of the American Colonization Society's efforts to send free blacks overseas to Liberia. This was more successful than a private fund-raiser for seamen's orphans held by the Female Charitable Society, many of whose wealthy "annual contributors" were moving out of town.

In the drawing rooms and lecture halls, some people ignored the circus of the murder trial. Reverend Charles W. Upham, secure at the First Church, was deeply engaged in researching Salem's witchcraft delusion of 1692, a topic that had become eerily relevant. He hoped to get at the truth of the causes of ancient madness and judicial murder and to relate his findings in a series of lectures, perhaps to be given at Salem's new lyceum, devoted to public education.

At the drowsing wharves, a few vessels came in from South America and the Caribbean and one from Amsterdam. The brig *Mexican,* under Captain J. G. Butman, arrived from Susu, Sumatra, in early July, and late in September the ship *Francis,* commanded by Captain Charles Wilkins, also came in from Sumatra, with a valuable haul of pepper for Joseph Peabody.[3] Most of the rest of Salem's shipping was sailing out of Boston or New York.

Benjamin Hawkes, recently the head of the Salem Mill Dam Corporation, advertised the sale of material docked at Collins Cove: various kinds of timber and stout plank in large lots, the remnants of a dream.[4]

Secret grand jury proceedings began at Salem on July 20. The jury men heard testimony from several witnesses, but no charges were brought against Selman or Chase. After eighty-five days in prison, they were free to go. At home in Marblehead, a collection was taken up to buy Colonel Selman new clothes; while he had been in jail, someone impersonating a court messenger had conned his mother out of much of his wardrobe.

On August 3, the Salem Court House was packed, and the streets were crowded as Frank Knapp stood trial on four counts of murder, in one of which

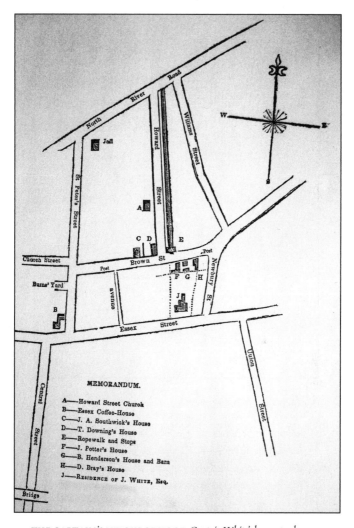

THE CAPTAIN'S NEIGHBORHOOD. Captain White's house stood on an
upscale stretch of Essex Street, next to and across from other merchants' large
houses, adjoining the home of his cousin Fairfield Gardner, whose invitation to
an evening party Captain White had declined on April 6. The property had a
rear garden extending toward Brown Street, from which the lights of the house
could be observed.

he was accused of being a principal in the second degree, present on-site aid-
ing Richard Crowninshield Jr. The prosecutors had prepared two illustrated
plans, one of the neighborhood and one of the grounds of Captain White's

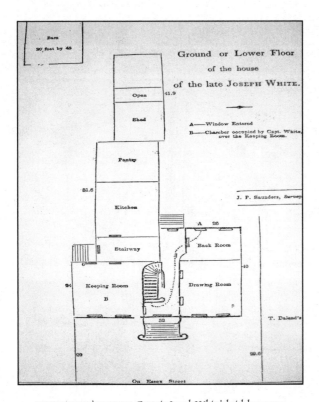

Ground or Lower Floor
of the house
of the late JOSEPH WHITE.

A——Window Entered
B——Chamber occupied by Capt. White,
over the Keeping Room.

Barn
90 feet by 45

Open   41.9

Shed

Pantry

51.6

Kitchen

J. P. Saunders, Surveyor

A   25

Stairway   Back Room

40

24   Keeping Room   Drawing Room

B

59   T. Daland's

29   29.6

On Essex Street

*THE KILLER'S ROUTE. Captain Joseph White's brick house was
nearly impregnable. It stood high on its foundation, and all doors and
windows were locked at night. This first-floor plan shows how the
intruder came in through the unlocked window in Mrs. Beckford's
parlor, proceeded to the front entry, boldly ascended the grand
staircase, and entered the bed chamber.*

house, showing the supposed route of the murderer from Essex Street through
the rear garden, into Mrs. Beckford's back parlor, and up into the captain's
bedchamber.

By law, Frank could not testify in his own behalf. George and Joe were considered accessories before the fact. As the visitors settled in, they were thrilled to
see the great Daniel Webster at the government counsel's table. He had been
hired as a special prosecutor by Stephen White for the fatal fee of $1,000. More
was felt than expressed, but Webster was clear in his understanding: neither of
the Knapps was to survive this judicial process.

The crowd had many outsiders, including Charles Sumner and other budding lawyers and college students up from Boston, along with a pack of journal-
ists reporting to a national audience about the crimes and disgrace of the most
respectable town in America. Young James Gordon Bennett would fill the columns of his New York paper, and others would fire off lurid descriptions to the
far corners of the nation.

The three prisoners attracted much attention: all were good-looking young
men from privileged backgrounds. Frank, Joe, and George appeared together
for arraignment and entered the box "well and rather genteely dressed," according to the reporter from the Massachusetts *Journal*. Frank moved with "a quick
and vigorous motion, more like a bound than a step"; Joe "followed rather lan-
guidly"; and George "came last, with a quiet and easy air." George was tall and
blond, with a broad face; Frank was solid and dark, taller than his slim older
brother. The reporter described Frank as "a well-made full-faced youth of 19
years of age and 5′ 7″ in height. He was dressed neatly in a grey frock coat and a
colored and fashionable breast-pin. His face was deadly pale showing . . . a very
coarse skin." He had "thick dark and straight hair, growing low, parted and
combed smoothly; the nose strong and blunt, the mouth rather large and cheeks
full but very pale. On entering the dock he folded his arms firmly, and assumed
a fixed, downward and sullen expression."

Joe, once notable for his talents as a dancer, was thought to be "about thirty"
(he was twenty-five), with a "not displeasing" countenance: "It is thin and pale,
and his hair long and brown, his nose sharp and his mouth small. His look is
intellectual, but I understand his mind does not correspond. He is a little shorter
and slenderer than his younger brother. He appeared to be more listless than the
latter, and was constantly biting something which he held in his mouth, probably a clove. Both the Knapps have dark eyes, both have been masters of vessels."

George impressed the reporter as "the tallest and best looking of the three.
His features are quite singular, but may be classed. His cheek bones are very high
and broad, his forehead narrower, though still ample, and somewhat sloping; his
hair bright flaxen and curly. His size is large, his limbs strong and moving grace-
fully; his eyes grey; his mouth small and delicate colored, and complexion florid
and fine. There was an air of more ease and freedom about him than either of the
others."

The prisoners were directed to hold up their hands while the indictment was read. Joe could not keep an open palm: "Unconsciously, I presume," he "gradually contracted his fingers until his fist became clenched and remained so."[5]

Webster's chances improved right away, as Joseph J. Knapp Jr. came to the stand looking awful—he had tried to starve himself. Joe would have to repeat his confession in court in order to claim the promised immunity. The attorney general approached him and asked if he was willing to testify. Joe hesitated, then shook his head no. Incredulous, the attorney general rephrased the question. Joe Knapp moved his lips but could not speak; against all advice, he nodded that yes, it was true that he would not testify against his brother. As Knapp was led away, the shaken prosecutor told him, "The peril remains on your own head."

At the end of the first day, Ben Leighton, a teenage laborer at the Beckford-Knapp farm, testified that he had been sitting in the sun by a high stone wall on a day late in March, when he had heard Frank telling Joe that he had seen Dick that morning. "When is he going to kill the old man?" asked Joe. Frank did not know, and Joe had said, "If he don't kill him soon I won't pay him." The boy's story went off like a bomb in the courtroom. He could not be shaken on cross-examination, and Daniel Webster helped him to recall that after the murder, Frank had begun carrying a dirk, which he would use on the boy, playing around, even when he was in bed, pricking him enough to draw blood. Ben had not come forward earlier because "if the Knapps get clear they will kill me."

That night or shortly after, Captain J. J. Knapp Sr. went down to his former warehouse on Union Wharf and was in the process of hanging himself when his son Phippen came rushing in and cut him down.

Next day, Reverend Henry Colman, the first witness, was quick to say that Joe had confessed in his presence. Frank's counsel objected, and the court ruled that confessions could not be introduced by a third party. Colman proceeded to describe how he had fetched the murder weapon out of the rat-hole under the church steps, where Frank had said it would be. Phippen Knapp was out-raged. Joe, not Frank, had said that—Colman was lying, making Frank seem to have confessed things that he had never said. Colman was followed by Palmer, who said that he had seen Frank at South Danvers at the time that the Crownin-shield brothers had asked him to join the Knapps' murder plot. Other witnesses testified about the letters by which the Knapps had tried to frame Stephen White.

Joseph Antony, White's spy, recalled that many months before he had encountered Richard Crowninshield Jr. at a tavern fondling a bone-handled dagger that he kept in his shirt and called his "nurse child." Then came the testimony of Southwick and Bray, the Brown Street observers, followed by a stable hand, Burns, to whom Frank had insisted that Stephen White was the killer.

Daniel Webster re-called Colman and again asked him about the forbidden matter of confession. Now the three-judge court reversed itself and allowed Webster to proceed. The clergyman said that Frank had confirmed Joe's statements that the murder took place between ten and eleven, that Richard Crowninshield had been alone in the house, and that he, Frank, "went home afterwards." Colman admitted that both Captain Joseph White and Senator Stephen White were his "parishioners and intimate friends" and that he felt toward Joe Knapp's wife, Mary, "as to a daughter."

Franklin Dexter and his co-counsel, William H. Gardiner,[6] put on an effective defense, shaking the stories of several witnesses. Phippen Knapp refuted Colman: Frank had never said anything about a murder plot or the bludgeon. As a lawyer, Phippen was thought to be risking his career; as a brother, he was admired. He could not help reporting, almost wistfully, an early rumor that Captain White had taken his own life "in his bed with a dagger in his side."

Henry Colman countered Phippen by repeating his version of the visits with Joe and Frank in their cells. Dexter hammered on Colman and his unusual role in the proceedings: "When a clergyman steps out of the sphere of his duty he becomes a man among men." Masquerading in his holy robes, that man might be "extorting questions which would condemn the prisoner." Dexter's implication was clear: Colman was a murderous hypocrite.

In the dog days of August, the two sides battled onward, with Dexter dueling

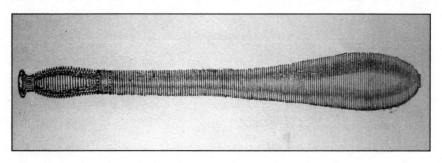

THE BLOODY BLUDGEON. The wooden cudgel used on April 6 was lovingly crafted by Dick Crowninshield on a lathe at his machine shop. It had a beaded grip and a lead insert in the barrel and was perfect for its purpose.

Webster for the life of Frank Knapp. The courtroom was crowded with men and women, locals and strangers, and the families of the dead and the living. Outdoors in the hot sun, hanging from open windows, sitting in the trees, thronging the square, everyone strained to hear Dexter as he opened at three thirty on August 10 and spoke continuously until seven. Next morning he started at nine, shredding Colman and his motives, discrediting those who had claimed that it was Frank Knapp in Brown Street, dismissing the notorious liar Palmer, and defending the honesty of Captain Knapp. Accusing Webster of a callous effort to "hurry the jury beyond the evidence and against the law," he closed powerfully in the half hour ending at eleven thirty.

Daniel Webster then rose to begin the case against Frank Knapp. Joseph Story had advised him in his efforts to overcome a ten-year-old ruling that would prevent his transforming Frank from an accomplice to a principal.[7] Webster gave a long, eloquent speech destined to become famous.[8] The crowd enjoyed hearing the great orator at work. His description of the murder, and its effects on the murderer, Dick Crowninshield, was a spellbinder. "At the blessed hour when, of all others, repose is soundest, the murderer goes to his work. In the silence and darkness, he enters the house. He does not falter—there is no trembling of the limbs, and his feet sustain him. He passes through the rooms, treads lightly through the entries, ascends the stairs, arrives at the door. There is no pause: he opens it. The victim lies asleep, his back is towards him, his deaf ear is uppermost, his temples bare. The moonlight plays upon his silver locks.

"One blow, and the task is accomplished! Now, mark his resolution, his self-possession, his deliberate coolness! He raises the aged arm, plunges the dagger to the heart—not once, but many times—replaces the arm, replaces the bed-clothes, feels the pulse, is satisfied that his work is perfected, and retires from the chamber. He retraces his steps. No eye has seen him, no ear has heard him. He is master of his own secret, and he escapes in secret.

"That was a dreadful mistake. The guilty secret never can be safe: there is no place in the universe, no corner, no cavern where he can deposit it and say it is safe. Though he take the wings of the morning and fly to the uttermost part of the seas, human murder to human vision will be known. A thousand eyes, a thousand ears, are marking and listening, and thousands of excited beings are watching his bloodstained step.

"The proofs of a discovery will go on. The murderer carries with him a secret which he can neither carry nor discharge. He lives at war with himself; his conscience is a domiciled accuser that cannot be ejected and will not be silent. His tormentor is inappeasable, his burden is intolerable. The secret which he possesses, possesses him, and, like the evil spirit spoken of in olden times, leads him withersoever it will. It is a vulture ever gnawing at his heart; he believes his very thoughts to be heard.

"His bosom's secret overmasters him, subdues him—he succumbs. His guilty soul is relieved by suicide or confession, and suicide is confession!"

Black Dan had given good value for Stephen White's blood money; but Frank's lawyer, Dexter, studying the jury men, thought that his client still had a chance. The twelve jurors retired at one o'clock, and a day later they were back in the courtroom. The town buzzed with news of a verdict, and people hurried to the courthouse. Webster turned in his chair to catch the dark, glittering eye of Stephen White. In open court, the foreman made his announcement to the judges: the jury had reviewed the case at great length, had discussed all of its aspects and allegations, and had concluded that there was no hope they would ever agree. Webster's artillery had scored direct hits on Richard Crowninshield's grave but had whistled past Frank Knapp. Some doubted, said the foreman, that Frank had been proved to be in Brown Street and that, if there, he was giving aid to the murderer as opposed to satisfying his curiosity. The angry judges sent the men of the jury back up to their chamber, but at the end of the day nothing had changed and the judges had to dismiss them.

Frank Knapp had not been found guilty. Despite the best work of Daniel Webster, despite the controversies and contradictions, despite the minister's damning allegations and the court's ruling on the confession, the jury had not been persuaded of the meaning of Dick's death or the case against Frank. However, this was not the end, for the law required that a new jury be impaneled to try the same cause. Frank's lawyers moved to postpone the trial until November, since "in the present state of public excitement it would be impossible to get an impartial jury in whose hands the fate of the prisoner could be safely trusted."

The court disagreed.

THE KILLING FIELD. Beneath the large granite block in the foreground was the White family tomb; in the distance, a temporary gallows was erected behind Salem Jail.

16.

DEATH AFTER DEATH

The second trial of Frank Knapp began on Saturday, August 14. Each side knew which witnesses would be called and what they would say; and the jury must have known a good deal of the story, too. Once again, the star witness for the prosecution was Reverend Henry Colman. The court ruled that Webster could not use Joe's confession but was free to use Colman's version of Frank's confession—the one that Phippen claimed had never been made. Colman's memory seemed to improve every time he took the stand, always with greater recollection of self-incrimination by Frank.

Mrs. Southwick testified that her husband, John, had said, on the night of April 6, that he had seen Frank Knapp at the Brown Street ropewalk. Others came forward to say that, come to think of it, they had seen him there, pulling down his cap as they went by. When Captain Daniel Bray agreed, the defense had court reporter Octavius Pickering testify that in the first trial Bray had not identified the person in Brown Street as Frank Knapp.

In his summation, Franklin Dexter addressed the passions of a community that had rejected the outcome of the first trial. He knew that he was up against public opinion, a fortune in reward money, cooked evidence, bloodlust, new witnesses for the prosecution, and the machinations of the Committee of Vigilance. Most of all, he had to overcome the influence of Stephen White, "*the source of favor* in this trial" and the implacable foe of "a helpless and friendless culprit, pursued by all the wealth and respectability of the town." Dexter ripped into the credibility of Leighton, the farmhand, and Palmer, the "mysterious stranger" and "unrepenting thief" suddenly released from jail and "made a free man on the stand."

Reverend Henry Colman was a liar, or Phippen Knapp, Esq., was a liar. The first jury, said Dexter, had seen through Colman as a faithless clergyman who had plunged into the "popular frenzy," living "in its focus and breathing its intoxicating air for months. No man in the community has been so excited by this horrible event as Mr. Colman. No man has taken a more active part in inquiring into its mysteries." Colman alone claimed that Frank had confessed. But Frank had put nothing in writing, had never tried to turn state's witness, and could not have been taken off guard. Frank was "a young but not a timid man. You have seen enough of his bearing at this trial to judge whether he would be likely to be surprised into a confession—and he was not surprised, for he had been examined and he had counsel."

Dexter reminded the jury to focus on Frank Knapp, not Dick or Joe. In the first trial, no one had placed him in Brown Street or at the White mansion. Further, the time of the murder had not been proven, so it was irrelevant as to where Frank Knapp was or was not on that night.[1]

Webster did not speak as long as before, for the evidence was now all against Frank. Nothing new had absolved the young shipmaster. It still came down to public sympathy for Stephen White and Henry Colman's word against Phippen Knapp's, with the ghost of Dick Crowninshield hovering close by and Joe's confession reverberating. The creepiness that Webster had earlier imputed to Dick he now aimed at Frank, using the crib sheet of the confession and evidence from witnesses whose testimony had been different in the first trial.

Webster concluded on the morning of Friday, August 20. Judge Putnam then gave his charge, which amounted to a brief for the prosecution. Five hours later, the jury pronounced a verdict of guilty on John Francis Knapp, twenty.[2] Frank grimaced and was led away. That night, his sister-in-law Mary Beckford Knapp again tried to kill herself. Once again, she was prevented.[3]

Many stories were told and letters written, but Nathaniel Hawthorne captured the moment best in a letter to a cousin in Ohio. He had grown up around the corner from the Knapps, and Joe was his exact contemporary. At the end of

August he wrote, "Frank Knapp's situation seems to make little or no impression on his mind. The night after his sentence, he joked and laughed with the men who watched him, with as much apparent gaiety as if he had been acquitted instead of condemned. He says, however, that he would rather be hung than remain a year in prison.

"It is reported, also, that he declares that he will not go to the gallows unless two women go with him. Who these women are must be left to your conjecture. Perhaps you have not heard that many people suspect Mrs. Bickford and her daughter, Joe Knapp's wife, of being privy to the whole affair before the murder was committed. I cannot say whether there are good grounds for these suspicions, but I know that it was daily expected, during the trial, that one or both of them would be arrested; and it is said that they were actually examined at the house of Mr. Brown the jailer.

"It is certain that Joseph Knapp's wife has twice attempted to hang herself. The first time was soon after her husband's arrest, and the second immediately after Frank was found guilty. Old Captain Knapp also made a similar attempt a little while ago and was cut down by his son Phippen. The poor old man is entirely broken in his mind and almost crazy; and it is no wonder that he should be so, when all sorts of trouble have come upon him at once. He and his son Phippen have injured their reputation for truth by the testimony they gave at the trial; but I have little doubt that they believed what they said; and, if not, they had as much excuse as there can possibly be for perjury. There seems to be an universal prejudice at present against the whole family—I am afraid Captain Knapp himself meets with but little real pity, and I believe everybody is eager for the death of his two sons. For my part, I wish Joe to be punished, but I should not be very sorry if Frank were to escape. It is the general opinion, however, that Joe will not live to be brought to trial. He contrives to obtain spirituous liquors in his cell, and is in a state of intoxication almost all the time. He is utterly desperate, and will not even wash and dress himself, and at one time he made a resolution to starve himself to death. I do not wonder that he feels unpleasantly, for he can have no hope of mercy, and it is absolutely certain that he will not be alive at the end of six months from this time."[4]

Frank Knapp lived a bipolar existence, alternating between spells "of stupor and levity," erratic, unpredictable. The Episcopal rector, Alexander Griswold, visited regularly to give Frank spiritual succor should he want it. The Knapp family minister, Reverend James Flint of the East Church, Unitarian, had visited once in June but had not returned, nor had he been asked to.[5] In the last week of September, Frank suddenly pulled himself together and faced his big day, Tuesday, September 28, with a gravity that was a relief to his visitors and handlers.

On Saturday evening, for the first time since arraignment, Joe and Frank Knapp kept each other company. The jailer took Joe from his third-story cell to Frank's on the first floor. Each was stunned at the other's appearance: Joe was feeble and emaciated; Frank looked better than ever. Joe asked if he was really as well as he seemed, and Frank said, "Yes, I can sleep as sound now on the soft side of a plank as I ever could." They chatted quietly, two young sailors on the last leg of a strange voyage, begun in stupid, drunken counsels in the unreality of the night world—and somehow never broken off. Now they enjoyed their brief time together, awaiting the impact of the coming storm and saying whatever might be said between two brothers, each of whom had refused to save himself at the cost of the other's life. Frank mentioned that his lawyers had tried to get a commutation from the governor, pleading that someone else was the instigator of the crime. With no evidence that this was so, the governor had passed. The brothers met again on Monday evening and concluded with poignant farewells.[6]

That night, with two guards in his cell, Frank woke at four, drank coffee, then fell back to sleep. Just before six he rose, washed, and dressed with care, saying that he hoped he would not lose his poise. Mr. Griswold reassured him, and he was granted an extra half hour with the man of God. At eight thirty, solemn and self-possessed, Frank left his cell and had his arms pinioned in the entry on his way to the scaffold that had been built behind the jail, adjoining a graveyard.

A concourse of about five thousand people, including several hundred women, had gathered in the sunshine to watch Frank Knapp die. He stepped as firmly onto the platform as onto a quarterdeck and stood looking out over the crowd looking back at him, expectant faces in hats and bonnets. The attendants tied his feet and snugged the noose on his neck. He took out a white pocket handkerchief and lifted his face to the sky. The hood was slipped over his head, and the new sheriff, Joseph E. Sprague, quickly read the death warrant.

At his signal, the drop fell, Frank clutched his handkerchief, and the crowd gasped and buckled: "Deep horror was visible in every countenance and a convulsive shudder was seen to agitate every frame."[7]

The guilty citizens rushed away to homes and places of business and left Frank's body hanging for nearly an hour. When it was taken down, Joe was allowed to leave his cell to be alone with his brother. A little shaky, he entered the passageway to the gallows. It was almost like being outdoors. In the afternoon light, he could see the lost world, with the green lawn of the burying ground and the still trees and houses beyond, and the clouds, moving in the sea breeze. On a rough table against the wall lay his brother's sheet-covered corpse. Fearfully, steadily, Joe approached it, lifted the linen to look at Frank's face, and fainted.

The *Friendship* arrived on the scorching coast of Sumatra at Kuala Batu, too late in September for the pepper harvest. Captain Endicott stayed to trade, laying out some specie and opium on a small lading of old-crop pepper, then departing early in November for the port of Muki. There he met other captains who warned him that the natives had been harassing Americans.[8] Endicott stayed cool; he was an old Sumatra hand and was not surprised that the ongoing Dutch war against the Malays was turning them against all Westerners.[9]

At the end of January the *Friendship* returned as far as Pulo Kio, the home of rajah Po Adam, friend of Americans, to wait for the spring pepper crop to be harvested and brought to Kuala Batu, two miles away. In his cabin, the cautious Endicott still had a trunk of specie and twelve chests of opium, as was well-known along the coast.[10]

On a hot, moonlit night at Pulo Kio, the men on the *Friendship*'s watch were chatting quietly when one noticed a dark shape astern. Others joined him and made out a native pepper boat—a large proa canoe—propelled with short, noiseless paddle strokes. The watch roused the captain. Endicott bounded up and observed the approach of what he decided was "a reconnoitering party, sent to ascertain how good a lookout was kept on board the ship, and intending to surprise us. . . ." Endicott ordered his first mate, Charles Knight, to call all hands to quarters. Leaning into the darkness, the captain challenged them in their own language, What do you want in the night, why do you approach like the tiger? "Instantly, all was life and animation" down in the water, with muffled cries and the splashes of back-paddling. After a minute a singsong voice called up, to say they were friends from Kuala Batu, with a load of good smuggled pepper. Pistol in hand, Endicott ordered them to stand off. After discussion with his officers, he called out that he would send men to inspect their pepper. If they laid aside their weapons and all went well, he would rig a whip upon the main yard to hoist their bags of pepper with one of their men allowed on deck.

The ship's boat went out. Sure enough, the proa had pepper, and the deal was made. Ever careful, Captain Endicott placed armed "sentinels on each side of the gangway" as the pepper came on board. The first mate, Charles Knight, not five feet tall, snorted at the captain's precautions and muttered to the second mate, John Barry, that Endicott was an old granny, afraid of shadows, cowed by these monkeys without tails. Smoothly, safely, sixty full bags of pepper were laded that night, courtesy of young Po Kuala, the ambitious son of a rajah of Kuala Batu.

Endicott could not be cowed or ambushed. For as long as he had been on the Pepper Coast—and none knew it better than the pink, portly maker of charts and speaker of Malay and Atjehnese—he had never forgotten that he was trading with violent men. No one ruled them; the rajahs governed themselves, largely by bloodshed and cunning, always with concern about rivals as well as the conquering Europeans. It was Endicott who had reported in 1826 on Dutch military incursions and native reprisals against British and American merchantmen; and matters had not improved. The rajahs were just as likely to turn on one another with "ferocity and barbarity," and even on the king of Atjeh, who really had no influence over these outpost pepper sultans holed up in their forts, maintaining their armies with Western drugs and specie.

Ashore in Kuala Batu, Endicott had a whiff of paranoia—violence and now opium addiction were rampant, two new forts had been built, bloody battles had recently been fought with outside natives. In this off-season for pepper, the supplies of opium ran low and gangs of battle-tested youths grew fierce. Still, he knew that hundreds of Salem vessels had voyaged to this place without problems.

The most powerful rajahs valued the pepper trade above all and held their people in check for the sake of commerce. Endicott spent much time with Po Adam, who warned his friend that he "must look sharp," for the rajahs were angry because of last season's falling pepper prices and because some captains had sailed away without making full payment.

In early February, Captain Endicott moved up to Kuala Batu to get the first lading of pepper. As yet, no other vessel had come on this part of the coast. He called the crew together and decreed no night boats and no more than two visitors on deck. The loading then began in the river-month and all went well as the pepper boats came out. On a stage affixed to the side of the vessel, the tallest sailors, John Davis and Charles Converse, caught the bulging bags of pepper swung up by the natives and in turn slung them to the men on deck to be stored in the hold.

One day, Po Adam came by in a canoe and said that there was trouble brewing on shore. Captain Endicott listened quietly. He turned over the ship to Mr. Knight and reminded him of his duties; and then he, the rajah, second mate John Barry, and four sailors set out on the three-quarter-mile trip upriver in the vessel's sturdy pinnace. At Kuala Batu, work went on as usual. The pepper arrived slowly and the weighing dragged on, but finally a native boat was full enough to start out for the *Friendship*. Endicott sent a couple of his men to watch at the beach while he and Barry continued to weigh the bags of pepper. After a while, he went to look for a brig that was said to be arriving but instead noticed that the distant pepper boat had twice as many natives on board as when it had left. Oh, said his lookouts, the original crew had been replaced by "youngsters" along the shore and from a ferry boat in midriver. What did this mean? Angry and worried, Endicott went back to the scales. He asked Barry whether Charles Knight would do right. To his shock, Barry said the truth was that the first mate held the natives in contempt and might let down his guard. The captain, noticing that a crowd was gathering nearby, sent Barry over to take another look down the river. He came sauntering right back, speaking low: "There is trouble on board, sir—men jumping over the side."

"Show no alarm," said Endicott. "Go slow, but get the men to the pinnace."

As they pushed off into the river, Po Adam suddenly sprinted down the wharf and jumped on board, screaming that the natives planned to kill them.

Endicott shouted, "Spring to your oars, my lads, for your lives—fall to, fall to, or we are all dead men!"

The oarsmen made the pinnace fly down the narrow river. As they rounded a point, hundreds of natives rushed yelling into the shallows. They had no artillery, but now a large war canoe came on to intercept them. Po Adam handed his cutlass up to Barry in the bow, and the men pulled on their heavy oars, "nerved with the feeling of desperation" to smash into the canoe. At the last possible second, the native paddlers backed off, and the Salem pinnace shot past the last point as the crowd of furious natives "ran into the water up to their armpits in their endeavors to intercept us, waving their swords above their heads and shouting at the top of their voices."

Pouring sweat in the tropical heat, the Salem men rowed on as their captain watched "the doomed ship laying tranquilly in the water, with sails furled and a pepper boat alongside . . . and high mountains in the background densely clothed with wood, and a long range of low thatched houses," like a painting in the Salem East India Museum, except on closer inspection there were "ten or twelve heads just even with the surface of the water," and a man dancing on the foretopgallant yard, and the deck swarming with natives. Clearly, the *Friendship* was lost; and now three more war canoes were coming up the river.

Po Adam urged the Yankees to make for Susu twenty-five miles away, and he pulled an oar with the rest until they were clear of their pursuers. When they arrived at Susu River, they dared not land and went along the coast toward Muki. Night fell, and a thunderstorm rolled down from the hills. Captain Endicott consulted the map in his head and stayed wide of the shoals. The storm blew by, and they made a sail out of gunnysacks, and finally they reached the roadstead and saw the looming black masts and rigging against the starry sky.

"What boat is that?" came the challenge of the watch.

"Pinnace of the *Friendship* of Salem, from Kuala Batu! Who are you?"

"The brig *Governor Endicott*, Captain Jenks, of Salem! Is that you, Captain Endicott?"

"Yes, and all that's left of us!"

Endicott boarded the *Endicott* and they were joined by Jeremiah Porter of Beverly and the ship *James Monroe* of New York, and Michael Power of Marblehead, master of the brig *Palmer* of Boston. All agreed to retake the *Friend-ship* next day, and by midafternoon the flotilla was off Kuala Batu, preparing to attack. A rainstorm intervened, and next morning the *Friendship* rode inside a reef, dangerously close to the beach. The Americans took out their telescopes. On shore were hundreds of natives "decked out in a white, blue, red, checked or striped shirt, or some other European article of dress or manufacture, stolen from the ship, not even excepting the woolen tablecloth belonging to the cabin, which was seen displayed over the shoulders of a native. All seemed quite proud of their appearance and strutted about with a solemn gravity and oriental self-complacency. . . ."[11]

The captains sent word to the rajah to surrender the vessel or they would begin firing on the vessel and the town. He answered that he would not give her up, so they blasted away at the *Friendship* and at the boats carrying plunder to the beach. Their fire was returned from the forts and from the guns of their former vessel, but the shots missed, and then a keg of powder exploded on the *Friendship*. Three boatloads of well-armed American mariners surged toward her, and the natives fled. Captain Endicott and his men boarded the *Friend-ship* and called out for their shipmates, but they found only silence and wreck-age and blood. Warily they went below. Every locker and closet had been emptied, but the bags of pepper remained. The missing crewmen, they concluded, were dead.

Next morning, a canoe with a white flag came from the shore with three Chinese who explained that they had rescued four wounded men. Ransomed from the rajahs for $10 each, and sent to the ship in a sampan, they were: Gregory Pedechie, formerly the yardarm dancer, unscathed; Lorenzo Mizell, the cook, and William Francis, twenty, the steward, both badly hurt but on the mend; and Charles Converse, "laid out at full length upon a board, as if dead," but also able to relate what had happened.

After Endicott and the others had left the *Friendship*, the large pepper boat had ranged alongside, full of unfamiliar natives. Each had on a white or yellow jacket, almost a uniform, and each had a new ivory-handled kris knife. They were, in fact, a ravening group of addicts, willing to kill or be killed to get their hands on the opium. When Mate Knight had allowed about twenty visitors on board, crewman William Parnell had objected; but Knight had told him to shut up and get back to work. Hearing this account, Endicott must have been stricken. No doubt he did not push it—Knight was dead, after all—but just a little humility from his handpicked first mate would have produced a very different result, and this incident, like so many in Salem's long history on the Pepper Coast, would have passed into scuttlebutt as just one more close call.

The men continued their story. While Knight had bossed the work of loading, the natives slowly spread out around the deck, and suddenly there was a convulsive attack. Two natives rushed the first mate, burying their knives in his back and side; he fought hard and would not go down. George Chester was killed outright and fell into the forward hatch. Inside the galley, Will Francis screamed as he was stabbed, and the deck was pandemonium as caged pigs squealed and screeched and unarmed sailors shouted and fell and got back up, cursing for weapons, trying to escape the slaughter. Knight broke free and ran aft to the quarterdeck to get a boarding pike out of the beckets. As Parnell helped him, the first mate cried, "Do your duty!" and three natives killed him with hatchets. Parnell sprang away to get down to the arms locker, but he and his shipmates were cut off. Defenseless and desperate, some jumped overboard, and Pedechie scrambled up into the rigging. Four of the strongest swimmers struck off for a distant point; closer in, natives cheered from the shore.

The men on the outboard stage, Charles Converse and John Davis, jumped into the canoe and were stabbed and speared before flopping into the water. Converse swam to the bow and clung to the anchor chains, unseen. His friend Davis got to the stern and held tight, begging for mercy as he was slashed to death. Pedechie, aloft, nimbly dodged as they shot at him. Seaman John Masury watched from his perch on the anchor. Stabbed in the side, he was in better shape than Converse below him, bleeding at the mouth from his internal wounds, holding up a hand that had been half cut off. When darkness came, Converse got on board and crept down the forecastle stairs and passed out. The natives tramped over his body all night, thinking him dead. They rejoiced in their victory over the Yankees and plundered the vessel with wild exuberance. A thunderstorm hit, and by its lightning they had loaded canoes with opium, gold, clothes, and furniture and tackled squealing pigs skidding over the bloody deck. The morning after, when all was quiet, the Chinese in their sailboat had brought off the survivors.

As the men finished their tale, Endicott saw another boat approaching, one of Po Adam's. It came alongside, with some natives and four others. Endicott stared at but did not recognize Parnell, Bray, Muzzey, and Warren, the swimmers, back from the dead, "their bodies crisped and burned in large running blisters, their flesh wasted away, and even the very tones of their voices changed." It seemed "impossible that in the space of four days men could, by any casualty, so entirely lose their identity. They bore no resemblance to their former selves, and it was only by asking their names that I knew any of them."[12]

After stripping off their clothes, they had swum to safety and then spent three days wandering in the jungle under a blazing sun, amid the roaring of tigers. On the third night they had sneaked into the town, jumped in canoes, and paddled out to Po Adam's headland. They'd hid until daybreak, wondering if the friendly rajah's fort had been overrun; then they had dared to show themselves, burned and famished white men emerging naked from the bushes, perhaps in the final act of their lives. Po Adam had "recognized them with the strongest demonstrations of delight, slapping his hands, shouting at the top of his lungs and, in the exuberance of his joy, committing all sorts of extravagances." Over a breakfast of boiled rice, he had told them of his own adventures, so they'd learned of the survival of Captain Endicott and the entire party that had gone ashore—a group that the sailors had thought must certainly have been slaughtered.

Endicott recorded the events in his logbook. The attackers were not pirates but "a set of opium smokers, rendered desperate by their habits." With regard to First mate Knight's fatal disobedience, Endicott wrote only that the *Friendship* was "risen upon by the crew of a Malay pepper boat who were permitted, contrary to the regulations of the ship, to come on board. . . ."

Three sailors were dead, three badly wounded. Po Adam helped Captain

Endicott to recover some of his nautical instruments and a few other items; and the *Friendship* sailed from Kuala Batu with the other American vessels, stopping in at South Tallapow, where news of their losses had preceded them. "When we landed at the place with other masters and supercargos," recalled Endicott, "we were followed through the streets of the bazaar by natives in great crowds, exulting and hooting.

"'Who great man now,' they taunted, 'Malay or American? How many man Malay dead? How many man American dead?'"[13]

PULLING FOR SUSU. As Salemites writhed in the flames of a moral and civic inferno, their ships kept sailing out into the world. On the Pepper Coast of Sumatra, Salem's Friendship was attacked and captured and the crewmen presumably slaughtered. Captain Endicott escaped with Po Adam and others in a whaleboat, rowing for their lives past war canoes and on through the tropical night twenty-five miles down the coast to Susu and three waiting American vessels.

17.

CONFLAGRATION

Captain Joseph Jenkins Knapp Jr., twenty-five, stood before the court, indicted for the same crime as his brother. It was November 9, and Joe looked as if he had already died.

Reverend Henry Colman came to the stand. Regarding the prisoner with a compassionate expression, he discussed his visits to Joe's cell and had begun to divulge the terms of Joe's confessions when the defense lawyers objected vehemently: the confessions had been obtained under the influence of hope and fear and a direct promise. The court adjourned until next morning, when Daniel Webster argued that Joe had chosen not to seek immunity.

The court ruled that Joe Knapp's confessions were admissible. Of course—Frank and Dick were dead, so Joe had little leverage. Colman, Joe's confessor, retook the stand, and the attorney general read the confessions aloud. The audience gasped at certain passages and even groaned—they knew the whole story but had not heard the details in the words of the prisoner. Then the Grant and Claxton letters were produced and attributed to Joe, and they too were read. Southwick and Bray were called, to describe their observations in Brown Street: the man wearing a glazed cap and a camlet cloak was Frank Knapp. Colman, sworn a third time, readily identified the club that he had taken from under the steps "on the day on which Knapp's confessions were made."

Franklin Dexter closed for the hapless defendant, speaking for three and a half hours. He was followed by Webster, who accused Joe of causing the deaths of Captain White, Dick Crowninshield, and Frank Knapp, with George

Crowninshield yet to be tried. "The unhappy man at the bar," he said, "is emphatically encompassed by a sea of blood." With rhetoric recycled from the earlier trials, Webster impressed the jury. "Whenever, in after times, our children shall read of this murder, they will shudder at the thought that the assassin and his confederates were all sons of New England, reared up under our religious and moral institutions and of respectable and affluent families. In whatever light we view this murder, we can find no bright spot about it: all is dark, dismal, and bloody."

Joe did not want to live. He was resigned to the verdict, which he had sealed by his confession, made to his minister and then turned into a legal matter in which he had refused to save himself at the risk of his younger brother. He was found guilty, and his execution was set for New Year's Eve.

That afternoon, George Crowninshield, twenty-four, was placed at the bar for trial. Fortunately for George, the hired killer Daniel Webster had completed his mission for Stephen White and had returned to his career as a distinguished statesman and advocate for the wealthy.

The usual evidence was presented, and then John Palmer was called to the stand. George smirked from his chair. Once they had been rip-roarers together in the bordellos of New Orleans, in the taverns of Charleston, on the road among the wolves. Now Palmer's testimony might hang him. He said that George had invited him to participate in a murder, explaining that Joe Knapp would destroy a will and they would kill the old gentleman as he returned from his farm. Palmer stepped down. Various witnesses said they had seen George near the White mansion on the evening of April 6, but then Mary Jane Weller, whorehouse madam, was called to testify. She said that a happy George Crowninshield was at her house by ten thirty to spend the rest of the night with Mary Bassett. Both Marys had been upset when they found a knife under his pillow next morning, but George had laughed it off—he had enemies. Next morning they had heard about the White murder, but George, she said, had been sick and stayed all day. That evening, though, when "he was called for," he had gone out "as usual."

At this point, George's lawyer, Samuel Hoar, suggested that it "would be absurd to attempt to defend a case made out like this, without a tittle of evidence to incriminate the prisoner except that given by Palmer, which was altogether unworthy of credit." Such a case, he said, "ought not to be suffered to go to a jury." George nodded. His other lawyer said that George had been doing "business relating to his mechanical trade, up to a late hour on the night of the murder." Then an out-of-town innkeeper attested to Palmer's having stayed at his place after the murder. Penniless, Palmer had left a silk handkerchief in pawn and signed the bill with an alias: George Crowninshield.

Next morning, Hoar and the attorney general gave their closing arguments. The jury took the case at one and retired to consider George's fate.

As the Crowninshield jury left, the court summoned Joe Knapp to appear and hear his sentence read. The miserable shipmaster shuffled in and stood silent.

"Before we perform the duty of sentencing," the judge intoned, "we are desirous of preparing your mind, so far as it is in our power, to meet the tremendous doom which awaits you. It is not to aggravate your sufferings that we address you, for your present wretchedness excites feelings of compassion and not of indignation. But we hope that by presenting to your review some of the horrible circumstances which have attended the crime for which you are to suffer, we may lead you to sincere contrition and repentance.

"The aged sufferer was a near relative to your wife. She was nurtured at his house, and loved and cherished by him as a child. You were admitted to partake of his hospitality—you availed yourself of the opportunities to visit at the house of the deceased, to prepare the way for the entrance of your hired assassin to the bed chamber of the victim. You were for months deliberately occupied in devising ways and means of his death. Horrible to think: while you were eating his bread, at his own table, you were plotting against his life.

"The execution of this awful conspiracy spread dismay, anxiety, and distrust throughout the country. Week after week passed away, and left the dreadful deed veiled in mystery. At length a discovery was made by means almost as extraordinary as was the crime. If such events had been set forth in a work of fiction, they would have been considered as too absurd and unnatural for public endurance. The story would have been treated as a libel upon Man."[1]

Joe was led out by deputies and taken back to his cell. In the hush of his leaving, doors opened and shut and opened again, and now fleshy George Crowninshield was escorted to Joe's place at the bar, smiling faintly, humming a little, fidgeting. In just one hour, in the time it took to reprove Joe Knapp and condemn him to the gallows, the jury had made its decision on this last case in the murder of Joseph White. The foreman read the verdict: George was not guilty. Some people cheered; their hero waved and bowed; his father, Richard Crowninshield, posted bail for him on a lesser charge and hustled him off in a carriage to the big house by the factory.

In the fall of 1830, Nathaniel Hawthorne stepped into the daylight. Hawthorne, the last of a once eminent family, had a great deal of vengeful pride and a pretty close acquaintance with the Knapps; and the trials' lurid revelations evidently had a liberating effect on the would-be author. For years he had been writing on dark themes, pondering the hypocrisy of bourgeois Salem and the evil of its lurid night world, combining his perceptions in impressionistic tales, sometimes in ancient settings, sometimes in modern settings with supernatural attributes, but always about the Salem that no one had wanted to see. Upon returning from a tour of the taverns of rural New England, he made arrangements with Caleb Foote of the *Gazette* to publish some of his creepy tales.

His first Boston publisher, Samuel Goodrich, met the elusive Hawthorne in 1830 and found the twenty-five-year-old to be "of a rather sturdy form, his hair dark and bushy, his eye steel-gray, his brow thick, his mouth sarcastic, his complexion stony, his whole aspect cold, moody, distrustful," as befitted someone who "plunged into the dim caverns of the mind and studied the grisly specters of jealousy, remorse, despair." Hawthorne was unsure of his talents. He considered *Fanshawe*'s failure "a fatal rebuff from the reading world," and he was thinking of taking up "a mercantile profession." Goodrich urged him to keep writing and slipped some of the anonymous tales to John Pickering, who found that "they displayed a wonderful beauty of style, with a kind of double vision, a sort of second sight, which revealed, beyond the outward forms of life and being, a sort of spirit world, somewhat as a lake reflects the earth around it and the sky above it." Pickering, however, "deemed them too mystical to be popular."[2]

Every two weeks starting early in November, the *Salem Gazette* ran pieces as obsessive and disturbing as dreams,[3] unsigned Hawthorne stories and sketches reflecting the morbid, shaky state of Salem in this season of murder, suicide, and execution. On the last day of Joe's trial, "The Hollow of the Three Hills" appeared on the *Gazette*'s front page. It seemed to revel in evil, spiting human nature, mocking the value of confession or forgiveness. In it a repentant woman seeks forgiveness for her sins, but in reaching out to those whom she has hurt, she is herself crushed and killed, almost for sport. It was a story that gave no comfort and seemed to foretell the last lurid events of this year of horrors.[4]

In the same month, a gang attempted to smash their way into the vault of the Salem Bank. As in a similar break-in at the Merchants Bank in 1829, the walls held firm against the onslaught. To those who claimed the incident betrayed further "deterioration of the public morals," some of the town elders claimed they had seen worse, and cautioned against overreacting. Attempted bank robberies and the killing of Captain White, they said, could not compare with the wholesale immorality and "irresistibly corrupting influence" of Revolutionary War privateering, during which Salem had been a wide-open naval base with the seaminess typical of such places. Since then, Salem's history had been one of constant moral improvement, so that "the habits and manners which lead to crime are less prevalent at the present time than they have been for fifty years before." If this was accurate, not many felt the truth of it.[5]

In late December, rumors swirled like snow flurries. As Joe Knapp waited to be executed at the end of the month, his wife and father were trying to see the governor to save him, while his mother-in-law, Mary Beckford, was doing all she could to have him killed, even going so far as to ask Stephen White not to become party to the effort to spare him.

White was appalled at the behavior of his adoptive sister Beckford. On December 17, while moving his family to Boston, he wrote to Webster: "Altho' we

are in our household in the very hours of removal, being in the midst of band-
boxes and bureaus, paper-hangings and paint, I cannot omit troubling you with
a line to speak of the renewed excitement in Salem regarding the wretched
woman Mrs. Mary Beckford. Suspicions, horrible as they are, have almost become certainty.

"Yesterday she sent me a private message intimating her wish that I should
not interfere to obtain a commutation for J. J. Knapp, Jr. The message said she
thought it better he should be hung. Now, I know she has been, with her daughter
Mrs. Knapp and Knapp's father, to Worcester to prevail on Governor Lincoln to
grant a reprieve or commutation, though she herself kept in the background by
remaining at the tavern incognito, doubtless with a view to induce [Joe] to believe she was interceding for him, while in truth she seeks his life *to smother
further investigation.*

"Dexter & Gardiner urged their request to the Governor and Council for
a commutation in Frank Knapp's case, chiefly on the ground that another person was at the bottom of the whole affair. . . . This, I know, will not take you
by surprise, for I have long seen where your suspicions pointed, but it horrifies
me, who have always thought her very weak but not wicked. She must be the very
devil."[6]

Stephen White was not alone in his assessment, for at the same time the
Salem Gazette was reporting strange news. Item: Captain White had been
poisoned, which accounted for "the *fit* of indisposition" he had suffered two
or three months before the murder. Item: Dick Crowninshield, that unquiet
intruder, had entered the White mansion on Sunday night, forty-eight hours
before the killing, but had lost his nerve and retreated a little before eleven,
when the watch men began making their rounds. Item: The governor was seri-
ously considering a pardon for Joe Knapp, or at least a commutation of the
death sentence. The governor, wrote editor Foote, understood that Joe was
not "the prime mover of the murder, but that there is another person, not yet
arrested, who plotted and originally instigated the commission of the crime.
Both Knapps have intimated as much; and all who are acquainted with them
know it was not in character for them to have planned it; they were too passive
and inert to have conceived or to have executed such an enterprise of their
own heads."

It was not that Frank or Joe ever claimed innocence. They never had, and Frank was quoted as having said, "No, I do not wish to live—from the first morning I awaked and found the murder was committed, I have been wretched, and have no desire to prolong my life."[7] It was strongly hinted that the real author of the plot was living in comfortable seclusion at the Pickering farm. Mrs. Mary Beckford had long been the subject of rumors, as the woman scorned by Captain White, as Stephen White's remaining rival, furious at losing her full share of the family fortune, goading her son-in-law Joe Knapp to do something about it. Palmer had testified that she was to be out of the house at the time of the murder; and indeed, on the afternoon of April 6 she had gone to Wenham.

The current of opinion had set strongly against her, as a Lady Macbeth, or as Hamlet's mother, Gertrude, betrayer of the king—in the *Gazette,* editor Caleb Foote dared to state that "further prosecutions will undoubtedly take place, whatever may be the condition in life of the offender, whether high or low, rich or poor, if the prosecuting officers obtain sufficient evidence." They should not, Foote said, follow the Ghost's advice to Hamlet, quoted, somewhat delicately, as follows: "Leave h—— to Heaven, and the thorns that in h—— bosom lodge, to prick and sting h——." In the original passage, the pronouns are feminine, and Hamlet's murdered father appears as a ghost urging him to vengeance, with one condition:

> But, howsoever thou pursuest this act,
> Taint not thy mind, nor let thy soul contrive
> Against thy mother aught: leave her to heaven,
> And to those thorns that in her bosom lodge,
> To prick and sting her.[8]

Joe Knapp, it was thought, had yielded to bad counsel in shielding his wife's mother, Mary Beckford. After three deaths, Joe might have traded her life for his; but Frank had not done so, and Joe too was likely to leave her punishment to heaven.

Besides, in this tragedy, Stephen White played the role of Prince of Salem, and he was no Hamlet: hearing the Ghost, he had been quick to revenge his father's foul and most unnatural murder.

Joe Knapp was comforted by a new minister from a different church. Reverend Henry Colman had long been a stranger at Salem Jail, where Reverend John P. Cleaveland of the orthodox Tabernacle tended to the haggard prisoner. In the depths of winter, Joe found what he had sought in springtime from Colman. As the fateful day approached—the last of the year 1830—Joe had turned into a Bible-devouring Christian; and some said he had been born again. He begged Cleaveland to warn young people about "the consequences of dissipation and sin." He accepted his sentence but craved the governor's pardon.

Then he received his death warrant, with no hope of reprieve. On the last night, his young wife, Mary, visited him, and her anguish was terrible. Innocent Mary, the beautiful dancer, had been his downfall. The hope of acquiring a fortune through this sweet girl, the desire to get his hands on what was not really his, a bad idea proposed to an eager younger brother—these things had already killed three persons and had brought him to the brink. The couple's final meeting left Mary stumbling as she departed. Joe prayed that she would forget him quickly and completely. He was weeping, and he wished it was morning. He composed himself, Bible in hand, and read for twenty minutes, then fell asleep. At five he rose for the day and put on his best clothes, a funeral outfit. He read some more, and ate breakfast, and welcomed Cleaveland at seven. The crowd was gathering, almost as many as for Frank, but fewer women. He stood at a window, appearing "composed and calm but completely absorbed and amazed by the scene before him." It was a cold morning, too cold for so many people to be standing outdoors.

Very pale and very thin, he looked twice his age. The murder had killed Joe; he had not known that he had a well-developed conscience and a guilty nervous system, overtaxed every day since April 6. At nine he was brought from his cell by Sheriff Sprague, his deputies, and Parson Cleaveland. They pinioned his arms and proceeded to the gallows beside the jail. Joe approached the scaffold and gazed out at the solemn faces. Unfortunately, Sprague was making a speech, and then Sprague was reading the death warrant in drawn-out theatrical fashion, and Joe began to tremble in the winter's chill and his whole body shook so much that Cleaveland had to prop him up. Sprague finally came to the end. With great relief, Joe stepped forward on the trap and accepted the noose and the hood.

Per the *Gazette*, "In a moment he was launched into the world of spirits." Not really: he did not go off like a flash, but died a hard and terrible death, for the fall did not break his neck, and for five minutes he struggled to stay alive, dancing and writhing as he slowly strangled.[9]

Witnessing the terrible spectacle not by choice but as a requirement of his position, old Justice Ezekiel Savage felt the full impact of the disaster. He had never been one of Salem's luminaries, not rich or famous, never a striver after laurels or an organizer of festivities; he had been a solid citizen and family man and a steady, thoughtful judge in the lowest of courts. As the magistrate, he spent his days wallowing in the crimes of desperate and abandoned people who were without hope and without work, inhabitants of the rottenness that had sprung out of Salem's shadows. Dozens of these cases, month after month, had grown up around him in a dark tangle of human misery.

To Savage, the turning point had come late in 1825 in the Mumford case, not just in the sordid incidents themselves, but in the morbid voyeurism of the crowds and in Choate's mesmerizing rhetoric—in the tawdry racial violence and the brazenness of the Crowninshields and the debasement of the public whom they fascinated. In all of this, the judge had felt a haunting evil, a moral failure that might become as devastating to Salem as "a dreadful conflagration."

Four years later, Savage saw the flames.

Early in the harvest of 1832, the fifty-gun frigate *Potomac,* disguised as an over-size Danish trading vessel, came onto the Pepper Coast. Using Endicott's elaborate charts, U.S. Navy commodore John Downes brought her to a mooring a few miles off Kuala Batu, at a fortunate spot: a hidden reef, missed by the Salem cartographer, lay just a few dozen yards away.

Downes was on a mission for President Jackson. The new American policy of Indian clearances—ordering the tribes to surrender their homelands and settle in the wilds of the western territories—was a fair indicator of the official attitude toward other peoples of the world. Downes had a good grounding in the precepts of white supremacy and military might, having served in 1813 in a brief war against natives of the Marquesas in the Pacific.[10]

On board the *Potomac* was assistant sailing master John Barry of Salem, former second mate of the *Friendship*. Also on board was Lieutenant Alex Pinkham, once Richard Cleveland's partner in adventures along the troubled coast of Peru. Barry was to pilot the ship in unfamiliar waters and identify the men involved in the taking of the *Friendship*. Pinkham was to lead the first division of Marines in a land assault, if ordered.

Upon arrival home in July 1831—a dry-goods clerk had led the Independence Day parade—Charles M. Endicott had related the *Friendship*'s misadventures to his owners, Silsbee, Pickman & Stone. He had a half cargo of pepper, but the opium and much of the specie had been stolen. Dead were seamen George Chester and John Davis and first mate Charles Knight. So too was Knight's brother Enoch, a teenage sailor on board the ship *Glide,* killed by Fijians with another Salem lad, Joshua Derby. The Salem brig *Fawn* had been wrecked there in a hurricane, with the whaler *Oeno*—lost with all hands—and rumor had it that the *Glide* had also been lost. Salem's faltering worldwide commerce, desperately extended into danger zones, appeared to be under attack.[11]

The *Friendship*'s owners had sent a letter to President Jackson, complaining that "piratical" Malays had killed three Americans and plundered their vessel for a loss to the owners of $41,000 in pepper, specie, and opium. No mention was made of Charles Knight's dereliction of duty or of the opium-addicted nature of the attackers. The Salemites had asked the president to take action to protect American commerce in that part of the world and to seek redress for the deaths and losses.

It had been a bold request. In the past, such disasters had been considered a part of the overall risk taken by merchants and mariners in their worldwide commerce. The death of three men, however tragic, was predictable, even typical, for a long voyage to the Orient. But co-owner Nathaniel Silsbee was now a

U.S. senator, and times had changed. President Jackson was willing to order the navy to use force against indigenous peoples overseas, just as he was willing to stand by as Georgia's governor and legislature defied the United States Supreme Court and invaded Cherokee homelands. White male America now had a mighty nation that insisted on fealty everywhere; and even before hearing from the *Friendship*'s owners, the planners at the Navy Department had been discussing the best way to avenge the insult to "lives and property."

Secretary of the Navy Levi Woodbury, a friend of Silsbee, had carefully prepared new orders for Downes, bound on a world cruise in the *Potomac*. He was to sail at once for Kuala Batu to "obtain from the intelligent shipmasters, supercargos, and others, engaged in the American trade in that neighborhood," information about "the government there, the piratical character of the population, and the flagrant circumstances of the injury" that had been done to the *Friendship* and her men. If it seemed that Endicott or his crew had provoked the natives, or if the people or their rulers showed contrition for "the plunder or murder," he was only to make a demand on the authorities, assuring them that "this government entertains no hostile feelings towards the people of Quallah Batoo or their governors, rajahs, or rulers of any kind." However, if he were to confirm the allegations of Endicott and the owners, he was to "demand of the rajah" restitution for the plundered property and the damaged vessel and to bring about "the immediate punishment of those concerned in the murder of the American citizens." If rejected or opposed, he had license to destroy boats, houses, and forts "near the scene of aggression."

Downes had not been sure what all of this meant. Just before sailing from New York, he had requested clarification from Secretary Woodbury as to the real expectations of the government. He would later claim that Woodbury replied, "Give the rascals a good thrashing."

There was something strange about the big Danish vessel moored so far out. When it sent in a boat, two hundred men and boys gathered on the beach, and the boat turned around. Ignoring his orders to consult with others along the coast and to parley with the rajah, Commodore Downes decided that "voluntary justice on the part of the Malays . . . was entirely out of the question."[12] From Downes, the people of Kuala Batu would get no warning or any chances for explanations, reparations, or negotiations. The *Potomac* was poised to inflict modern warfare on a bamboo village.

That night, at two, about three hundred sailors and marines, armed with muskets, pistols, crowbars, and boarding pikes, took off in six whaleboats. Downes ordered them to land about a mile north of the town, take the five forts, and capture the rajahs. At daybreak, the Americans began to cross the beach. The people in the first fort were terrified to see a small army of white men advancing through the gloom, for reasons unstated and unknown. Inside the fort, Po Mahomet rallied them, men and women, to turn back the infidels. The Americans' cannon fire and musketry was met by the flight of javelins and spears. The soldiers kept coming, firing with deadly precision, blowing holes in the dirt walls of the fort. Po Mahomet was cut down, but his people battled on against the superior foe. "The fort was stormed and soon carried; not, however, till almost every individual in it was slain," many of them women, many run through by bayonets.[13]

The second fort fell, too, with terrible losses to the defenders. Lieutenant Pinkham, leading the attack on a fort in the jungle behind the village, trained his cannon on people trying to escape upriver and blew them apart in the proas and on the beaches.[14] In the course of two and a half hours, the flimsy forts were wrecked, the rajahs killed or driven off, the people shot down and stabbed, and Kuala Batu "leveled to the dust." There was nothing more to be done, so the buglers played the national anthem, "Yankee Doodle";[15] and the American fighters, with two dead and a few wounded, embarked in their boats, rowing back to the *Potomac* as the flames consumed the trees and the rubble of the village.

Next morning, the mighty warship came within a mile of the shore, to make "an indelible impression on the minds of these people of the power of the United States" in defense of commerce.[16] It seems that it did not occur to Downes that his rogue actions were certain to diminish that commerce for many years and that his failure to carry out orders to treat with the rajahs meant that the owners of the *Friendship* would never receive any reparations, which was, after all, the main point of his mission. Downes ordered that the *Potomac*'s larboard guns be run out; and for the next hour, thirty-two-pound shot rained on the remaining earthen fort. "In performing this service there was a fine opportunity of observing the great proficiency the gun crews had made in that highly important part of their profession, loading and firing."[17]

Finally, a man with a white handkerchief appeared on the beach. Downes allowed him to paddle out to the mighty *Potomac*. In broken English, the man said "a great many had been killed on shore, and all the property had been destroyed." He did not know why this had happened, but he made a plea for an end to the assault. Downes proudly recounted that he told him "that I had been sent to demand restitution of the property taken from the *Friendship* and to insist on the punishment of those persons concerned in the outrage committed on the individuals of that ship. Finding it impossible to effect either object, I said to him that I was satisfied with what had been done, and I granted him the peace for which they begged."

The world had a new enemy. In the seas where Americans had long been welcomed as friendly traders, the U.S. Navy had taken charge, just as the European navies and monopolies had always taken charge; and a different kind of American appeared, murderous and imperious, looking for a fight in a planet filled with troublemakers. The lessons and advantages of commerce had been lost, as they had been lost on the merchants who had made opium their medium of exchange, and on men like first mate Charles Knight aboard the *Friendship*, contemptuous toward people who were different. It was a sea change in America's relations with the non-Western and the nonwhite world, consistent with the final solution that Jackson and Congress had applied toward America's own native peoples: a policy of intolerance, lies, violence, forced removal, and genocide. Eventually it would require the permanent presence of armies and navies on the frontiers, at home and abroad, to crush the enemy and the would-be friend.

The people of Sumatra and the archipelago, already beset by the British and the Dutch, already addicted to the Westerners' opium, now understood that

America too had great war machines that would deal out massive destruction. What Salem knew, what it had learned in decades of interactions with other peoples, was a needlessly complicated and quaintly outdated set of understandings. Its genius had been for exploring the unknown and making contact with new peoples, for self-reliance and self-defense while initiating and sustaining mutually beneficial commerce. Salem mariners had always regarded the approach of native canoes with a certain amount of anxiety, and the natives had always been capable of the treachery and violence by which they had long preserved their independence. If vessels had sometimes been attacked, the sultans and the rajahs, as merchants and guarantors of commerce, had prevented a recurrence, and the world had kept turning.

No longer: overkill and military intervention were the new standards for dealing with danger, which is to say dealing with the world. The period of openness and positive exchange, of forty years of friendship around the globe that Salem had helped to make—of a world in which a young shipmaster might, in one voyage, make connections for a lifetime of honorable trade—that world had come to an end, in the thunderous, pointless broadsides of the *Potomac,* and in the bodies of men and women strewn lifeless across the white sand, and in the clouds of dark smoke rolling up from the burning town.

GETTING CLEAR. Stephen White, merchant, had long dealt with the effects of death and shipwreck as inescapable hazards of commerce. He soon moved on from the disaster at Salem and began life anew in Boston with his adoring children, a huge fortune, and a vision of America's maritime greatness.

PART FOUR

BLOWN AWAY

O Christ! To think of the green navies and the green-skulled crews!

—HERMAN MELVILLE, *MOBY-DICK*

WHITE HAVEN. As the head of the East Boston Timber Company, Stephen White went to the Niagara River in New York to find old-growth forest for use in shipbuilding. On Grand Island above the Falls, he developed the largest steam-driven sawmill complex in the world and conducted highly profitable lumber and shipbuilding operations.

18.

THE MAGNATE

Living in splendor at the Tremont House, Stephen White and his three daughters enjoyed their lives in the city and stayed clear of Salem. He had inherited the lion's share of Captain White's estate, including the forgiveness of about $50,000 in debt, which gave him a fortune exceeding $200,000.

As his vessels arrived from their voyages, he shifted them to their new home port. In Boston he was elected to the state senatorial delegation, and he joined the richest Bostonians at their seacoast summer colony at Great Nahant. Some holdings he chose to manage, some he decided to sell. The first to go was his own Salem homestead, the big brick house and stable on the Common at Washington Square, which he sold in March 1831, for $7,000 to John W. Rogers, a partner in N. L. Rogers & Brothers. His sister-in-law Eliza Story White sold her Washington Square house to a Silsbee and also moved to Boston, where her three daughters were the wives of wealthy young men.

Stephen White sold the Knapp homestead to a Boston merchant for $3,000. He sold his own Salem wharf, with its buildings; and the rest, the property formerly of Joseph White, he kept. To Jedediah Lathrop, the tenant farmer, he leased out Cherry Hill Farm. There, in the balmy weeks of September and October, Stephen would enjoy the pleasures of harvest season with friends and family. Daniel Webster came for long visits, and the two men and their sons spent their days gunning, sailing, and fishing.[1]

In downtown Salem, the Joseph White mansion—haunted in the public mind, more famous than the East India Museum, more fearful than Salem Jail or Gallows Hill—was occupied by Reverend Alexander Griswold, the Episcopal bishop who had comforted Frank Knapp at the end.

In the aftermath of the murder and the failure of the Salem Mill Dam Corporation, Salem lost many more of its leading citizens.

Reverend Henry Colman, forty-six, continued briefly in the pulpit at Barton Square. His daughter Sarah was the wife of a Boston lawyer, and daughter Anna was married to Pickering Dodge Jr., scion of one of Salem's last prosperous merchants; but Mary, fourteen, remained at home with her parents through the many difficulties of the year 1830. In mid-December, two weeks before the scheduled hanging of Joe Knapp, Mary Colman suddenly fell ill and died. By the end of 1831, her heartbroken father could not go on in his role as the leader of the flock.

His congregation had been generally supportive, but some saw Colman as stained with the blood of the Knapps. Joe had been a member of his church, and Joe's lawyer had vividly portrayed Colman as a minister turned executioner in service to the vengeful White. One year after the hanging of Frank Knapp, Henry Colman resigned his pastorate. In his valedictory sermon, on December 4, 1831, he acknowledged that "misfortune and death have been busily at work among us. The removal of families from the town, who were once connected with us, has been almost unprecedented. The bereavements of death have been numerous and most afflictive." In saying good-bye, he warned that "the future is veiled in darkness. The connections of life at the longest must be short. Time places his rough hand upon us all. Parents, children, friends, neighbors, fellow men, one after another, take their leave and depart. Time permits no man to pause or linger, but continually impels us forward."[2]

Colman was impelled to sell his Swampscott farm for a large profit to his son-in-law Pickering Dodge Jr., a rich man devoted to horticulture and literature, gentlemanly pastimes that Henry Colman himself wished to pursue. Leaving Salem, he abandoned his career as a parish minister. For a few months he was a lecturer, and in February 1832, he addressed the Salem Lyceum on the subject of eloquence. Then he became an "agriculturalist" and moved seventy

miles west to a farm in Deerfield. His friends secured for him the position of
commissioner for the Agricultural Survey of the State. Like his old enemy Timothy Pickering, he ardently promoted scientific farming. He was not really a
plowman, however; he edited publications and compiled agricultural studies
before crossing the seas in 1842 to write about castles, vineyards, great farms,
and the grand boulevards of Paris. After spending 1848 in Salem, he went to England to haunt the drawing rooms of the landed nobles. He remained their favorite American until the last year of his life, when he published a book about
the lifestyles of Britain's rich and famous, who complained that their charming
visitor had betrayed them.[3]

Salem was lost to the Honorable Benjamin W. Crowninshield, who did not
wish to continue to reside there or to represent it in Congress. His nephews had
disgraced his family, sullying his famous name and ruining forever the pleasures
of life in his ancestral town. He sold his Essex Street mansion and moved with
his family to Boston, where he set up as a lawyer, as did his talented son Francis
B. Crowninshield, partnered with fellow transplant Rufus Choate, the legal
wizard of the Committee of Vigilance, who had first achieved recognition by
representing Dick and George in the Mumford case. Benjamin's brother-in-law
Nathaniel Silsbee served in the United States Senate with Daniel Webster. In 1835,
Silsbee would retire to Salem, to be succeeded in the Senate by Rufus Choate.
With Silsbee's resignation, Salem was finished as a national political power.

William Fettyplace, the pillar of several Salem institutions, moved to Boston
and remained close to his brother-in-law White. Pickmans, Ropeses, and many
more joined the Grays, Cabots, Higginsons, Pickerings, and Bowditches already
established in Boston. Others went bankrupt and had to go west to start over.
Frederick Bessell moved to Ohio. Stephen's younger sister Mary and her husband, Nathaniel West Jr. of Chestnut Street, hoped for a revival of commerce; but
even West's great fortune gave out, and they moved to Indianapolis. Stephen's sister Eliza Hodges coinherited Captain White's block of town houses on LaGrange
Street in the south end of Boston. Her husband, George A. Hodges, musician and
merchant, failed in business, after which they moved to various places with her

mother, Phebe, and handicapped brother, Francis.[4] By the late 1830s, they resided in the industrial city of Lowell.

Stephen's brother John White, master of the *Franklin* at Saigon, had retired
to the farm in Lynn. He had never made much money as a sea captain, and his
naval career, begun late in the War of 1812, had not continued; nor had he kept
writing after the rejection of his book on commerce in 1825. He and his family
moved to Boston by 1830, summering in Lynn until he sold the farm in 1833
for $2,350 and began residing full-time in Boston with his wife and daughters,
Phebe and Elizabeth. There, at last, he would be raised to the naval rank of
commander.

John White was plagued for years by the elephantiasis he had contracted in
Vietnam. There was no cure, and in 1840 it would kill him.[5] His *History of a
Voyage to the China Sea*, edited by John Pickering, was among the earliest and
best American contributions to the literature of the sea.[6]

George Crowninshield, lightly wearing the mantle of sole survivor of the indicted killer-conspirators, remained an unrepentant roué. His father, Richard, had his hands full: his other son, Edward, had begun to lose his mind,
and the daughters complained that their chances of a good marriage were
ruined. George kept up his old habits. In September 1831, Nathaniel Hawthorne
noted that "the talk about Captain White's murder has almost entirely ceased.
George Crowninshield still lives at his father's, and seems not at all cast down by
what has taken place. I saw him walk by our house, arm-in-arm with a girl,
about a month since."[7]

Mary Beckford invested her inheritance from Joseph White and lived
quietly at the Pickering farm. Hawthorne, a good gossip, reported that her
daughter Mary Beckford Knapp, Joe's suicidal widow, "is said to be engaged to
a lawyer in Boston. She lives at Wenham with her mother, who is believed by
everybody to have had a hand in the murder."[8] Young Mary was by no means
finished: she did marry the ambitious attorney Edmund Kimball, an associate
of Daniel Webster, and with him had several children and a respectable middle-
class life.

The surviving Knapps fled Salem in different directions. Most went to New York City, where their Brooklyn relatives, the Lows, who had left in 1829, were well established in trade. William H. Low and wife Abigail Knapp resided at the port of Macao, China, with his wife and their niece Harriett Low of Salem. There, William pushed vast quantities of opium into China through a network of smugglers. Phippen Knapp chose a different path. The redoubtable young lawyer moved across the harbor to practice law at Marblehead and run the local lyceum. He visited his father and brothers in Manhattan and corresponded warmly with Harriett Low in Macao.

Harriett had been astonished to hear of the murder in August 1830. Her news from America was always four months old, so she had no idea who the suspects might be: "I cannot find words to express the horrors of it. Who could it have been and what for? Old White dead, not much lamented we suppose, poor old gentleman."[9] It was far more horrific to learn, a few weeks later, that her lovely aunt Abigail Low's two shipmaster brothers had plotted the assassination and would be executed for it. That news, traveling around the world, rocked the Yankee community there and provoked some of her uncle's rivals to smear him and his family. Not surprisingly, Harriett found no spouse among the eligible American and British merchants at Macao, and when her uncle fell ill she sailed for home in 1834.

In Salem, Harriett learned that her friend Phippen Knapp, Esq., had given up on both New England and the law. In a trajectory exactly opposite that of Rev. Henry Colman, Knapp reacted to the traumas of 1830 by embracing religion—specifically, the teachings of Bishop Griswold, the tenant of Captain White's mansion. In 1833, Knapp became an Episcopal priest and took back his name, Nathaniel; and in 1836 he married and moved to New York. After his wife died, he went to Alabama and wandered off into the wilderness. No one knew him there, and no one knew of his thwarted ambitions and his hard losses and his connections to Frank and Joe, and his court battles with Henry Colman, and the tragic scenes at Salem Jail and its prison yard. After a few months of missionary work, he answered a call to the pulpit in Tuscaloosa. He remarried, and years later he went to Montgomery; and finally he would settle in the feverish port of Mobile. He survived an epidemic of yellow fever, during which he ministered to the sick and dying like a saint. Reverend Nathaniel P. Knapp ended his career as the beloved rector of Mobile's Christ Church, and a volume of his sermons would be published after his untimely death in 1854 at the age of forty-eight.[10]

John Forrester, Stephen White's next-door neighbor in Salem and the husband of his wife's sister Charlotte Story, would fail in business spectacularly in 1833, with no hope of recovery. His large family of little aristocrats crowded into an apartment in the half-house owned by the Storys' elderly mother, Mrs. Mehitable Story, on a side street behind the former Stephen White mansion. She would move away to Boston, but not the Forresters. For decades, they lived there in genteel poverty, the girls growing old as teachers in a little private school, the boys going off, half-educated, to the South, to meet early death or return to the quietude of Salem.

Frank Story remained in Salem for a while, in his solitary brick mansion out on Bridge Street, overlooking the calm waters that were to have supplied the power for the mill dam project. When he married, he moved to Boston and began a successful career in business. His older half-brother, Captain William Story, for many years a distinguished shipmaster and then a merchant, went bankrupt and had to resume his career at sea, finally retiring to an office at the Salem Custom House. He put his son Augustus through Harvard, and for many years he would reside with Gus, an insurance company president, on Bridge Street, across from the house formerly Mary Beckford's.

Judge Joseph Story remained in Cambridge, growing melancholy on the bench of the Supreme Court. Early in 1830, the state of Georgia had invoked "nullification" in claiming the right to ignore federal laws and treaties in dealing with its Indians; but the Supreme Court upheld the Cherokees' right to remain in place. Defying the Court, the governor of Georgia had sent the state militia to dispossess the Indians, and President Jackson had done nothing to intervene. In one blow, the Cherokee nation had been destroyed and the United States Supreme Court had been stripped of its constitutional power. In May 1830, a federal Indian Removal Bill was passed, barely. For the first time, Congress abandoned the concept of assimilation in favor of total separation of the two races, white and red, with white in complete control. America's enslaved people, chained to the immense power of the cotton growers, were in worse shape than in 1820; and the Creeks and Cherokees and other civilized tribes faced the likelihood of forced removal to the desert territories of the West. In these events, Joseph Story could feel the principles of the national republic crumbling.[11]

Chief Justice John Marshall died in 1835, and Story, the ablest of his disciples, was bypassed as his successor in favor of Roger B. Taney, slaveholder of Maryland. Diminished in his role on the Court, Story would become famous for his work at Harvard Law School and his magisterial *Commentaries on the Constitution.* He wrote occasional pieces for the public but lost his taste for oratory. At times he would glance at the poem he had published in his youth, "The Power of Solitude," and he wrote a memoir of growing up in Marblehead and of Salem's glory days, when the Crowninshields ruled the world and he ruled the Crowninshields. From time to time he would visit his hometown, and chat with the Grand Banks fishermen in the crooked streets, and hike out to the highland pastures where he had stood as a boy, gazing across the harbor at the promised land of Salem.

Like Bowditch and Pickering,[12] Story continued to participate in the governance of Harvard. It prospered under President Quincy, and he watched with great interest as Salem's Benjamin Peirce, of the class of 1829, became a college professor, headed for eminence as a philosopher and mathematician. Story busied himself in various learned societies and associations and prepared for a very long stay in Cambridge, where he led the group that developed Mount Auburn Cemetery, landscaped with hills and fountains, trees and flowers, shrubs and statuary and pathways, to be enjoyed as a park and a place for long walks and quiet reflection.[13]

Protected by his anonymity, Nathaniel Hawthorne inhabited Salem without any stake in it, confirmed in his dark outlook and even in his night habits, as if sunlight and society were part of a pretense, a false civility that was at odds with the truth of human nature. He would stay on in Salem, living obscurely with his mother and sisters for years to come, writing more tales, avoiding a novel. His aim was profundity, not popularity, yet he cherished a dim hope of fame.

In 1830, publisher Samuel Goodrich bought two Hawthorne sketches, "Sights from a Steeple" (unsigned) and "The Haunted Quack" (by "Joseph Nicholson"), the latter a short story about a journey in a Niagara canal boat, in which a passenger overhears the words of another, muttered in the midst of a nightmare. He wakes the young man, a patent-medicine dealer, who is haunted by the ghost of an old woman whom he believes he had poisoned with his "curious mixture," an "antidote to death"; and now he is returning to the scene of his crime to be hanged. As the boat pulls into the dock, he is greeted by a crowd of people who inform him that his concoction had knocked the granny into a swoon but then had brought her back, better than ever; and he was hailed as her savior, a "smart doctor who had a power of larning, but gave severe doses," like Hawthorne himself.

Goodrich bought five more Hawthorne pieces in 1831. In that year, the writer made his usual summer tour of New England's up-country taverns, and he thought about running off to New Hampshire to join the Shakers. He did not but moved back to his boyhood room in the Manning house on Herbert Street in Salem and kept writing into his thirties, still anonymous, still deferring a decision on a career. In 1832, his friend Reverend George Cheever was publicly beaten in Salem for having written a temperance pamphlet aimed at Salem's distillery-owning deacons; and in 1835, Hawthorne witnessed another flare-up of Salem fires in the furor over a newspaper excerpt from *Lectures on Salem Witchcraft*, by Reverend Charles W. Upham of the First Church. Many in Salem and vicinity remained as deeply ashamed of the events of 1692 as of 1830. "Who Is Safe?" asked a writer in the *Gazette*, regarding Upham's revelations of ancient scandal and tragedy: "If such things are tolerated, there will be no safety and no peace for any family in the town. We shall all be overwhelmed in a torrent of calumny and cruelty. Every man will be armed with a dagger to pierce the breast of his neighbor. The decencies of civilized life will be destroyed, and human society will degenerate into a savage horde, no better than the 'scaly scape-jail blue devils' whom a certain sanctified personage has just introduced to our city of Peace."[14]

Hawthorne's themes, even when presented by Upham, still had great power to disturb; but he had dwelled long enough in morbid realms, and in Salem. He moved to Boston when Goodrich helped him get a job as compiler of the *American Magazine of Useful and Entertaining Knowledge*. Most of the dreary content was hacked out by Hawthorne himself; but his sister Ebe helped him from Salem, and he reprinted some selections verbatim, including an up-the-river passage from John White's *History of a Voyage to the China Sea*.[15] Hawthorne's name would first appear in print on a collection of tales in 1837, but his writing would earn him no fame or money until he was forty-six, in 1850, as he left Salem for the last time, soon after publication of *The Scarlet Letter*, rendered locally scandalous by his portrayal of the Salem Custom House and the habits of its denizens.

In the fall of 1830, John C. R. Palmer Jr., the betrayer of his friends the killers, finally moved out of his cell at Salem Jail. His truthful testimony had been discounted, and he had been unable to establish his innocence. Public opinion found him guilty of attempted extortion of the Knapps and of membership in the Crowninshield gang.

He stayed on in Salem, petitioning for the reward money, put off by Stephen White. Palmer roomed in a boardinghouse and did a lot of writing and a little traveling. On April 6, 1831, the first anniversary of Captain White's murder, Stephen White was at his office in Boston when there came a knocking at the countinghouse door. It was Palmer, angry and desperate. With nowhere to hide, White faced him down and told him that the reward money was gone, given to Dr. Barstow and the Committee of Vigilance. Defeated once more, Palmer reflected that for rich men like White, "honour pledged to inferiors is only a jingling of words, and words are only wind if they are uttered by those far above you in point of property."[16]

Through the summer of 1831, Palmer kept writing—it was a race against time. Like John White, he hoped to reinvent himself as an author, but he owed nine months of back rent, and then he slandered his landlady. Back he went to a cell at Salem Jail.[17] Someone, perhaps Stephen White, bailed him out.

Determined to redeem himself, he pressed forward and published his book in Boston in August 1831. He had begun *Explanation* intending to relate his adventures and how he had tried to trap the Knapps into admitting their guilt; but it had turned into his confession, a book of raw feelings and painful disclosures and outrage against the fate that had made him a pariah. The pressmen took the liberty of inserting disclaimers as to spelling and punctuation, but it was a good read nonetheless. Its motto is one of Palmer's own quatrains:

> *Fiercely gleam'd the planet infamy,*
> *Lighting up the path of misery;*
> *Urging on a fearful destiny—*
> *Loudly roar'd the tempest's revelry.*

The first part of *Explanation* is a buoyant, humorous, picaresque, often moving account of a state-of-Maine sailor boy gone wrong in the big world, sometimes rambling through unfamiliar landscapes, calling out to be rescued from sinking sailboats and bad company, always in peril, always slipping away— until he is befriended by Needham and Crowninshield.

With the description of his incarceration in 1827, Palmer's narrative turns dark. Henceforth, he would be locked up in rooms and cells and dungeons, oddly without will but ferociously himself. It was a bitter irony that Stephen White, progressive, was a leader of the Society for Prison Reform. Palmer, a veteran of Thomaston Prison, had nothing but contempt for aristocrats ignorant of prison realities, of trauma and humiliation. In *Explanation,* he blasted away at White's misguided ideals: "Search every state prison in the country; follow every convict to his dying bed, and there ask *him* what good his first state imprisonment did him, and he will tell you, It was his ruin . . . and they will tell you they have been the means of contaminating others who, but for their poisonous example, might have been reclaimed."[18] Palmer called for real prison reform, aimed at rehabilitation.

Explanation and its "innocent peculiarities" received a sarcastic review in Salem, in the same issue of the *Gazette* in which Nat Turner's "insurrection of

Africans in the slave-holding states" was described as imparting "a thrilling interest to everything relative to their projects for self-emancipation."[19] Despite his attempt to write his way to redemption, John C. R. Palmer Jr. seems to have vanished by the end of 1831. Perhaps he followed the advice that his uncle had once given, to choose an alias and light out for the territories.[20]

Stephen White invested heavily in the future of the National Republican Party and put forward his friend Daniel Webster as its leader. White bankrolled Senator Webster's campaigns, put him on legal retainer, and even gave him a beautiful yacht, christened *Calypso* and moored at Green Harbor off Webster's estate at Marshfield, south of Boston. One of White's first acts as a Bostonian was to hire the editor Samuel L. Knapp (second cousin to the Salem Knapps) to write Webster's biography. White soon published *A Memoir of the Life of Daniel Webster* to boost him for the presidency—and to address the White murder. "The crime produced the most astonishing excitement ever known in that peaceful community . . . ," it began.[21] "The prime mover of the whole scene" was Joe Knapp, "a wicked and shallow man who attempted to pursue a bold course to screen himself and his associates by scattering rumors and by forging letters to draw suspicions on others, and particularly on the favorite nephew of the deceased, the Hon. Stephen White, who had been brought up, as it were, in the old man's bosom. These rumors were not believed for a moment by those acquainted with that gentleman. He had from his early youth been a favorite with the people among whom he lived as well as with his uncle. . . ."

After covering the trial, the narrative veers into the backstory and the Salem characters: "A grand-niece of Mr. White's, Miss Beckford, had married a Captain Joseph J. Knapp, Jr. He had been in Stephen White's employment as master and factor of a ship, but the owner, finding that [Knapp] wanted[22] capacity in his profession, did not continue him in his service. This probably excited some heart-burnings, which were not allayed by any subsequent intercourse among the family connections. The mother of Knapp's wife, Mrs. Beckford, was housekeeper to Mr. White. Of course the prime mover of this murder had access to this house as he chose. He was living in idleness; the affairs of his father were falling into embarrassment, which fact was probably well known to him. Captain

White, though old, was healthy, and seemed formed to live some years, if no accident should take him off; and even when he might die, it was understood that much of his property would go by will to Stephen White, and he was an object of his envy and resentment."

Of the "moral turpitude" that marked the murder, "it is to be forever a dark and terrible story, it will be the ground-work of a hundred legends. Its criminality cannot be exaggerated, nor will its moral ever be lost; it will show the guilty that there is but little security and no peace for them; it will teach the public that justice is often much indebted to talents and professional skill in bringing rank offenders to a just judgment."

Thus did White's money produce a biography that included his public version of the Salem events—a version that was soon suppressed, for reasons now unknown, but which were probably political. Stephen collected 450 unsold copies and kept twice as many in sheets. In the 1835 edition of the book, not a word appeared about Stephen White or the Salem murder.

In promoting the career and candidacy of Daniel Webster, Stephen White was far-seeing. White himself served in the fall of 1832 as chairman of the first statewide convention of the National Republicans, which in 1834 would morph into the Whig Party.[23] The convention nominated Henry Clay as its presidential candidate against Jackson. Webster hung back, hoping to forge an alliance with the Hero; but that proved futile.

The White-Webster friendship, sealed in the blood of the Knapps, had ripened into something deeper still. In 1831, the first of the three White Witches was married to a Boston beau: Stephen's beautiful daughter Harriet Story White, twenty-two, became the wife of J. William Paige, thirty-nine, Daniel Webster's brother-in-law. The Paiges would reside on Summer Street, Boston, in a mansion provided by Stephen White. No doubt a large marriage portion was settled on Harriet. Her sisters, Caroline and Ellen, were ardently pursued by Boston beaux and enjoyed a very active social life. Stephen's son, Joseph—the sole surviving White male in his generation—continued his studies across the river at Harvard.

FINAL VOYAGE. In September 1835, at East Boston, the first of Stephen White's new line of large ships was launched. Christened Owanungah *(Indian for Grand Island), the ship was designed to carry 460 tons of cargo and was built entirely of timber cut into ship-parts at Grand Island and barged down the Erie Canal for transport to Boston. After three vessels, White built no more; but in his former shipyards would rise the hulls of the greatest sailing vessels ever known.*

19.

THE MIRAGE

Stephen White lived well on Beacon Hill, with good returns from his investments in financial institutions and manufacturing companies.[1] He figured prominently in the capital as a governor's councilor and state senator, and he enjoyed the company of Webster and the Boston Brahmins and the Salem Bostonians as he guided his children into the upper reaches of high society. Possessed of an immense fortune, he grew restless as an investor and rentier but did not dare to engage too heavily in shipping. He enjoyed his many outings with Webster, and he maintained a keen interest in politics and traveled often to Washington to influence policy and promote Webster's career and the interests of the new Whig Party. This kept him busy, but he did not find a new wife, and he yearned for something great to do, something that would put him on top of the world, as in the good old days. Although he kept up his romance with ships and the sea, it was something else that carried him into the current of possibilities and finally into an enterprise worthy of a huge fortune and a new beginning.

Railroads were as yet unseen in America, but it was understood that the economic future would someday ride on their tracks and gather at their terminals. As the head of the legislative committee reporting on the feasibility of Boston railroads, Stephen White was often courted by potential investors; and in 1831 he agreed to meet with General William H. Sumner.[2] Sumner wanted to be sure that any railroad built from Boston to points north and east would begin on his island—he was an owner of 660-acre Noddle's Island, just across the harbor channel. White brought out a bottle, and Sumner admitted that he wanted much more and had already been to New York to see investors. He intended, he said, to build nothing less than a brand-new city, to be called North Boston. The empty island was perfect for development, with direct access to the sea, a north shore close to the mainland, an open expanse for residential development, and a southerly and westerly waterfront perfect for shipping. Done right, the grand project would absorb much of the growth of Boston proper, already bursting the confines of its original peninsula.

White, the man who had tried to rebuild Salem as a modern city, saw redemption in North Boston: parks and avenues and neighborhoods on the slopes, factories and hotels and large vessels in the shipyards, and tall ships along the shore, all shining and beckoning just a half mile across the water from the overcrowded old city. North Boston would be the next step for the great metropolis.

Throughout 1832, the men put together the financing and the legal structures to make their vision possible. By 1833, the real work commenced. White and Francis J. Oliver, president of the American Insurance Company, joined Sumner in founding the North Boston Company to develop the city, arrange for the railroad, and establish a ferry service. To ensure sufficient resources, they took in three new partners and incorporated with about forty shareholders.[3] Stephen White had found his leviathan, capable of absorbing his energy, ambition, and imagination. Looming largest in his imagination was the opportunity to build great ships. Since the 1790s, as far back as he could recall, his family had built vessels—and now, on the shores of East Boston, he had the opportunity to build them bigger, better, and faster, capable of surpassing the preeminent British and achieving ascendancy for the United States. White intended to make Boston the shipbuilding center of the world.

Joseph White, nineteen, graduated from Harvard in 1833 and entered his father's countinghouse on State Street. Two of Joseph's college classmates, John B. Joy and Fletcher Webster, courted his sisters. John was the scion of a rich Boston family; Fletcher was the son of Daniel Webster and nephew of William Paige, husband of Joseph's sister Harriet. In the spring of 1833, Stephen White and

Daniel Webster, best friends, went off together, no doubt with a case of Stephen's wine, to make a tour of the West, starting at Albany and proceeding to Buffalo. With Webster making speeches and building political support for their new party, they stormed into Ohio and down to Cincinnati, headed for Clay's Kentucky and Jackson's Tennessee.

Webster was greeted with enthusiastic crowds as the defender of the Constitution. In the recent congressional fight over South Carolina's "nullification" in refusing to adhere to the tariff laws, Webster had supported President Jackson's threat to use federal force. White and Webster never made it to Kentucky, where cholera caused them to turn back. White spent some of the return trip at Niagara Falls and vicinity, boating on the river among the great stands of primeval forest above the Erie Canal. Webster, gratified by his reception in the upper West—he had invested heavily in western lands and urged his son to settle in the new districts of the nation—began planning for a presidential run.

White did not encourage his son, Joseph, to pursue a profession; instead, he made him his partner in business.

In applying for incorporation, the investors found that the name North Boston had been taken, and so it was the East Boston Company that laid out a grid of streets, all straight and wide, Webster Street and White Street and many others. A large hill was the first to be subdivided, with Stephen White taking three lots, Oliver two, and one each to Sumner, Daniel Webster, and J. William Paige, among others.[4] In the fall of 1833, the East Boston Company built the Maverick House, a large resort hotel, near the new ferry wharf.[5] The company also built two large steam ferries, the *East Boston* and the *Maverick,* to make regular runs across the channel.[6] At the Maverick House, the flamboyant Major Barton attracted crowds of smiling visitors to his living tableaux and galas of all sorts. By day, guests could ride the steam-powered island monorail; after dark, there were balls, parties, concerts, and moonlight cruises. Stephen White sold off Cherry Hill Farm and his Nahant summer colony property and moved into the Maverick House for the season, as did other notables—John Downes, commandant of the navy yard, included—so many that in its third season, it would be doubled in size, with a dining room served by fifty waiters. East Boston was off to a splendid start.[7]

White never lost track of his main purpose, which was to build sailing ships on a new scale—ships never seen before, enormous vessels that would dominate global commerce and transportation. Large steamers were now venturing out on the oceans, but White's sailing ships would be so large and so fast that nothing could outrace them. He remained a keen student of naval architecture, as the top shipwrights of Boston, New York, and Baltimore improved their designs and provided ever-larger vessels for the packet lines to England and the opium shippers of the South China Sea.

In the fall of 1833, White organized the East Boston Timber Company, with investors from Boston and New York. Another island now came into play: White had been deeply impressed by his visits to the Buffalo area and the primeval forest of Grand Island. Twelve miles long, situated about ten miles above the falls in the middle of the Niagara River, Grand Island contained the largest stand of old-growth oak in North America, perfect for battleships and world-class freighters. Shipped to East Boston, the lumber would attract shipbuilders, manufacturers, and workmen as new residents.[8]

The East Boston Timber Company directors elected Stephen White president. The investors shared his vision and urged him to pursue the goal of worldwide shipping supremacy. Among the owners were Webster, Oliver, Sumner, Dr. Gideon Barstow of Salem, J. William Paige, who served as clerk and treasurer, and William Fettyplace, superintendent.[9] Using New York agents, White purchased all eighteen thousand acres of Grand Island oak, and he consulted engineers about using the steam technology that had been overlooked by the wise men of Salem. This time, there would be no drawn-out process of permission seeking and stock subscription and newspaper controversies.

Grand Island would require a lumbering and milling operation bigger than any ever attempted. It would also require a great deal of courage in the face of economic conditions, for America was headed into a recession. The Bank War raged, and the nation's capitalists agonized, as Jackson tried to dissolve the Bank of the United States, while Clay, Webster, and Calhoun led the charge in its favor, believing that it was fundamental to the nation's financial system. When bank chief Nicholas Biddle responded to Jackson by curtailing loans, a panic ensued and bankruptcies piled up. White proposed that Webster introduce a bill to create a new national bank, with substantial state authority for the branches.[10] Despite many small victories, the anti-Jackson forces—now organizing as the Whigs—ultimately had to relent. Money was released into the marketplace, and projects like the East Boston Timber Company went forward.

In 1834, Stephen White sold the Captain Joseph White mansion in Salem for $7,000 to David Pingree, a newcomer merchant with large timber holdings in Maine. Pingree's Salem was a very different place from the Salem of the 1820s. South Salem industries were expanding, but the waterfront was quiet. Eight Salem vessels had been converted to hunt whales,[11] as an antidote "to the present state of business in Salem, [in which] our young men are emigrating, or their hearts are corroding with the miseries of idleness."[12] Francis Peabody built up his lead mill, added whale oil candle factories, and kept up his experiments; and he was followed in these courses by Caleb Smith and Eben Seccomb, South Salem whale oil refiners. The new trade with East Africa and South America continued to supply raw materials to the manufacturers of leather, shoes, and chemicals.[13]

Salem would be incorporated as a city in March 1836: Leverett Saltonstall of Chestnut Street, former Federalist, was elected mayor, along with a board of aldermen. They adopted a seal depicting a natty mandarin holding a parasol near a palm tree, with a ship sailing in the distance and a dove with an olive branch, encircled by the anachronistic motto *Divitis Indiae, usque ad ultimum sinum,* roughly, "To the farthest cove of the rich Indies."

In the fall of 1838, Salem's status as a suburb of Boston would be made official with the arrival of the first locomotive, chugging up from East Boston on the brand-new tracks of the Eastern Railroad, on its way toward other fading seaports: Beverly, Newburyport, Portsmouth, and Portland. By then, one of Stephen White's former captains, Nathaniel Griffin, was managing a new industrial enterprise in Salem. Greatly surpassing the ambitions of the Salem Mill Dam Corporation, the Naumkeag Steam Cotton Company would draw on much of the city's dwindling mercantile money. Over the course of eight years, in South Salem, on the site of the wharf of Pickering Dodge, the company would erect the largest steam-powered textile plant in the United States.[14]

Old Joseph Peabody stayed in his mansion on Essex Street and continued his trade with China, exchanging cash and opium for tea and silks; and he and others continued to send their ships to Java for coffee and Sumatra for pepper. Sumatra's Pepper Coast remained agitated by war with the Dutch and opium addiction and cultural incursions, and the devastation wrought by the *Potomac* in 1832 had no effect as a preventive. In 1834, two American missionaries ventured into the interior of northern Sumatra to bring Jesus to the Batak people, who killed and ate them.[15]

Po Adam, friend of Americans, suffered for his loyalty. After the *Potomac* had done its worst and sailed away, the king of Atjeh had stripped Adam of his property. He fled down the coast to Susu and went up the river to build a new fort. When he heard that Americans had arrived, he would appear with his man Suchie and a gift of fruit. One of his favorites was Charles Wilkins, master of Joseph Peabody's bark *Eclipse,* loading pepper near Muki in the summer of 1838. Without warning, the natives rose up and killed Wilkins and four of his men; but the crew fought back and retook the *Eclipse,* and Po Adam assisted them in escaping, although her Salem cook stayed in Sumatra, "living among the Malays far down the coast, as happy as any of the natives."[16]

U.S. Navy battleships eventually arrived to retaliate. At first nothing much was done—some desultory shelling of the coast. With his dark-stained lips and black teeth, Po Adam smiled nervously and told his naval friends, "This little fire only make mad that Malay man: they kill Po Adam when the big ship go, and they kill more American captain. But s'pose plenty men land for make fight, Malay all run, hide, dig hole in mountain. . . . Then Po Adam be great man—he speak true."[17] Commodore George C. Read listened and had his men run out the long guns and level the town of Muki, after which he had no trouble in exacting tribute from the rest of the rajahs.

The Dutch, who had been fighting their way up the coast for decades, intensified their war but had few victories. Finally, in 1910, after a decade-long intensive campaign of genocide, they became the overlords of the people of Atjeh

and so would remain—with eruptions and rebellions—until the creation of Indonesia.

Early in 1834, Ellen White became engaged to marry John B. Joy, her brother's
classmate. John received title to various Joy properties, while Stephen made the
couple a gift of money and a furnished mansion in Boston.[18] By the time of Ellen's wedding in February 1835, her sister Caroline had become engaged to
Daniel Webster's son Daniel Fletcher Webster, twenty-two, studying to become
a lawyer.[19]

Stephen White downsized, moving in 1835 from a Beacon Hill mansion to a
house near Bowditch below Boston Common. East Boston called to him, and
Grand Island, or Owanungah. After acquiring an East Boston parcel as the timber company's lumberyard and dock, White, forty-eight, and his son, Joseph,
twenty-one, headed for Niagara. With them went Jedediah Lathrop, once the
foreman at Cherry Hill Farm, and Benjamin F. Delano, a young shipbuilder who
brought his two brothers and twenty skilled shipwrights.

At Grand Island, they found industry and achievement. On its eastern
shore, at the new town named White Haven, stood the largest sawmill complex on
earth. Although surrounded by swift-moving water, it was powered by steam—
the steam that Salem had ignored. House-sized stacks of blond planks—local
oak and pine from Canada—occupied the waterfront, fodder for fifty canal boats
and a number of sloops bound for the Erie Canal and down the Hudson to the
shipyards of New York. The sawmill, with sixty roaring saws and rising clouds
of steam, was fed by gangs hauling logs up to seventy feet long.[20] Teams of oxen
and their drivers constantly arrived at the mill, amid the work of laborers, blacksmiths, carpenters, and sailors.

Shipwright Benjamin Delano gaped at the immensity of the White Haven works.
Jedediah Lathrop agreed to manage Grand Island for the company, which had
financial agents in Manhattan and Buffalo. Delano and crew went to work and built
three large schooners in the spring and summer, including the three-hundred-ton

Milwaukie, launched on the Fourth of July.[21] They also got out all the white-oak timbers for a good-sized vessel and sent them down the Erie Canal. Upon returning to East Boston, they built a handsome ship, 460 tons burthen, the first sailing vessel to rise on the shores of the city of the future. Christened *Owanungah* (the Indian name for Grand Island), she was launched on September 24, 1835, as a crowd celebrated with rum, firecrackers, gunfire, and band music.[22] White intended for many more to follow.

Delano returned to Niagara with his men in 1836 and hewed out the parts for dozens of new vessels. At the same time, Stephen White purchased a fifty-acre island near White Haven and named it White's Island. He and his son, Joseph, returned to Boston before the new year, to assist in Daniel Webster's halfhearted presidential campaign, part of an uncoordinated effort in which several Whigs ran as regional candidates against Jackson's successor, Martin Van Buren. Webster won only in Massachusetts. White remained worried about the financial condition of the country: the Bank of the United States had not been rechartered, and no other source of fiscal control, like the Federal Reserve, then existed. In December 1836, Stephen wrote to Webster scoring "the crack-brained old chief," President Jackson, for suppressing the supply of money: "If I mistake not, however, the time is at hand when the people *by great suffering* will be awakened to the absurdity of this policy. . . ."[23]

Unfortunately, White was correct. The Panic of 1837 began with bank refusals in the spring, followed by the collapse of the Liverpool cotton market and worldwide recession. The East Boston Timber Company was hard-hit by the massive contraction of credit. Grand Island's main customers, the shipyards of New York, closed down or cut back, and White and his stockholder associates, personally liable for losses, were forced to borrow large amounts from banks in Buffalo, Manhattan, and Boston. White was not overly concerned. The downturn could not last, and White Haven would resume its highly profitable operations. He had at last found a wife, evidently at the Maverick House; and in December 1837, he married Mrs. Mary Matthews, a steamboat captain's widow. Upon receiving the news, his daughter Caroline Webster, in Illinois, sighed and told her husband, "I hope she will make him a happy and contented man, for he has been very uneasy for a long time."[24]

White had built a wonderful house on White's Island. Beachwater, as they named it, overlooked a formal garden that took in an Indian burial mound. People came from miles around to stare at the grand foursquare mansion and its beautiful grounds. That summer, the Whites resided at Beachwater and Stephen did some amateur archaeology upriver, exhuming part of the frame of an old French warship. He sent for his handicapped brother, Francis, who came to live with them. White's Island became an oasis for the happy couple, a bastion of pleasant unreality.

Stephen's son, Joseph, twenty-four, returned to Boston to confer with his father's business manager about the difficulties of the timber company. The economy was now depressed, and East Boston's galas were held no more. Along the shoreline, as quiet as in the days of Noddle's Island, White's shipyards were still only empty beaches. By June, Joseph was residing at the Maverick House, but something happened. Evidently he suffered a breakdown and entered McLean Hospital for treatment. In the first week of July 1838, as Bostonians celebrated the anniversary of independence, Joseph White killed himself.[25]

Perhaps as a way of remembering Joseph, Stephen White engaged in one more in a lifetime of idealistic endeavors. The Erie Canal had attracted many runaway boys and orphans who drifted up and down the canal and the river, hustling and stealing, without homes or families to look after them. In Buffalo, a group of citizens and clergy founded an asylum for the canal boys, and in the fall of 1839, Stephen White gave them a site on Grand Island for the Institution for Destitute Boys, a success for many years.[26]

The Depression continued, and the mills of White Haven lay silent. White did not return to Massachusetts, where creditors sold off the timber company's property in East Boston. He spent much of his time in Buffalo, trying to arrange financing. His health was gone, and he suspected he was dying. From Beachwater, at ten o'clock on the night of January 26, 1840, he wrote to Daniel Webster to relate his latest illness-related encounter with absurdity—he had left his hotel in Buffalo and retreated to his island mansion "just as this most savage winter set in, since which snows, blows, and storms have been the order of the day. . . ." He was very sick with liver disease, and the physicians had prepared two remedies. One was iron powder, to be drunk with brandy and water; the other was a vial of toxic chemicals to be dissolved in water and applied in a compress to his side. By accident, he mixed the toxins into his brandy and drank it down—not unlike Hawthorne's Niagara potion maker.

"The dose I took made wonderfully good punch, and on telling my wife what an agreeable beverage the doctors had prescribed, she was horrified at my mistake and sent off express to Buffalo for my physician. Meantime, my appetite, of which I had not the slightest experience for six weeks, revisited me; the vomiting, which had constantly followed the taking of food, left me; and here I am, waiting the event, and employing myself in my nightgown, writing to you, my dear sir, perhaps the last scrawl I shall ever indite."

As with Captain Joseph White, poisoning would not kill him. In the spring of 1840, however, he received the news that his brother John had died at Boston and his mother, Phebe, at Lowell. And then the last of the East Boston Timber Company blew down in a high wind of lawsuits and foreclosures.

Stephen and Mary returned to the Maverick House by December. Having set aside his ambitions and surrendered his hopes for a great shipbuilding enterprise, Stephen was amazed to find a thriving shipyard on the site of his East Boston lumberyard. Samuel Hall had already built and launched the fine ship *Akbar,* 460 tons burthen, commissioned by a merchant for use in the China trade. Hall now had other vessels up on the stocks, with fair hopes for continued operations.[27]

By the spring of 1841, the country's economy was in recovery, but things continued dismal for White. His fifty-one-year-old brother, Francis, had died at Beachwater in February. Stephen saw no end to his problems. Illness plagued him, and financial difficulties carried him away from Boston. By summer he was in New York City, talking to bankers, perhaps consulting liver specialists, perhaps just taking treatments of laudanum. On August 10, he died, aged fifty-four; and the big-city newspapers noted the passing of Stephen White, Esq., "formerly an eminent merchant of Salem, Massachusetts."

White's widow, Mary, retreated to Beachwater and would live there for many years. It is not clear how much he had saved from the wreckage of the timber company. In New York, he had sheltered some property; in Massachusetts, his entire estate came to $55, most of it in fifteen hundred unbound copies of the first edition of *A Memoir of the Life of Daniel Webster*. In his will, he gave everything at White's Island to Mary and all the rest to his three daughters, with a few exceptions: to Daniel Webster's wife, Caroline, he devised his signet ring, which she had given him; and to Daniel he gave his musket and fowling pieces—mementos of good times spent gunning together with their sons.

Stephen made a final bequest: "To evince the deep affection and high veneration which I entertain for my late benefactor Joseph White Esq. of Salem, Massachusetts, I hereby direct my executors to appropriate and expend a sum not less than five hundred dollars for the erection and construction of an appropriate monument in his memory at Mount Auburn in the town of Cambridge, Massachusetts, with a suitable but simple inscription commemorative of his virtues and the time and manner of his melancholy fate."

Stephen White had dared greatly in linking the resources of the frontier and the money and skills of the East. He came very close to achieving his vision of building a merchant fleet that would dominate global commerce for America as Salem once had in the days of neutral trade. Like many other highfliers of that period, he had been brought low by the nation's financial collapse—the very same that he had predicted to Senator Webster.

The moment was wrong, but it turned out that White had not been mistaken in his ambitions. Nine years later, as bands played for jubilant crowds, the builder Donald McKay launched from his shipyard the first of the magnificent clipper ships—*Flying Cloud, Great Republic, Daniel Webster, Chariot of Fame, Sovereign of the Seas,* and many others—that would be the wonders of the age and the pride of the nation. Moving out from East Boston under towering masts and acres of canvas, they were the largest, fastest, and finest vessels ever to sail on the oceans of the world.

ACKNOWLEDGMENTS

A book has many midwives. To all librarians everywhere, I extend sympathy and gratitude, and especially to Kathy Flynn of the J. D. Phillips Library and to Aimee Primeaux, formerly of the Massachusetts Historical Society. Thank you, people of Salem and Boston, for your excellent libraries, and thanks to Mystic Seaport for digitizing the Salem Crew Lists and to Danny Vickers for his work in maritime history and for bringing the Crew Lists to my attention.

Thanks also to Google Books and other digitizers of old volumes and newspapers, by whom I have been spared thousands of miles, dollars, and hours. To the folks at Cornerstone Books in Salem, now defunct, thanks for your noble efforts and hospitality, and to Maggi and Jim Smith-Dalton, musical and historical prodigies, blessings for interest and companionship. To Racket Shreve and Ellen Booth, many thanks for your talent and creativity; and to Ned Schimminger of the Historical Society of the Tonawandas, to Michael J. Tucker, blogger and teacher extraordinaire, and to Robert Leonard and Pat Gruttemeyer, White descendants, thanks for kindness and encouragement.

To Saunders Robinson, editor, thanks for your generosity. To Tris Coburn, exemplary literary agent, thanks for bearing with me through skull fractures, flaming chassis, weather takedowns, and flying jibes. Joel Ariaratnam, thanks for seeing the big picture. And to Pete Wolverton, Peter Joseph, and Margaret Smith at Thomas Dunne Books, many thanks for keeping the project on track.

Finally, I thank my sister Molly and my mother for unflagging enthusiasm. And I thank my wife Vicki and our children for love and patience during the course of a long voyage.

ENDNOTES

PREFACE

1 Malcolm Gladwell, *Outliers: The Story of Success* (Boston: Little, Brown & Company, 2008), 61.
2 The early U.S. federal government had no presence in the Orient. In 1786 Congress turned away both an English merchant, John Wingrove, who proposed the formation of an American East India Company, and John O'Donnell, a merchant of Baltimore who wished to establish commercial treaties abroad. Congress decided that trade in the Orient was entirely a matter of private enterprise to be conducted with enough prudence that federal resources would not have to be devoted to protection or to reprisals if things went wrong. So it remained for decades, except for the occasional appointments of expatriate American merchants as consuls in a few ports.
3 John Crawfurd, *History of the Indian Archipelago*, volume III (Edinburgh: Archibald Constable & Co., 1820), 252.

I: AT WAR

1 In June 1814, Bentley noted the close-in cruising of a frigate and ship-of-the-line *HMS Bulwark*, seventy-four guns, and the burning of about twenty American coasting vessels. William Bentley, *The Diary of William Bentley*, volume IV (Salem: The Essex Institute, 1914), entries June 9, 15, 1814.
2 In May 1814, Nathaniel Silsbee, Robert Stone, and Stone's nephew Andrew Dunlap departed on a meandering journey to Washington, D.C., and other points south and west, per Bentley's *Diary*, May 30, 1814.
3 Salem's great wealth was generally conceded in the newspapers of the day, and was related to the duties on foreign trade tallied at the Custom House. Salem had a population of about 13,000; Greater Salem, consisting of the contiguous harbor towns of Marblehead, Salem, and Beverly, had a population of more than 20,000.
4 Boston's voters had just passed a similar resolution.
5 Leverett Saltonstall, speech to Federalists during War of 1812; in 1819, Judge Joseph Story would cite this concept in the case of *U.S. v. Rice*, 4 Wheaton, 276.
6 Bentley's *Diary*, Jan. 28, 1813.
7 The Whites' brig *Mary & Eliza,* built as a freighter in the happy days of neutral trade, was also pressed into service; trading in France when war was declared, Captain John White, the owners' brother, had her refitted at Cherbourg as a sixteen-gun privateer. With goods in the hold and a

fifty-man crew he set sail in November 1812 and soon encountered a British naval vessel. After an exchange of fire, White dumped some cannon, pressed on all sail, and pulled away. John White took no English prizes, but he did perform a rescue when, a few days from home, he came upon the mastless hulk of the Connecticut vessel *Carolina,* with her crew just barely alive after forty days adrift. White saved them and arrived in Salem in mid-January with a rich cargo consigned to his uncle, Captain Joseph White.

8   Caleb Foote, *"Autobiography of Caleb Foote"* in Mary W. Tileston, editor, *Caleb and Mary Wilder Foote: Reminiscences and Letters* (Boston and New York: Houghton Mifflin Co., 1918), 307–8.

9   Bentley's *Diary*, Sept 11, 1814.

10   Ibid., Sept. 15, 19, 1814.

11   Per Bentley's *Diary*, B. W. Crowninshield's appointment was first cleared with Joseph Story, who evidently had veto power. Bentley disliked Story, and noted that he took over Crowninshield's office as president of the Merchants Bank of Salem in January 1815 upon Crowninshield's departure for Washington.

12   Richard Crowninshield's bankruptcy lawsuit, *Sturges v. Crowninshield,* eventually became the test case for a national bankruptcy law.

13   Sarah Savage may have been inspired by the opening of the first local textile factory by Gen. Gideon Foster in 1814 in Danvers (now Peabody), Massachusetts.

14   Thomas B. Lovell, "Separate Spheres and Extensive Circles, Sarah Savage's *The Factory Girl* and the Celebration of Industry in Early Nineteenth Century America," *Early American Literature* 31, No. 1 (1996), 1–24.

15   Joseph Story to Nathaniel Williams, letter of Feb. 22, 1815, William W. Story, editor, *Life & Letters of Joseph Story* (Boston: Charles C. Little & James Brown, 1851), 254.

2: THE LOST PRINCE

1   In shipping, a ton was not a measure of weight but of volume, forty cubic feet.

2   For ethnicity and race of sailors, see Salem Crew Lists at Mystic Seaport, The Museum of America and The Sea; see also William Bentley's *List of Parish Deaths.*

3   Caroline H. King, *When I Lived In Salem* (Brattleboro, Vt.: Stephen Daye Press, 1937), 30.

4   A supercargo sailed on a merchant vessel as the owner's business agent for sale and acquisition of cargoes.

5   Name pronounced *Bough-ditch,* not *Bo-ditch.*

6   Nathaniel Bowditch's work was never surpassed; today, after many revisions, it remains the standard guide to navigation and seamanship, published by the U.S. Navy.

7   Bentley's *Diary*, Sept. 23, 1788.

8   John D. Whidden, *Ocean Life in the Old Sailing Ship Days* (Boston, Little, Brown, & Co., 1908), 2.

9   Richard J. Cleveland, *A Narrative of Voyages and Commercial Enterprises, Vol. One* (Cambridge, Mass.: John Owen, 1842), x.

10   Joseph Story opinion in *Brown et. al. v. Lull*, Charles Sumner, *Reports of Cases Argued and Determined in the Circuit Court of the United States for the First Circuit, vol. II* (Boston: Charles C. Little & James Brown, 1837), 449.

11   Amasa Delano, *A Narrative of Voyages and Travels* (Boston, for the author, 1817), 30.

12   John H. Reinoehl, "Some Remarks on the American Trade: Jacob Crowninshield to James Madison 1806," *The William and Mary Quarterly* (third series, 16), 83–118.

13   Ibid.

14   Of the many accounts of Salem's early trade with Sumatra, the only reliable one is that of James W. Gould, "Sumatra—America's Pepperpot, 1784–1873," *Essex Institute Historical Collections* (92, 1956), 83–152, 203–251, 295–346.

15   The Atjehnese standard term for Caucasian visitors was "white devil."

16 George Nichols's difficulties in finding Muckie—another example of the uncharted world that Bowditch tried to describe correctly—are mentioned in Jeremiah N. Reynolds, *Journal of a Voyage of the United States Frigate Potomac* (New York: Harper & Brothers, 1835), 208.

17 George Nichols in Martha Nichols, editor, *A Salem Shipmaster and Merchant* (Boston: Four Seas Press, 1921), 58.

18 Ibid., 55.

19 Now Djkarta, Indonesia.

20 Franz Bessell was the older brother of Friedrich Bessel (1784–1843), a top astronomer of Europe, well known to Nathaniel Bowditch.

21 Reference to brick buildings in *Salem Gazette,* Feb. 4, 1806. Salem had about two thousand buildings, of which about fifty were built entirely in brick.

22 See Ebenezer Francis's advertisement in the *Repertory* (Boston), Sept. 22, 1807.

23 Joseph Story in William W. Story, editor, *Life & Letters of Joseph Story* (Boston: Charles C. Little & James Brown, 1851), 29.

24 Joseph Story to William Fettyplace, Feb. 25, 1808, W. W. Story ed., *Life and Letters*, 165–66.

25 Jefferson considered Story a traitor to the Republican Party. See John P. Foley, editor, *The Jeffersonian Cyclopedia* (New York & London: Funk & Wagnalls, 1900), 290, 840.

26 Marianne C. D. Silsbee, *A Half Century In Salem* (Boston: Houghton Mifflin & Co., 1888), 15.

3: WHITE HEAT

1 John Crawfurd, *History of the Indian Archipelago, vol. III* (Edinburgh & London, 1820), 278.

2 Ibid., 341–43.

3 Joseph Story, author of 1816 Salem memorial to Congress, quoted in Henry Lee, "No. 11, The Inequality of the High Duty System," pp. 10–11, in *An Exposition of Evidence in Support of the Memorial to Congress* (Boston: Boston Press, 1832).

4 Thomas Morris's report quoted in H. Niles, editor, *Niles' Weekly Register*, vol. XI, issue of Jan. 25, 1817 (Baltimore, editor, 1817), 366.

5 Joseph Story, *The Miscellaneous Writings* (Boston: James Munroe & Co., 1835), 495–510.

6 Bentley's *Diary*, Jan. 22, 27, 1816.

7 Salem was the only town in America in which the majority of the traditional congregations had converted to Unitarianism.

8 Sarah A. Emery, *Memories of a Nonagenarian* (Newburyport, author, 1879), 300–09.

9 John Crawfurd, *Indian Archipelago, vol. III*, 518.

10 Two Boston firms, T. H. Perkins & Co., and Langdon & Coffin, had agents in Smyrna. The Perkins firm, which also dealt in Bengal opium and had an office in Canton, was engaged in the larger business of the so-called Boston Concern, a group of several merchants whose key London agent was Samuel Williams, originally of Salem, cousin of Timothy Pickering.

11 Tyler Dennett, *Americans in Eastern Asia* (New York: Macmillan Co., 1922), 68–73; also Jacques M. Downs, "American Merchants and the China Opium Trade, 1800–1840," in *The Business History Review* (42, 1968), also R. J. Cleveland, *A Narrative, vol. I (1842), v.*

12 Richard J. Cleveland, *A Narrative of Voyages and Commercial Enterprises,* vol. II, 83.

13 Ibid., Richard J. Cleveland alludes to the "animation and hilarity always observable with seamen when on the point of arriving home," 213.

14 Francis B. C. Bradlee, "The Steamboat Massachusetts and the Beginnings of Steam Navigation in Boston Bay," *Essex Institute Historical Collections, vol. L, No. 3* (Salem, Essex Institute, 1914), 1–20.

15 In fact a sea serpent, or plesiosaur, about eighty feet long with a horselike head, appeared frequently on upper Salem Bay during the summer of 1817, per Bentley's *Diary,* newspapers, and eyewitnesses. It eluded all attempts at capture.

16 David L. Ferguson, *Cleopatra's Barge: the Crowninshield Story* (Boston: Little, Brown, 1976).

17 Bentley's *Diary*, April 8, 1819.

18 See Daniel Vickers with Vince Walsh, *Young Men & The Sea* (New Haven & London: Yale University Press, 2005), 187-89.

19 The Medici trope was not rare among American merchants, influenced by William Roscoe of Liverpool, a merchant who had published a very popular biography of Cosimo de Medici, the Renaissance merchant and art patron.

20 Bentley's *Diary*, Nov. 14, 18, 1818.

21 William Bentley, *Essex Register,* Oct. 17, 1818.

22 James T. De Kay, *Chronicles of the Frigate Macedonian* (New York: W.W. Norton, 1995), 172.

23 Brig *Mary & Eliza* cleared for India Oct. 13, 1818; arrived Salem Aug. 12, 1819, 113 days from Mingin, Sumatra, with 2800 piculs pepper to S. White Esq. & others, per *Essex Register* Aug. 14, 1819.

24 Brig *Eliza & Mary,* Proctor, went to sea for East India from Charleston Oct. 17, 1818, per New York *Daily Advertiser* Oct. 26, 1818; she would return to New York in late September 1819, and arrive 8 days later on Oct. 7, 1819, at Salem, Captain J. Ropes, per *Salem Gazette,* Oct. 8, 1819.

25 *Essex Register,* June 18, 1817 (*Albatross* cleared); Ibid., Aug. 30, 1817, sailed from Isle of May July 22; wreck described, *Salem Gazette,* Oct. 13, 16, 1818, Essex *Register* Oct. 14, 1818, New York *Daily Advertiser* and American *Daily Advertiser* (Phila.), both Oct. 19, 1818.

26 *Britannia* was refitted and sailed Dec. 14, 1819 for Europe, Captain Abiel Wardwell, first mate Nathaniel Ingersoll, second mate John Beckford, 20, Mary's son, per Mystic Seaport records.

27 *Wallace* sailed Dec. 8, 1818, for India, Captain Joseph L. Lee, mate James Brown, Jr., 46, second mate Joseph Cheever, 22, and seventeen-man crew, per Salem Crew Lists at Mystic Seaport. Frederick Story had sailed March 24, 1818, on *Adaline,* Capt. Joseph Felt, for Europe, Ibid. *Franklin* sailed Jan. 1, 1819, for India, Captain John White, boy John R. Becket, crew of twelve; Aug. 1820 Christopher Babbidge, Salem Justice of the Peace, took testimony that three men had died and three had shipped in their places; she arrived Salem August 31, 1820, per Captain John White.

4: PANIC

1 Salem Moral Society report.

2 Bentley's *Diary,* vol. IV, June 15, 1819.

3 On April 24, 1820, Nathaniel Silsbee made his speech in the Revision of Tariff debate in House of Representatives. *Annals of Congress, 16th Congress, 1st session*, 1987–1997.

4 Bentley's *Diary*, Feb. 13, 1819.

5 Many years later, Story would preside at the famous *Amistad* case, upholding the actions of some Africans who killed their seagoing captors and gained their freedom by sailing to a northern port.

6 Committee members were Joseph White, Joseph Peabody, B. W. Crowninshield and Pickering Dodge, Dudley L. Pickman and Willard Peele, with Nathaniel Hooper from Marblehead and Thomas Stephens from Beverly.

7 Salem's inbound Sumatra trade in 1819 consisted of the arrival of six vessels, three of them owned by White.

8 James Brown to Stephen White, letter of Dec. 24, 1820, from Etaples, France, printed in Boston *Daily Advertiser,* March 16, 1821. Other newspaper accounts of the wreck of the *Wallace,* given earlier, were inaccurate. Joseph L. Lee's brother-in-law, General Henry A. S. Dearborn, had a monument erected at Lee's grave in France.

9 Josiah Quincy's Report on Pauper Laws would be published by the state early in 1821.

10 Henry Baldwin, speech in April 1820 introducing tariff bill, *Annals of Congress, 16th Congress, 1st session*, 1978.

11 Anonymous, *Biographical Sketch of the Celebrated Salem Murderer . . . by a Resident of Danvers* (Boston: for the author, 1830), a pamphlet by one "has known him and his confederates for many years."

12 This John Beckford was the cousin of the John Beckford, son of Mrs. Mary Beckford; nine of the ten crewmen resided in Salem.

13 During the period that the U.S. Custom House in Salem was commissioned and built, the Port's Customs duties on imports declined from $650,369 (1818) to $455,070 (1819), out of total U.S. Customs revenues of $21.83 million (1818) and $17.12 million (1819), per "Memorial of Chamber of Commerce of City of New York to Congress," 1821, and "The Revenue" by the House Committee of Ways and Means, 1821, in *American State Papers, Class III, Finance, Vol. III, December 1815 to May 1822* (Washington, D.C., Gales and Seaton, 1834, 641, 664).

14 Bentley's *Diary*, May 31, 1812.

15 In his speech of April 1820, in the House of Representatives, Henry Baldwin gave a figure of more than $850,000 in forfeited duty-credit bonds in 1818 in New York, whereas in Salem the figure was $4,400. *Annals of Congress, 16th Congress, 1st session*, 1978.

16 Nathaniel Silsbee's speech, *Annals of Congress, 16th Congress, 1st session*, 1987–1997.

17 Cleveland Amory, *The Proper Bostonians* (New York: E. P. Dutton Co., 1947), 38.

5: LOST AT SEA

1 Nathaniel Hathorne (1804–1864) adopted the surname Hawthorne in 1826 or so, before he became a published author. In Salem, the surname was usually pronounced Har-thorn.

2 See theatre story and advertisements, April 1820, Salem newspapers.

3 Nathaniel Hawthorne, quoted in Julian Hawthorne, *Nathaniel Hawthorne . . .* , Vol. I, 108.

4 Essex *Register,* Oct. 25, 1820.

5 Ibid., Oct. 28, 1820.

6 Joseph E. Sprague in Essex *Register*, Feb. 20, 1823. Dr. Gideon Barstow, Republican, was eventually elected.

7 Story and Webster correctly assessed the conservatism of the electorate, for the Massachusetts voters turned down a few of the convention's reform-oriented recommendations.

8 John White, *History of a Voyage to the China Sea* (Boston: Wells and Lilly, 1823).

9 Four if one counts the *Merrimack Packet,* which he may have owned (newspapers indicate that he did, but there is no record in A. Frank Hitchings, *Ship Registers of the District of Salem & Beverly* (Salem: Essex Institute, 1906), 121.

10 Brigantine *Washington*, 178 tons burthen, built New Hampshire 1800; registered Nov. 2, 1816 to J. J. Knapp, James C. King & W. Shepard Gray, Captain Jonathan Skerry (Isaac Knapp also master), per A. F. Hitchings, *Ship Registers*, 39.

11 Schooner *Fame*, 95 tons burthen, built Duxbury 1801, registered for foreign trade in 1804 to Joseph White and Joseph White Jr., Captain Joseph Felt; registered Nov. 4, 1805 to J. J. Knapp, owner & master., etc., lost 1825 at St. Pierre, West Indies, per Ibid., 39.

12 Joh. B. Von Spix and C. F. Philip Von Martius, *Travels in Brazil, 1817–1820*, vol. I (London: Longman, Hurst, Rees, Orme, Brown, and Green, 1824), 136.

13 Anonymous, *The Modern Traveller,* vol. IV (Boston: Wells & Lilly, 1830), 134.

14 Captain John Beckford's letter of July 25, 1821, quoted in *Essex Register.*

15 Ibid.

16 Bentley's *Diary*, May 27, 1819, "Several of our friends have returned from Siam. Voyages have been made before, but the enterprising spirit of our countrymen will search anywhere for commerce. They are cautious in relating their first adventures, as commerce they think overdone by the many who embark to every port in which voyages are successful . . ."

17 *Essex Register* Nov. 28, 1821, elegy of Mathias J. L. Bessell.

18 John Crawfurd, *Journal of an Embassy from the Governor-General of India to the Courts of Siam and Cochin China, vol. I, second edition* (London: Henry Colburn & Richard Bentley, 1830), 112.

19 Ibid., vol. II, 160–67.

6: THE PROPHET

1 Anonymous, *Biographical Sketch of the Celebrated Salem Murderer . . . by a Resident of Danvers* (Boston, for the author, 1830).

2 Stephen M. Clark, of Newburyport, 16, was convicted of arson and executed in Salem in 1821.

3 Henry Whipple, "History of the Salem and Danvers Association for the Detection of Thieves and Robbers" in *Essex Institute Historical Collections* (8, 1866), 65–72.

4 Richard Crowninshield Jr. on brig *Persia,* sailing Sept. 1822, per Mystic Seaport Salem Crew Lists. In signing the ship's papers, he lied about his age and claimed residence in New York.

5 Among English speakers, the Italian port of Livorno was known as Leghorn.

6 *Persia* voyaged from Salem August 1822 to Mingin, Sumatra, loading pepper there in March 1823, in June passing the Cape of Good Hope and St. Helena, then at Leghorn about July, 1823; thence evidently back to Sumatra and on to Salem arriving July 1824, per newspaper reports June 18, July 22, Aug. 18, Nov. 7, 1823.

7 East Chelmsford/Lowell described in *Salem Gazette,* August 13, 1824.

8 Ibid.

9 For New Hampshire Iron Factory, see James L. Garvin, *Chronology of Development of the New Hampshire Iron Factory Company From 1805 to 1884* (Concord: New Hampshire Division of Historical Resources, 1994); also, see Massachusetts Historical Society papers, Joshua Goodale pledges two shares in New Hampshire Iron Factory as collateral on note from Joseph White, 1811. The plant was located near a vein of iron at Franconia, N.H., in the White Mountains.

10 Francis B. C. Bradlee, "The Salem Iron Factory," in *Essex Institute Historical Collections*, vol. 54 (Salem, Essex Institute, 1918), 97–114.

11 Harrison Gray Otis to George Harrison, letter 21 March 1823, quoted in Samuel E. Morison, *The Life and Letters of Harrison Gray Otis, Federalist,* vol. II (Boston and New York: Houghton Mifflin, 1913), 289.

12 Bentley's *Diary,* 1818, reference to possibility of a tidal mill for industry at Collins Cove.

13 Vote on dam proposal "indefinitely postponed" per Salem Town Records, March 17, 1823.

7: WHITE HOPE

1 Robert S. Rantoul of Beverly reported that John Quincy Adams's candidacy had been launched at the Whites' Cherry Hill Farm at a meeting of money men and politicos. R.S. Rantoul, "Some Notes on Wenham Pond," in *Essex Institute Historical Collections,* vol. VI (Salem: Essex Institute, 1864), 151.

2 In Salem, imports dropped from $2.007 million (1821) to $1.767 million (1824), and exports shrank from $2.922 million (1821) to $1.893 million (1824). *Salem Gazette* Aug. 9, 1825, commercial statistics for 1821–1824.

3 Story and Beckford seafaring data from Salem Crew Lists at Mystic Seaport.

4 *Salem Observer,* Feb. 14, 1824.

5 Daniel Vickers & Vince Walsh, *Young Men & The Sea,* 174–77.

6 Vessel count as of January 1823, per Joseph B. Felt, *Annals of Salem, volume II* (Salem: W. & S. B. Ives, 1849), 349.

7 "A Hamiltonian," *Salem Gazette,* Feb. 18, 1823.

8 Writer to *Salem Gazette,* Feb. 25, 1823. In New York, a Workingman's party was making the case for more direct political representation of the interests of the working class; and by 1825 in Boston the various types of artisan had organized to push for economic and political power per *Columbian Centinel,* April 20, 23, 1825.

9 Anne Royall, *Sketches of History, Life, and Manners in the United States by A Traveller* (New Haven, for the author, 1826), 363.

10 Harrison Gray Otis quoted in Robert A. McCaughey, *Josiah Quincy, 1772–1864, The Last Federalist* (Cambridge, Mass.: Harvard University Press, 1974), 94.

11 Ibid., 117.

12 Newspaper references to the many losses of vessels in 1823–24.

13 "Timothy Pickering" in *Essex Register*, Oct. 28, 1824.

14 The five merchants announced their defection on May 15, 1824.

15 John Andrew served as straw in May 1824 (when the newspapers announced the purchase) and conveyed the property to the Hall Corporation in July.

16 *Salem Gazette* Oct. 22, 1824, 4.

17 Ibid., Aug. 10, 1824, "Mr. Dixon's Steam Apparatus." Joseph Dixon, of Marblehead, who had demonstrated his steam apparatus in Lynn in February, had since moved to Salem to work with Frank Peabody on steam technology.

18 *Annals of the Lyceum of Natural History of New York City*, vol. V (New York: H. Bailliere, 1852), xx.

19 *Salem Gazette* July 13, 1824, Female Charitable Society, Justice's Court.

20 Lynn H. Parsons, "'A Perpetual Harrow Upon My Feelings': John Quincy Adams and The American Indian," *The New England Quarterly* (46, Sept. 1973) from 348.

21 *Salem Gazette* July 27, Aug. 5, 1824. One Salem publisher decided that the success of the textile industry called for a second edition of Sarah Savage's ten-year-old Salem novel, *The Factory Girl*.

22 Which, many years later, would make it possible for one to "kiss the lips that kissed the lips that kissed the lips of the girl who kissed La Fayette."

23 *Eliza* arrived Salem Aug. 17, 1824 from Cronstadt, per *Salem Gazette* Aug. 17, 1824.

24 Susan S. Bean, *Yankee India* (Salem: Peabody Essex Museum; Chidambaram: Mapin Publishing, 2001), 183–184; also, Oct. 22, 1824 *Salem Gazette* for arrival of *Emerald*, Captain J. B. Briggs.

25 See *Essex Register* Feb. 21, 28, 1825, and March 14, 1825.

26 Henry Pickering (1781–1838) published two books of well-reviewed serious verse, in 1822 and 1824; a bachelor merchant, he lost his money by 1826 and eventually moved to Newburgh, New York.

27 Philip C. F. Smith, *East India Marine Hall: 1824–1974* (Salem: Peabody Museum of Salem, 1974), pamphlet.

8: CELEBRATIONS

1 *Salem Gazette*, July 18, 1825.

2 Salem Mill Dam Corporation Report of 1826, 3. Among the underwriters were (in order) John Andrew, Robert Stone, Stephen Phillips, Joseph Story, Stephen White, John H. Andrews, Gideon Barstow; and it also included Wm. F. Gardner, J. W. Treadwell, S. C. Phillips, Wm. Fettyplace, J. S. Cabot, F. H. Story, J. E. Sprague, et. al.

3 Frederick Howes, also appointed, had dropped out early.

4 *Salem Gazette*, August 16, 1825.

5 Ibid., Nov. 15, 18, 1825.

6 *Salem Gazette*, Aug. 1, 1825, reporting on Stone's visit to Boston and on "Riots at Boston."

7 *Salem Gazette*, July 15, 1825.

8 Ibid., account of the earlier bacchanal at Mumford's and police action.

9 Edward G. Parker, *Reminiscences of Rufus Choate* (New York: Mason Bros., 1860), 38–9.

10 June 1825 letter of Mary Williams explaining that "many have left (St. Peter's Church) and joined the new society of Mr. Colman among them both Mr. Whites and their families and connections and also Mr & Mrs. Johonnot," *Essex Institute Historical Collections*, vol. 36 (Salem: Essex Institute, 1900), 239.

11 Ibid., 239–42.

12 *Essex Institute Historical Collections*, vol. 74.

13 Ibid.

14 Henry White Jr., 48, having lost his wife and only child, died insolvent on Feb. 6, 1826.

9: JUBILEE

1 Anonymous, *Biographical Sketch of the Celebrated Salem Murderer . . . by a Resident of Dan-vers* (Boston, for the author, 1830), pamphlet.

2 The liability limitation held that individuals were not answerable for the company's debts until manufactures were actually established there, after which the individuals would not be liable for any longer than one year after they shall have ceased to be members, so that if the capital stock were to be paid in, the individual is protected "from the serious consequences to which he is exposed by the general laws" respecting manufacturing corporations; see John Pickering et al, *Report of Committee on Practicability and Expediency . . .*, 15.

3 Ibid., 17.

4 Ibid., 19.

5 Committee Report of March 29, 1826, *Report of the Committee Appointed to Enquire into The Practicability and Expediency of Establishing Manufactures in Salem* (Salem: Salem Mill Dam Corporation, 1826), 13 Ibid., 20.

6 Ibid.

7 *Essex Register*, Jan. 23, 1826, quoting Boston *Daily Advertiser*, quoting a writer to the *Register*.

8 July 10, 1826 letter of Mary Williams, *Essex Institute Historical Collections*, vol. 36, 242.

9 White's reference to Mary Beckford as "weak" in letter to Daniel Webster, Charles M. Wiltse, and David G. Allen, editors, *The Papers of Daniel Webster: Correspondence, 1830* Ibid., *1834*, vol. 3 (Hanover, Mass.: University Press of New England, 1977), 90–91.

10 Moses Endicott's report, "Shipping News" in *Essex Register* June 26, 1826.

11 George Nichols, *A Salem Shipmaster and Merchant*, 94–96.

12 Susan N. Pulsifer, *Witch's Breed: The Peirce-Nichols Family of Salem* (Cambridge, Massachusetts: Dresser, Chapman & Grimes, 1967).

13 George Dangerfield, *The Awakening of American Nationalism* (New York: Harper & Row, 1965) 149–62, 260–65.

14 Nathaniel Hawthorne, quoted in Julian Hawthorne, *Nathaniel Hawthorne and His Wife*, vol. I, 96.

15 Elizabeth Hawthorne, quoted in Ibid., 124.

16 "The Ocean" in *Salem Gazette* Aug. 26, 1825, identified by George P. Lathrop, Hawthorne's son-in-law, as an early Hawthorne poem.

17 Dick Crowninshield quoted in Anonymous, *Biographical Sketch of the Celebrated Salem Murderer . . .*, a pamphlet by one "has known him and his confederates for many years." The accuracy of the story is impossible to confirm, as is the time-span in which Dick was in Charleston.

10: DREAMS OF NEW BLISS

1 Needham was evidently not his real surname, per John C. R. Palmer Jr., *Explanation* (Boston, for the author, 1831), 74.

2 Ibid., 14.

3 *Salem Gazette*, Oct 3, 1826.

4 1036 shares to 581.

5 *Salem Gazette*, Oct. 20, 1826, also *Boston Newsletter* Oct. 28, 1826.

6 Testimony of Joseph Fisher regarding Palmer and Crowninshield at Lafayette Coffee House.

7 Joseph Fisher, 17, of Salem, was imprisoned in Dec. 1827 (or so) on a four-year sentence for larceny. Per the prison parson, Fisher, "an interesting young man in his appearance; his demeanor modest and respectful," at 16 "ran away with two other lads of the town; went to Portland where he stayed 6 months till his father went and brought him home. Continued wild, run after bad women and gambled, was profane, and finally committed a larceny which sent him here." Philip F. Gura, editor, *Buried from the World* (Boston: Massachusetts Historical Society, 2001), 89.

8 *Essex Register*, Aug. 23, Sept. 10, 1827; *Salem Gazette* Sept. 11, 1827.

9 Dixon eventually created the standard pencil, still produced by the Dixon-Ticonderoga company.

10 Joseph Story to Bushrod Washington, letter July 4, 1827, from W. W. Story, ed., *Life and Letters*, 571.

11 Joseph Story to Daniel Webster, letter June 10, 1827, Story Papers.

12 Joseph Story, poem titled *Reflections On Life*, 1827, from W. W. Story, ed., *Life and Letters*, 572.

13 *Salem Gazette*, Sept. 21, 1827.

14 Timothy Flint, letter to Rev. James Flint from Cincinnati, Sept. 1825, in Timothy Flint, *Recollections of The Last Ten Years* (Boston: Cummings, Hilliard & Co., 1826), 382–9.

15 Ship *Suffolk,* 314 tons burthen, had sailed March 3, 1827, owned by Pickering Dodge, William Manning, Samuel & Timothy Endicott; she was sold 1828 at Rio de Janeiro; see Mystic Seaport for Salem vessels and F. A. Hitchings' *Ship Registers*.

16 Reference to abuses of Europeans toward the Atjehnese in the pepper trade were evidently common; American abuses are acknowledged (and justified) in accounts by Charles M. Endicott and others.

17 Joe Knapp's failings as a captain and factor are mentioned ("he wanted capacity in his profession") in Samuel L. Knapp, *A Memoir of the Life of Daniel Webster* (Boston: Stimpson & Clapp, 1831), 79. Stephen White paid for publication of the book.

11: TWILIGHT

1 See Gale & Seaton's *Register of Debates in Congress,* May 9, 1828, pp. 750–61.

2 *Salem Gazette*, May 31, 1828.

3 Miss Clemmons' poem, BR/821/C62 in collection of J. Duncan Phillips Library, Peabody Essex Museum, Salem, Mass.

4 D. Hamilton Hurd, *The History of Essex County, Mass.*, vol. I (Philadelphia: J. W. Lewis & Co., 1888), 16.

5 *Salem Gazette*, June 24, 1828.

6 Ibid., July 25, 1828.

7 Ibid., Sept. 12, 1828.

8 *Historical Sketch of the Salem Lyceum* (Salem: Salem Gazette, 1879), 15–6.

9 L. Lincoln, N. Hale, S. White, et. al., *Report to Massachusetts Legislature Jan. 16, 1829 of Board of Directors of Internal Improvements of the State of Mass. on the Practicability and Expediency of a Rail-road from Boston to the Hudson River and from Boston to Providence, with Annexed Reports*.

10 Outside of his family, the other Hathornes kept the traditional spelling of their name.

11 Nathaniel Hawthorne, *Fanshawe*, in Norman H. Pearson, editor, *The Complete Novels and Selected Tales of Nathaniel Hawthorne* (New York: The Modern Library, 1937), 14. This is a good self-description at the time.

12 Hawthorne would not write another novel for more than twenty years.

13 Charles W. Upham, editor, *Life of Timothy Pickering*, vol. IV (Boston: Little, Brown & Co., 1873), 470.

14 *Salem Gazette* March 27, 1829.

15 "Veracity" in *Essex Register,* April 1, 1830.

16 Francis B. C. Bradlee, "The Suppression of Piracy in the West Indies, 1820–1832 (continued)," *Essex Institute Historical Collections*, vol. 58 (Salem: Essex Institute, 1922), from p. 297; also Corregan's Feb. 26 statement, printed in the Philadelphia *Gazette* and copied elsewhere, including *The Bee* (New Orleans) for April 1, 1829.

17 Account of farewell dinner to Joseph Story from *Salem Gazette*.

18 See list of foreign trade vessels and corrections, *Salem Gazette*, Jan. 19, 1830; also Ibid., Jan 1, 1828, list of vessels registered for foreign trade. In two years, nine ships had been added, to replace eight sold off, one lost in a wreck, and two broken up as no longer seaworthy. Salem's large fleet of brigs had suffered a major decline—32 disappeared in two years: 13 lost in wrecks, 17

sold, and two broken up. The net loss in brigs between the end of 1827 and the end of 1829 was ten, with an additional net loss of seven large schooners.

19 Fiji trade in Charles S. Osgood and Henry M. Batchelder, *Historical Sketch of Salem* (Salem: Essex Institute, 1879), 168–71.

20 Joseph J. Knapp's voyages taken from Mystic Seaport's collection of Salem Crew Lists and Salem newspapers; see especially *Salem Gazette* for Dec. 19, 1828, Jan. 6, 1829, Sept. 22, 1829.

12: NIGHTFALL

1 *Fifth Annual Report of the Board of managers of the Prison Discipline Society of Boston* (Boston: Prison Discipline Society, 1831), 60; also, White, S., Leland, S., and Sumner, B., Mass. legislative report Jan. 12, 1827, commissioned March 3, 1826, *The Discipline of Prisoners and the Compensation of Officers in the State Prison at Charlestown* (Boston: True & Greene, 1827).

2 Russell Lynes, *The Tastemakers* (New York: Harper & Brothers, 1955), 83.

3 Samuel L. Knapp, *A Memoir of the Life of Daniel Webster*, 179.

4 Massachusetts Historical Society, MS N-1529 White Papers, "I am determined not to put my estate out of my hand," wrote Joseph White.

5 In trial of J. Francis Knapp, testimony of Benjamin White (son of Nicholas).

6 Joseph White, funeral instructions, from Massachusetts Historical Society collections, MS N-1529.

7 February 1830, night at Dick's gambling den, per testimony of Pendergrass, Hatch, and Quiner.

8 Stephen White advertisement in *Salem Gazette*, 6 April 6, 1830; "balsam copavi" in ad means "balsam copaiba," used in making varnishes and medicinally as an expectorant, etc.

9 Nathaniel Hawthorne, "The Hollow of Three Hills," *Salem Gazette*, Nov 12, 1830.

10 John D. Lawson, editor, *American State Trials*, vol. VII (St. Louis: F.H. Thomas Law Book Co., 1917), 616. Joe Knapp told Barstow & Phillips that George Crowninshield had said "he had Palmer locked up in his room about a week—that he had been passing counterfeit money and so forth."

13: THE SALEM MURDER

1 John C. R. Palmer Jr., *Explanation* (Boston: for the author, 1831), 104, 107.

2 Joseph Story to Daniel Webster, letter April 17, 1830, *The Works of Daniel Webster, Correspondence*, vol. VI, 11th edition (Boston: Little, Brown, & Co., 1858), 56–7.

3 Hatch used the alias Hall (under which he was jailed in New Bedford) and Stewart.

4 John C. Quiner was a distant relative of Captain Joseph White's mother.

5 Antony testified that the Crowninshield brothers planned to go to Portland to run a gambling con.

6 Letter of Richard Crowninshield Jr., May 15, 1830, quoted in Dover (NH) *Gazette*, Aug. 3, 1830.

7 Howard A. Bradley and James A. Winans, *Daniel Webster and The Salem Murder* (Columbia, Mo.: Artcraft Press, 1955), 23.

14: CONFESSION

1 John C. R. Palmer Jr., *Explanation*, 105.

2 Benjamin Merrill, "The Murder of Captain Joseph White," *The Works of Daniel Webste*, vol. VI, 48.

3 Nathaniel Hawthorne letter to John S. Dike, Sept. 1, 1830, referring to Mary W. (Beckford) Knapp's attempted suicide soon after the arrest of her husband. Thomas Woodson, L. Neal Smith, Norman H. Pearson, editors, *Nathaniel Hawthorne, The Letters, 1813–1843, vol. 15 of*

the Centenary Edition of the Works of Nathaniel Hawthorne (Columbus: Ohio State Univ. Press, 1984), 207–8.

4 The sequence of Colman's actions comes from his testimony in Joseph J. Knapp Jr.'s Trial.

5 *Salem Gazette,* Aug. 31, 1830 for N. Phippen Knapp's statement.

6 Henry Colman's testimony, Joseph. J. Knapp Jr.'s trial.

7 Several members of the Committee of Vigilance were Colman's parishioners, including the secretary, Stephen C. Phillips.

8 Joe Knapp's first (May 29, 1830) confession, John D. Lawson, editor, *American State Trials,* vol. VII (St. Louis: F.H. Thomas Law Book Co., 1917), 611–4.

9 Ibid., 614–6. Two days later, on May 31, Joe Knapp received a visit from Gideon Barstow and Stephen C. Phillips of the Committee of Vigilance. Without clergyman or lawyer present, they pressed him hard; and he spilled a bit more.

10 Ibid., 598.

11 Ibid., 611.

12 Ibid., 612.

13 Ibid., 616.

15: IMPS OF HELL & DEVILS ROAM

1 John C. R. Palmer Jr.'s testimony, first trial of J. Francis Knapp.

2 "Salem Outrage," *Essex Register,* July 1, 1830, reference to "a most daring, a most infamous, and a disgusting affair."

3 On her next voyage the *Mexican* was attacked by pirates and set on fire but Captain Butman and crew saved themselves and their vessel. Captain Wilkins, in 1837, would be killed with five sailors on board the *Francis* at Sumatra.

4 *Essex Register,* July 1, 1830, *Salem Gazette* July 6, 1830.

5 "Portraits of the Salem Prisoners," *Marblehead Register* Aug. 21, 1830, copying the Massachusetts *Journal.*

6 William H. Gardiner of Boston took the place of the young Salem lawyer Robert Rantoul, who had been Dexter's co-counsel but was not licensed to practice in the Supreme Judicial Court.

7 Aug 6, 1830, letter of Daniel Webster to Joseph Story, *Works of Daniel Webster* (1857), 85.

8 Webster later rewrote and polished his oration, and published it. In books of lawyerly rhetoric well into the twentieth century, his written version was held up as a model of courtroom oratory; and in 1955 two Dartmouth professors of rhetoric published a whole book about the White murder, focused on Webster's performance, *Daniel Webster and The Salem Murder* (Columbia, Mo.: Artcraft Press, 1955).

16: DEATH AFTER DEATH

1 Franklin Dexter's summation, second trial of J. Francis Knapp.

2 Rufus Choate, who had advised Webster during the trial, later admitted that Frank had been found guilty on trumped-up evidence, and that his death was little more than judicial murder.

3 Nathaniel Hawthorne to John S. Dike, letter Sept. 1, 1830, refers to Mary W. (Beckford) Knapp's second attempted suicide immediately after Frank Knapp's being found guilty, *Nathaniel Hawthorne, The Letters, 1813–1843,* 207–8.

4 Ibid.

5 James Flint, quoted by Margaret Moore, *Salem World of Nathaniel Hawthorne* (Columbia, Mo.: University of Missouri Press, 2001), 163.

6 *Portsmouth Journal & Rockingham Gazette* (NH), Oct. 2, 1830.

7 *Salem Gazette,* Oct. 1, 1830.

8   Joshua Leavitt, ed., *The Sailor's Magazine* (New York, 1831), vol. III, 7, reference to Feb. 26, 1831 "appeal to government for protection against the natives in those seas" from seven shipmasters and a supercargo at Muckie.

9   Charles M. Endicott refers to the role of opium in this incident, memorial dated Feb. 26, 1831. *American State Papers, Naval Affairs,* No. 485, 22nd Congress, First Session, 154–55.

10 The story of the *Friendship*'s disastrous experience in February 1831, on the coast of Sumatra, is most accurately told by those who were there at the time: Charles M. Endicott in his own ship's log, and Endicott and seven other Americans at Muckie in their memorial dated Feb. 26, 1831 when the incidents were fresh. No mention is made of "pirates" or "piracy" in these accounts. Other accounts were written in 1832 by Francis Warriner and by Jeremiah N. Reynolds, who were not on-site in 1831 but who may have interviewed a survivor(s). Long (twenty-one years) after the incident, in the summer of 1852, Endicott published an account in the Boston *Courier;* and on Jan. 28, 1858, twenty-seven years after the incident, he read a paper, *Narrative of the Piracy, and Plunder of the ship Friendship, of Salem, on the West Coast of Sumatra, in February 1831, and the Massacre of Part of Her Crew; Also, Her Re-capture out of the Hands of the Malay Pirates,* at a meeting (Jan. 1858) of the members of the Essex Institute, which published that paper, with interpolations from the 1852 newspaper article, in its *Essex Institute Historical Collections* (1859), vol. I, 15–32. Endicott's later versions are quite different from his logbook entry, not least in their politicized use of the terms piracy and pirates, which he never uses in 1831.

11 Ibid.

12 Ibid.

13 Captain Charles M. Endicott, Statement, *American State Papers, Naval Affairs,* No. 485, 22nd Congress, First Session, pp. 154–55. "We subsequently learned," wrote Endicott, "that the pepper boat exchanged her crew of fishermen at the river's mouth, for a set of opium smokers, rendered desperate by their habits, and to these men added, also, others of the same class, taken from the ferry boat."

17: CONFLAGRATION

1   John D. Lawson, editor, *American State Trials,* vol. VII, 636.

2   Samuel G. Goodrich, *Recollections of a Lifetime,* Letter XIV (New York and Auburn: Miller, Orton, and Mulligan, 1856), 272.

3   Hawthorne's tale "The Hollow of Three Hills" appeared anonymously in *Salem Gazette* Nov. 12, 1830, alongside a very full account of Joe Knapp's trial. Hawthorne's "An Old Woman's Tale" appeared in the *Salem Gazette* for Dec. 21, 1830 alongside "The Salem Murder" piece implying that Mary Beckford was behind the assassination. Two other Hawthorne sketches appeared in the *Gazette* in 1830: "Ann Hutchinson" and "William Phipps."

4   *Young Goodman Brown* was written in the mid-1830s evidently, as was Hawthorne's *Mr. Higginbotham's Catastrophe,* a cynical, amusing fiction about the reported murder of a town patriarch.

5   *Salem Gazette,* Nov. 12, 19, 23, 1830.

6   Daniel Webster, *Works of Daniel Webster* (1857), 90–1.

7   *Salem Gazette,* Dec. 21, 1830.

8   "Salem Murder," *Salem Gazette,* Dec. 21, 1830; see also William Shakespeare, *The Tragedy of Hamlet, Prince of Denmark,* I: v: 84–8.

9   "Execution of Joseph J. Knapp Jr.," *Salem Gazette,* Jan. 4, 1831.

10 In 1813, Capt. David Porter, commanding the Salem-built frigate *Essex,* sailed into the Pacific and destroyed many British whalers there, then sailed to the Marquesas Islands and became embroiled in tribal warfare, during which Downes, master of the *Essex Jr.,* was twice wounded. Before returning to the South American coast and losing the *Essex* in battle, Porter claimed the Marquesas for the United States—the first instance of attempted conquest by an American. The U.S. government did not approve, and refused to take possession of the Marquesas.

11 The *Glide* sank in a hurricane at the Fijis in May 1831, along with the Salem brig *Niagara*. The crews escaped with their lives. The voyage of the *Glide* was the subject of two narratives published by survivors.

12 Jeremiah N. Reynolds, quoted in George G. Putnam, editor, *Salem Vessels & Their Voyages*, vol. I (Salem: The Essex Institute, 1922), 96.

13 Francis Warriner, *Cruise of the United States Frigate Potomac Round the World* (New York: Leavitt, Lord, & Co., and Boston: Crocker & Brewster, 1835), 88–9. He is a reliable reporter of the fighting at Kuala Batu, in which the women were as brave as the men. Jeremiah N. Reynolds, in his *Voyage of the United States Frigate Potomac* (New York: Harper & Brothers, 1835), also describes the invasion and fighting, but he was in Valparaiso at the time (and his version was probably corrected, if not drafted, by Captain Downes). Warriner's sympathy for the Sumatrans earned him vilification and his book disparagement by certain critics. In most other versions, for decades to come, the Kuala Batu massacre was treated as an American triumph of arms rather than a crime in which a professional military force slaughtered terrified villagers without any warning.

14 Charles M. Endicott, quoted in George G. Putnam, op. cit., 90.

15 "Yankee Doodle" was then the national anthem, or considered so by John Downes and his men.

16 Jeremiah N. Reynolds quoted in George G. Putnam, op. cit., 106.

17 Ibid.

18: THE MAGNATE

1 Fletcher Webster, ed., *Private Correspondence of Daniel Webster,* vol. I (Boston: Little, Brown & Co., 1857) 520–1.

2 Ibid., 330–2.

3 Henry Colman (1785–1849) died of typhus at Islington, outside of London, England, on Aug. 14, 1849, aged 64 years. His last book, *European Life and Manners,* was published in 1850, at the same time as Hawthorne's *The Scarlet Letter.*

4 Stephen paid the expenses of Phebe and Francis.

5 When John White (1782–1840) died in Boston, the recorder of vital records referred to the cause of death as "gout" although it was almost certainly the elephantiasis he had contracted in Vietnam.

6 Long after John White's death in 1840, his grandson Frederick G. Eldridge married Alice, the daughter of Hawthorne's first publisher, S. G. Goodrich; and Eldridge, a great pal of J. P. Morgan, became a leading New York banker. See June 23, 1889 *New York Times* obituary of F. G. Eldridge.

7 Sept. 9, 1831, letter of N. Hawthorne to John S. Dike, in *Nathaniel Hawthorne, The Letters, 1813–1843*, 217. George Crowninshield eventually moved to the Roxbury section of Boston, where, affluent and eccentric, he died in his eighties.

8 Ibid.

9 Harriett Low to sister Molly, letter Aug. 3, 1830, quoted in Rosmarie W. N. Lamas, *Everything in Style* (Hong Kong and Aberdeen: Hong Kong University press, 2006), 118.

10 Nathaniel Phippen Knapp died on Feb. 17, 1854 (aged 45) at Mobile, Alabama, per Reverend William Johnson, editor of *Select Sermons of The Late Rev. N. P. Knapp, A.M.* (Philadelphia: Herman Hooker, 1855), viii.

11 Lynn H. Parsons, "'A Perpetual Harrow Upon My Feelings' . . ." *The New England Quarterly* vol. 46, 360–3.

12 Bowditch died in Boston in 1838, aged 65; Pickering died in Boston in 1846, aged 69.

13 Judge Joseph Story (1779–1845) died Sept. 10, 1845 and his remains were buried at Mount Auburn Cemetery. His son William, a distinguished lawyer, became a famous poet and sculptor in Italy.

14 "Who Is Safe," *Salem Gazette,* Feb. 6, 1835, by "Social Order."

15 John White, "The Trumpet Fish," in Nathaniel Hawthorne, editor, *American Magazine of Useful & Entertaining Knowledge,* vol. II, (Boston: Boston Bewick Co., 1836), 418.

16 John C. R. Palmer Jr., *Explanation,* 172–3.

17 *Salem Gazette,* Aug. 2, 1831.

18 John C. R. Palmer Jr., *Explanation,* 87.

19 *Salem Gazette,* Sept. 9, 1831.

20 John Carr Roberts Palmer Jr. was born in Augusta or Belfast, Maine, the son of J. C. R. Palmer and his wife Mary Sherburne. His grandfather, Jonathan Palmer of Wakefield, NH, had been an officer in the Revolutionary War. J. C. R. Palmer Jr.'s brother Israel Thorndike Palmer, went west in 1844 and became a prosperous Detroit shipmaster. They had at least four sisters. A genealogical memoir of 1871 implies that I. T. Palmer was at that time the only surviving brother.

21 Samuel L. Knapp, *A Memoir of the Life of Daniel Webster,* 173–84. The murder-related section of this book (paid for by Stephen White, who probably had the final say on matters of content), is the closest thing to White's own version of the killing and related events.

22 "Wanted" in the old sense of "stood in want of" or "lacked."

23 The convention was held at Worcester in October 1832.

19: THE MIRAGE

1 *Niles' Register,* Nov. 5, 183, vol. 41, No. 1050 (Balto.), 190. Stephen White was a Massachusetts delegate to a New York convention of "agriculturalists, mechanics, manufacturers, and others favorable to the protection of the national industry."

2 The first Massachusetts railroad company, the Boston & Lowell Railroad, chartered June 5, 1830, would not finish building its beds and tracks and go into operation until 1835.

3 William H. Sumner, *A History of East Boston* (Boston: William H. Piper & Co., 1869), 442.

4 Ibid., 458, 461.

5 Into the mid-1600s Samuel Maverick, a genial host, lived on the island and disturbed the Puritans with his independent ways. In 1831 the ferry wharf was built by the only two Irishmen among the proprietors.

6 W. H. Sumner, op. cit., 690. The ferries were built for the East Boston Ferry Company, with a third ferry following.

7 Ibid., 467, 503, 505n.

8 Ibid., 670.

9 Ibid., 671.

10 Maurice G. Baxter, *One and Inseparable: Daniel Webster and the Union* (Cambridge: Harvard University Press, 1984), 558. Letters of Stephen White to Daniel Webster, Jan. 9, 21, 1834.

11 Frances D. Robotti, *Whaling and Old Salem* (New York: Bonanza Books, 1962), 76–87. Evidently the bark *Izette,* in 1831, was the first to go whaling from Salem.

12 *Salem Gazette,* Nov. 12, 1830.

13 John Bertram (pronounced "Bartram" in Salem) would become a great merchant through his trade with east Africa, a continuation of that begun by the Rogers Bros. and Charles Forbes at Madagascar in 1820.

14 The Naumkeag Steam Cotton Company went into production in 1847 with the largest textile factory in America, situated on the waterfront in South Salem. It proved profitable and long-lasting as the industrial centerpiece of the city. Most of its cheap cottons were sold overseas to people in the tropics—a complete reversal of Salem's original oriental trade in the cheap cottons of Bengal.

15 The missionaries, Munson and Lyman, had sailed from Boston in 1832, and had made their way up the pepper Coast from Padang before taking a fatal turn inland.

16 Anonymous (Robert Burts), *Around the World: A Narrative of a Voyage in the East India Squadron under Commodore George C. Read,* vol. II (New York: Charles S. Francis, 1840), 52.

17 Ibid., 59

18 Suffolk County, Mass., *Land Records: Deed Book 672,* 298–302, for 1834 Joy-White marriage settlement.

19 Caroline Story White married Daniel Fletcher Webster at Portsmouth, NH, at Thanksgiving 1836; the couple soon moved to Detroit, where Fletcher hoped to establish a law practice and manage his father's western lands. They eventually returned to Massachusetts. In the Civil War, Colonel D. Fletcher Webster was killed in action at the Second Battle of Bull Run.

20 Henry A. S. Dearborn, 1838, "The Dearborn Journals" in *Publications of the Buffalo Historical Society,* vol. VII (Buffalo, 1904), 50.

21 The freighter *Owanungah,* was the first three-masted schooner on the Lakes, later altered to a hermaphrodite brig, per "Old Salt," note of Feb. 6, 1885, in Martha J. Lamb, editor, *Magazine of American History,* Vol. XIII, Jan.–June 1885 (New York: Historical Publishing Co., 1885), 304.

22 Benjamin F. Delano (1809–1882) is credited as her builder in D. Hamilton Hurd, *History of Plymouth County, Mass.,* vol. I (Philadelphia: J. W. Lewis & Co., 1884), 439–40. W. H. Sumner, *A History of East Boston,* claims (p. 690) she was built by Brown, Bates & Delano at "Central Square," East Boston. Brown & Bates was a Boston shipbuilding firm; perhaps Delano had become a partner. See also L. Vernon Briggs, *History of Ship Building on North River, Plymouth County, Mass.* (Boston: Coburn Brothers, 1889), 226–27.

23 Daniel Webster, *Daniel Webster Papers,* vol. 4, 165.

24 Ibid., 266–67.

25 The remains of young Joseph White (died 1838) were interred in the Story tomb at Mount Auburn Cemetery.

26 Grand Island Institution for Destitute Boys in entry for Oct. 11, 1839, *Prison Discipline Society, 15th Report, 1840* (Boston, 1840), 472–60.

27 L. Vernon Briggs, *History of Ship Building on North River,* 357. Samuel Hall (1800–1870), later a builder of first-rate clipper ships, had begun building at East Boston in April 1839. See also D. Hamilton Hurd, *History of Plymouth County,* Vol. II, 1169.

INDEX

Page numbers that are *italicized* indicate illustrations and captions

ILLUSTRATIONS